I never played to many posh dances…

Scan Tester, Sussex musician, 1887 – 1972

Reg Hall

Rollston Press

2024

I Never Played to Many Posh Dances:
Scan Tester, Sussex Musician, 1887-1972
by Reg Hall

ISBN-13: 978-1-953208-22-4

Originally produced and published in 1990 as
Musical Traditions Supplement No. 2
(ISSN 0265-5063)

Editor: Keith Summers
Design and desktop publishing: Graeme Kirkham
Cover design: Tony Engle
Cover photograph: Brian Shuel

Reprinted and reissued by Rollston Press, 2024
Editor/Publisher: Gary Coover

To my late mother, Peg, and my wife, Claire.

ROLLSTON PRESS
1717 Ala Wai Blvd #1703
Honolulu, HI 96815
USA
www.rollstonpress.com

Contents

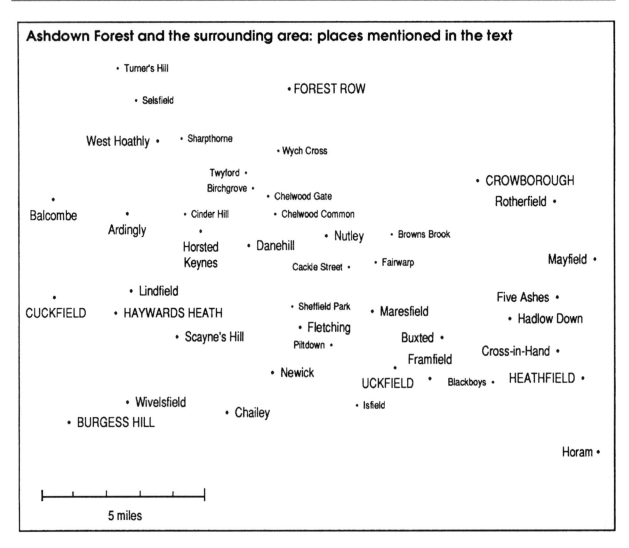

Ashdown Forest and the surrounding area: places mentioned in the text

The area shown on these maps is covered by Ordnance Survey
1:50 000 sheets 187,198 and 199.

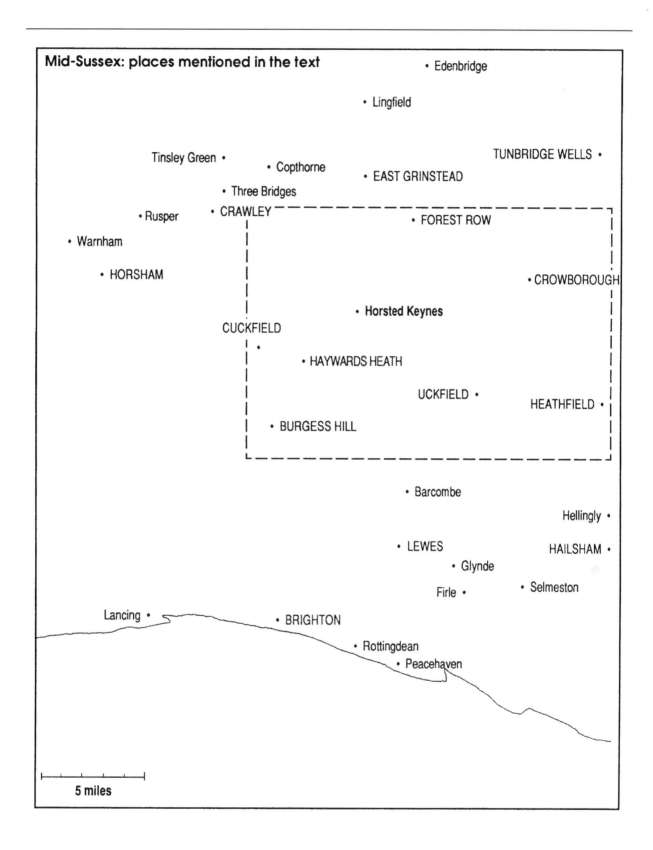

Mid-Sussex: places mentioned in the text

• Edenbridge

• Lingfield

Tinsley Green •

• Copthorne

• EAST GRINSTEAD

TUNBRIDGE WELLS •

• Three Bridges

• Rusper

• CRAWLEY

• FOREST ROW

• Warnham

• CROWBOROUGH

• HORSHAM

• Horsted Keynes

CUCKFIELD

• HAYWARDS HEATH

UCKFIELD •

HEATHFIELD •

• BURGESS HILL

• Barcombe

Hellingly •

• LEWES

HAILSHAM •

• Glynde

Firle •

• Selmeston

Lancing •

• BRIGHTON

• Rottingdean

• Peacehaven

5 miles

— — — — — Shown on the map opposite

5

Daisy Sherlock, Scan Tester
and Reg Hall at a party given
by Mervyn and Doë Plunkett
Wes Hoathly, Sussex
2 November 1957.

Preface

This view of Scan Tester and his music, which is published in conjunction with the double album on Topic Records, is essentially my own. Objectivity is a difficult stance to maintain and, inevitably, my own biases and value judgements about music and dance in general show through. Other people making a selection might have produced something quite different.

My relationship with Scan was based on friendship and music-making, and it never occurred to me, during his lifetime, to make Scan the subject of a project, nor did I ever record him or interview him with that in mind. In fact, I shied away from questioning him too closely as I felt, perhaps mistakenly, it would have been a breach of our relationship. I did, however, hope sometime to make a record of him, and Scan was quite happy about the idea. The recordings were made informally in private homes and public houses, as a bonus to what were first and foremost social events. None valued our music-making more than Scan, who consciously recalled old tunes when he knew the machine was running, and once exclaimed at the end of a session with his daughter, Daisy, and me, 'Cor, we're better than Jimmy Shand!"[1]

However fine and remarkable Scan was as a musician, he was not unique. He acknowledged other musicians he had known and played with, and, if he appeared to be a major figure in the music-making of his locality in the latter part of his life, it was largely because his old mates were dead and gone or had given up playing in public. Scan was not simply a musician; cricket, football, gardening, friendships and his family were all important to him, and, although he was not particularly mechanically minded, he could turn his hand to pretty well anything practical to earn his living. His life was spent within the culture of workers and tradesmen in a small area of the Sussex Weald and I will comment on this social background.

To a large extent, I have allowed Scan to speak for himself. His recorded conversation, transcribed verbatim with the minimum of editing, reveals more of his personality and values than I could hope to capture in dry prose. The tapes of Scan speaking were made by Mervyn Plunkett, David Nuttall, Alan Waller, Vic Smith, Rod and Danny Stradling, Hilda and Hugh Gibson and me, and I have used our initials at the end of each quotation to indicate the source.[2]

It is now too late to gather much first-hand evidence of Scan's early days, but I have tried to verify and expand upon what he told me with documentary evidence. My searches in archive material have included parish registers, licensing registers, census returns, *Parliamentary Registers*, *Kelly's Directory of Sussex* and the *Sussex Express*,[3] held in the East Sussex Records Office in Lewes, Brighton Reference Library, the University of Sussex Library and by the Registrar General of Births, Deaths and Marriages at St. Catherine's House in London, and in local churchyards.

I am grateful to Vic Gammon and Keith Chandler for encouraging me to organise my material for publication. I particularly wish to acknowledge the former, for the electric shock given to my dormant thoughts on the nature of English vernacular music by his doctoral thesis, Popular Music in Rural Society: Sussex 1815-1914, and for the advice and criticism he has offered so freely. David Nuttall has shared with me everything he noted during his association with Scan in Scan's last few years, and has discussed Victorian and twentieth-century popular music with me in the context of his collection of printed dance music. Phil Lucas from Danehill, a local historian with his feet set firmly in the working life of the area and with close family and neighbourhood connections with Scan's associates, has been very generous with his material and suggestions. Scan's daughter, Daisy, and her husband, Arch Sherlock (who sadly died a year or so before publication), have been enthusiastic about this production and have given me much biographical and anecdotal material. Numerous others, including Scan's relatives, friends and neighbours, have contributed factual information, photographs, advice and practical help.

Most of all, I remain deeply indebted to Mervyn Plunkett for introducing me to Scan, his brother Will, and Daisy, and for our shared experiences pubbing in the villages and small towns around West Hoathly from the mid-1950s to the early 1960s. Beneath the gentrification that was all too evident in Sussex even then, there was still a country, popular culture, its roots unbroken, but beginning to take a hammering from vast social change. There were plenty of marvellous old singers about and a few musicians, too, but they tended to keep their heads down. Mervyn had the imagination, sensitivity and motivation to meet them on their home ground. As a direct consequence of his activities, my rubbing shoulders with those old boys left me marked for life. In recent years Mervyn pondered upon the nature of Scan's style and repertoire and he intended writing a section of these notes. His unexpected death in December 1986 deprives us of his stimulating and inevitably contentious contribution.

The focus throughout this book is on music and dancing, and the text represents three distinct perspectives. The first two sections of the biography (chapters 2 and 3) reconstruct Scan's musical activities in the context of his own home environment and are based largely on verbal accounts, supported by documentary evidence. Chapter 4 introduces me as one of the leading actors, and thus creates an in-built problem of how to maintain objectivity. I have chosen therefore to write it in the first person, to avoid any pretence that it is anything other than a personal memoir.

The rest of the book, chapters 1 and 5 - 14, sets Scan in a much broader context, namely that of traditional music-making and dancing in southern England and further afield over two centuries. It is a remarkable fact that English traditional instrumental music has escaped the attention of historians and ethnomusicologists. My intention in engaging in what I consider to be a tentative exploration of the subject has been to propose an agenda for debate and to put down markers for future research.

Reg Hall

NOTES

1. Shand's hit record, *The Blue Bell Polka*, was played frequently on the radio in the late 1950s. Scan had just seen Shand's Band on television

2. Plunkett's interview was recorded on 9.2.1958 and I worked from his transcription. My recordings were made on 19.8.1964, 21.7.1965 and 22.7.1966, and Waller's in October 1966, and I worked directly from the tapes. The Gibsons' was made on 1.4.1967 and Nuttall's on 13.10.1968, and I worked from the latter's transcriptions. The Stradlings' interview was recorded late in the summer of 1968 and Smith's dates from 20.8.1971, and I worked from their transcriptions; the former appeared in edited form in *Folk Roots*, 31 (Jan., 1986), pp. 11-13, and the latter was edited for publication in *Traditional Music*, 4 (1976), pp. 4-10.

3. I decided upon ten-year sampling of the *Sussex Express* (1900 incomplete, 1910, 1920 and 1930 incomplete), skim-reading each edition, and focusing on village reports. I also directed attention at events (the Diamond Jubilee, the end of the Boer War and George V's Coronation and Silver Jubilee), a jazz-age year (1927) and an unsuccessful attempt at finding evidence of dancing at *Nutley Inn* (1905). (*Sussex Express*, Feb. - July 1897, Oct. 1900 - May 1902, 1905, Nov. 1909 - Dec. 1910, Feb. - July 1911, 1914, May April 1921, 1927, Jan. -May 1930and Jan. -May 1935.)

Chapter 1:
The 19th-century Sussex background

The area of the Sussex High Weald we are most concerned with in considering Scan's social background embraces the typical Wealden villages of Horsted Keynes and Fletching, the Ashdown Forest villages of Nutley, Fairwarp and Forest Row, and Chelwood Common and Chelwood Gate lying on the borders of the forest. In earlier times three social formations were quite distinct, the communities in the Wealden villages engaging in mixed farming, iron smelting and glass manufacture, the foresters living off the forest and the commoners at Chelwood asserting their grazing and gathering rights on the forest while living outside its boundary. Differences in social values and attitudes are discernible to the locals even now.[1] The last hundred years have blurred these differences, but the high degree of social and economic interaction masks a measure of social tension.

Mick Reed has challenged the general historical view that, in the early and mid-nineteenth century, England was predominantly a country of large landlords, cultivated by tenant farmers working the land with hired labour. He concludes that the 'social formation of the English countryside was a complex one, rather than the simple polarisation favoured by historians generally…'[2] In the Sussex High Weald perhaps a majority, but at least a large minority of farmers worked small acreages using family rather than hired labour. This might be seen as the survival of an English peasant economy.

Although London's growing demand for food provided a ready market for the produce of the Weald, the general consensus of opinion among early and mid-nineteenth century observers was that farming in the Weald was 'overwooded, ill-ploughed, chronically backward and worst of all, too reliant on hops… [which] farmers steadily overproduced.'[3] The situation was compounded by strong resistance to improved methods, and much farming was at little more than subsistence level. Most working people earned their living in multiple employment, often partly self-employment. Tradesmen supplemented their income by some involvement in agricultural production and waged labourers usually rented a small plot of land for their own immediate needs and relied to some extent upon common grazing.

Economic depression followed the Napoleonic Wars and, in spite of a degree of independence amongst working men, 'to have been a rural worker in the nineteenth century must have been to have had an existence of appalling toil, privation and precious little Joy'; 'until quite late in the century rural living was extremely squalid.'[4] The oppressive New Poor Law of 1834 was resisted by the poor and some Guardians alike, often pushing farmers and tradespeople into collusive alliances with labourers, as many of those operating the Poor Law relief system were only marginally better off than the paupers themselves. The Swing Riots of 1830, characterized by 'collective bargaining by riot', threats and the destruction of threshing machines, were followed by more covert forms of protest, often widely organised and practised, the commonest being poaching.

Mick Reed points out, however, that there were other forms of conflict between labour and capital: working men and women protected their economic interests by undertaking piecework rather than day work, which gave them some control over their own working conditions; the common practice among farm and indoor servants of changing their employer annually, with most hirings taking place on the door-step, gave servants some advantage in negotiating wages and conditions.[5] An exchange system of barter and credit operated alongside the normal flow of cash, with running, two-way accounts periodically settled by services or goods. Interest free loans and gifts were made to the poor by neighbours scarcely more affluent than themselves, and 'tradespeople and small farmers might depend on the poor for labour at crucial times or for the supply of raw materials for their various enterprises.'[6]

The remote, impenetrable Weald, mud-sodden in winter, was opened up by the eighteenth-century turnpike roads. East Grinstead and Lewes, centres of commercial activity, were linked by coach roads, first the long way round through Uckfield, which required a coaching stage at the *Nutley Inn*, purpose-built in the 1750s.[7] A generation later, the shorter route through Danehill was constructed, with the *New Inn*, later renamed the *Sheffield Arms*, provided at Fletching in 1786 by the Earl of Sheffield. Danehill, with the *Red Lion Inn* at Chelwood Gate, thus became a staging post for the old Wealden manors of Horsted Keynes and Fletching.

The process of gentrification began with the turnpike and continued with the railways. The rapid exploitation of the Southern coast for leisure and pleasure was made possible by the London and Brighton railway line, opened in 1841, and the creation of a completely new suburban dormitory town at Haywards Heath was possible only because of the railway.

> [B]y the end of the century no village or farm was more than ten miles from a station ... [which] disgorged not just passengers, but milk churns, seed catalogues, agricultural machinery and commercial travellers.[8]

Wealden bricks, once carried slowly by barge on the River Ouse, were now easily transported to London and Brighton to meet a growing demand. In 1882 Horsted Keynes station was opened on the Lewes to East Grinstead line. Completion of the link with the London and Brighton line the following year stimulated Scan Tester's father to move five miles westward, abandoning the turnpike road system for the advantages the railway could provide for his fish business.

Ashdown Forest was enclosed as a royal deer park in the fourteenth century. The Enclosure Award of 1693 sketched the framework of landownership for its subsequent evolution, with 6676 acres remaining as common-land, and the rest, some 7000 acres, the property of individual landowners.[9] By late Victorian times much of the privately-owned forest was divided into estates with large country houses, owned by London businessmen and members of the gentry. These provided work for house, garden and estate workers - woodmen, sawyers and builders - and some estates had 'bothies' for their unattached male staff.[10] Small farms had dotted the Forest, 'carved out of the wilderness at a very early date.'[11] Until the Ashdown Forest Act of 1885 put an end to the practice, squatters encroached on common land. They graduated from branch and turf shanties covering hollows dug into the side of a bank, to corrugated iron shacks, before finally building in brick. Crofters grazed livestock, dug building stone and gravel for sale, lifted mould for manure and turf for

burning, and cut litter (sedge grass and heather) for cattle feed, bracks for cattle bedding and dogwood for charcoal burning.[12] The more prosperous woodmen might buy a 'cant' of wood, the right to crop timber from a piece of woodland. Common land on the forest, remote from villages and farms, afforded some protection and freedom from harassment to families of gypsies, and there was regularly an encampment half a mile or so north of Fairwarp.

At the end of the nineteenth century, a large proportion of the working population in this part of Sussex were tied to their own property. There had been a slump in farming from the 1870s, brought about by cheap produce from the New World and the introduction of refrigerated transport, and the consequent decline in land values made it possible, for a short time, for some working men to buy or rent land of their own (and incidentally made it possible for town people to buy country properties). The main crops of the area remained wheat, oats, barley, mangolds, swedes, beans and hops with large areas of pasturage; sheep were driven up from Romney Marsh in September, fattened and returned in March.[13] There was also some enterprise in new ventures, such as poultry cramming and the development of the loganberry.

Labourers' average wages in Sussex have been estimated at 13s. 4d. in 1872, 13s. 6d. in 1882, 12s. in 1892 and 14s. in 1898.[14] Average real income, however, can not be readily pinned down, as many working men were fully or partly self-employed and those that were full-time employees usually had an extra side-line; in any case many aspects of exchange did not take place within the cash economy. While rural life was inevitably based on land, agricultural pursuits were not necessarily dominant. Rural industries, domestic service and estate work, service trades and a host of minor by-employments provided a living for a large proportion of the population. It is significant that while many of Scan Tester's associates in music and dancing were employed on the land for some of their working lives, none can be identified as having been primarily a farmworker or agricultural labourer.

Between 1801 and 1901 the population of Sussex as a whole increased by nearly 400 per cent, from 160,000 to about 600,000. There was some drift from the countryside to service industries in Brighton and other coastal towns, and to work on the railways. There were brief invasions of navvies - some Irish, but most from the Midlands and East Anglia - during the construction of the railway lines, but once the work was done they moved on. No analysis has been made of migration patterns within the area where Scan Tester spent his life, although local history studies show the persistence of many families over several centuries.[15] In the period 1891-1911, the population of Forest Row increased from 2137 to 3035, and in Nutley from 990 to 1109. In Danehill the total fell from 1214 to 1131, and in Horsted Keynes it remained constant at about 930. Fatalities during the Great War made a substantial demographic and social impact; in Fairwarp, for example, 25 were killed from a total population of about 700.

The village pub, much more than the church, had increasingly become a focal point for all aspects of the cultural life of country working men. At the beginning of the nineteenth century, commercially-brewed beer was available in urban taverns and alehouses, and inns sited strategically round the country provided food, drink and accommodation for bona fide travellers, most of whom were not working men. In the country, apart from home-brewed beer, cider and wine, beer was produced for sale by hucksters for consumption off the premises - to be drunk at home or in the fields - and it seems very unlikely that country working men spent much time or money in premises set aside for drinking. The flowering of country pub culture, although based on much earlier roots, was largely the product of the 1830s. The Beer-houses Act of 1830 permitted any rate payer to sell beer for consumption on or off the premises, and the effect was that 24,000 beer-houses opened in England and Wales before the year was out, followed by a further 22,000 within the next six years.[16]

By a strange irony the government had provided a greatly increased number of congenial meeting places for working men in the year of the Swing Riots, at the very time they feared insurrection. One consequence was the neglect and abuse of some wives and children by those who spent all day in the pub, but the 1830s also saw the beginning of a popular move-ment towards rationality and respectability in the countryside, embracing slate clubs, horticultural societies and sports clubs. Working men organized themselves or were organised by their respectable social superiors.

Village bands, first formed in the early nineteenth century, owed their existence to public subscription, upper-class patronage and/or the efforts of work-ing men themselves. The same motivating concepts of self-help, spiritual uplift and temperance devel-oped further in the second half of the century with the provision of reading rooms, recreation rooms and working-mens' club rooms. Horsted Keynes reading room, erected by the curate in the 1860s, was supplied with newspapers, magazines and a baga-telle table, and had an upstairs room capable of seating 150 for concerts, entertainments and vestry meetings.[17] In all the villages round about, working men were involved in cricket, football and quoits and young women in the far from genteel game of stoolball; local interest in cricket was strengthened by the appearance of W.G. Grace and the Australian touring team at Sheffield Park in the 1880s and 1890s.

But, if by the end of the century it was no longer largely true that 'rural life was extremely squalid,' it was still hard going for the working man and his family; living was for many still frugal, hazardous and uncertain. A pointer to changes that were on the way was the position and status of Stephen Clark (1850-1942), neither a working man nor a member of the gentry, but school master at Horsted Keynes. At the turn of the century he undertook additional duties for the community as secretary of the friendly society and the football club, church organist and as-sessor and collector of King's taxes. By 1909 he was also an insurance agent![18]

NOTES

1. Some local people offer a 'racial' explanation for perceived social differences, in the belief that the old Chelwood families are descended from pre-Saxon settlers.

2. Mick Reed, 'The Peasantry of Nineteenth-Century England: A Neglected Class?', *History Workshop*, 18 (Autumn 1984), p. 71.

3. John Lowerson, *Victorian Sussex* (1972), p. 43.

4. Mick Reed, 'Social Change and Social Conflict in the Nineteeth Century. A Comment', *Journal of Peasant Studies* (Oct. 1984), p. 121; Lowerson, *Victorian Sussex*, p. 10.

5. Reed, 'Social Change'.

6. Reed, 'Peasantry', pp. 62-3.

7. The turnpike road construction was authorised by Act of Parliament in 1753.

8. Lowerson, *Victorian Sussex*, p. 19.

9. Roy Millward and Adrian Robinson, *The High Weald* (1971), p. 174.

10. The word 'bothy' is used locally for the communal living quarters of estate workers.

11. Millward and Robinson, *High Weald*, p. 179.

12. The term 'crofters' is used locally to refer to these established squatters. Bracks is the local word for bracken.

13. Information on local agriculture derived from vari ous volumes of *Kelly's Directory of Sussex* for the late nineteenth and early twentieth century, and from oral sources.

14. Lord Ernle, *English Farming Past and Present*, quoted in Lowerson, p. 45.

15. See *Danehill Parish Historical Society Magazine*, 1978 - present.

16. Brian Spiller, *Victorian Public Houses* (1972), p. 9.

See also Brian Harrison: '[B]y paying two guineas a year, any householder assessed to the poor rate could obtain from the excise a licence to sell beer for consumption on or off the premises. The conditions of tenure, specified in the licence, were very similar to those for innkeepers, but closing hours were much more strictly defined.' Opening hours were 4 a.m. - 10 p.m. in 1830, 5 a.m. - 11 p.m. in 1834, and 5 a.m. - 11 p.m., or 10 p.m. if the population was under 2500, in 1840. (Harrison, *Drink and the Victorians: The Temperance Question in England 1815-1872* (1971), p. 79.)

17. *Kelly's* (1895).

18. *Kelly's* (1899, 1903, 1909).

The Green Man, *Horsted Keynes 1971*
Scan's parents bought the pub in 1891 and Scan lived there in early childhood.
(Photograph: Hamish Black)

Part I:

Biography

A portrait of Scan's parents, Will and Sally Tester, taken by the Nutley photographer, Arthur 'Daddy' Francis, between 1908 and 1915.
(Courtesy Daisy & Arch Sherlock)

Chapter 2:
1887 - Great War

Lewis Tester was born at the crossroads at Chelwood Common, Sussex, on 7 September 1887, though for most of his life he believed he was born in 1886. Whether this was a mistake or a deception, the effect was that he was able to leave school and contribute to the family income a year earlier than he should have done.[1] His parents, Will and Sally Tester, were married in 1870 and brought up eight children: Jinny (Jane, born 1872), Trayton (30 January 1875), Harriet (1877), Fred (Alfred, 1881), Bert (Albert), Minnie, Lewis and Will (1888). The three oldest, at least, were born at Horney Corner, halfway between Nutley and Maresfield. The family moved to Chelwood, then briefly to Maresfield in 1888, and then back to Chelwood. From there they went to Forest Row for the next three years, before buying Leamland, a plot of land and a house at Cinder Hill, from Arch Sherlock's grandmother, and the *Green Man*, a public house in Horsted Keynes, in 1891.[2]

Will and Sally Tester earned their living in a variety of enterprises. The pub was a source of steady income, supplemented seasonally by the sale of ponies bred in the paddock at the back of the pub, but the family was already involved in two well-established trades. It was the fish-hawking business that brought the family to Horsted Keynes:

> **Scan:** That's how we first come here; we had a fish-hawking licence. We used to go to pubs and fairs with whelks and oysters. We were known by it all around Sussex. My father had forty years going back and forward to Brighton fish market, so he knew a bit about it. I used to know most of the fishermen in Brighton. There used to be an old chap there, and he used to be what they call a picker-up; he used to pick up for these big fish buyers, but he used to fill his

Brighton fish market; undated.

BRIGHTON FISH MARKET AND BEACH.

[own] box up and, do you know, he had one of the finest fish rounds in Brighton. He was quite an elderly man then, and I can see his old go-cart now, that he used to push his fish out on. It was just like a pair of old bike wheels on a frame, and wire round to keep his baskets in there. You see, his fish was always fresh and good and cheap. Well, we bought it, and we didn't have to pay for it to come up by rail, because it came up with us, you see. There used to be a station here. Well, it used to be a junction and at that time of day it was very busy. We had a horse and cart come down to the station to meet us and we used to separate the stuff out into two or three carts and away we used to go. [VS]

Oh, we were known for it for years, my father was. And we'd got gentleman's places; we had to get there for lunch, and one of my brothers used to have to drive on in front and call at these places, and get the stuff there ready for lunchtime. We used to have to go out all around, one one way and one another, and sometimes, if we'd got a glut of herrings or anything like that caught off Brighton anywhere - well, we'd got a herring deese at the *Green Man* and we could keep them in there for very near a week – fresh.[3] So we'd always got plenty of fresh herrings, and then we used to dry a lot for bloaters. Perhaps you'd get four or five for a penny - with buying a lot like we used to buy. Well, you hang them up in the herring deese, and then sell them penny a time. It don't sound a lot, but if you got half a cart-load hanging up there, thaws ever so many pennies. [VS]

Yes, we used to do a good trade then. And now, well, you do see a fishmonger in the village; he comes from Haywards Heath, but I've told him, I says, 'I don't know how you people make a living.' I says, 'I've carried more stuff over one arm than you carry on your whole pony cart!' I've carried that much over my arms in baskets, that you had to stop and have a rest, you know, and have another go. Then if you went to two or three places and they didn't want none...Cor! But we used to travel all round the outskirts. We never used to go in the villages much. Well, round the outskirts they don't go in a shop to buy their stuff.

If they got some fish that they knew was all right come to the door, well, it saved them going out. We used to sell a lot of stuff like that.[4] [VS]

Will Tester was also a brickmaker, supplying J.J. Saunders & Sons of Brighton with pipes and tiles, as well as bricks from his three brickfields: one by the station at Horsted Keynes, another behind the *Green Man* and a third near the *Bricklayers' Arms* between North Chailey and Newick. This was essentially a family concern, operating almost at a domestic level, with the father and sons doing most of the work throughout the year and additional itinerant labour taken on in the summer months.

Arch Sherlock remembered the details of brickmaking: clay was dug and mixed with London ashes during the winter; this was known as curfing. Then in the better weather it was pug-milled in a pan and rollers driven by a horse or small engine. It was knocked up by hand in moulds and trimmed to size with cheese wire, and the wet bricks were then placed into a hack to dry, before going into the clab, a wood-fired oven, for firing and burning. A man could make 200 or 300 bricks a day and there might be four or five men working at a time. These travelling brickmakers made good money and it used to be said, 'Father paid the men their wages and mother got it back over the counter in the *Green Man*.'[5]

MUSIC IN THE FAMILY

In the bar at the *Green Man* there was a large wooden table where, besides dominoes, they played a guessing game called Ups for a gallon of beer, and there was music, singing and stepdancing in the evenings when Lewis was a boy.[6] His parents were not musicians, but his eldest brother, Trayt, was 'a bloody knockout; he could play any instrument' [DN], including the cornet, though he was primarily a concertina-player and stepdancer.[7] He was a young man when Lewis was a boy and Lewis looked up to him and paid great attention to his music. Their maternal uncle, Tom Shoebridge, a shoemaker in Nutley, was much older, having been born around 1829; he played a tambourine about two feet across with three tuned bells strung on a wire on the inside, and was so skilled 'he could knock hell out of the tambourine' [RH] and at the same time sound whichever bell he chose.[8]

Trayt learnt the concertina, probably during his teens around 1890, from a local lad five years older than himself, Joe Marten (1870-1959), the son of a small-holder at Chelwood Gate. Joe's son, Will Marten, recalled:

Scan Tester as a teenager; undated.
(Courtesy Daisy & Arch Sherlock)

When grandfather was alive I think Dad used to be the general dogsbody ... He was the youngest one of the family. As a matter of fact he was lame; he damaged his foot as a child, so he didn't really go out a lot. I think he stayed at home and looked after the pigs, cows and everything.

Joe was a practical man, good with his hands, and he set himself up in 1895 as a cycle dealer and repairman. He cut hair, run the slate club in the *Red Lion*, and drove a wagonette – 'take people to the station'.[9] According to Bert Wood, he was a good blacksmith as well. He married at the age of 40 in 1910 or 1911, and his sister-in-law, Fanny Lander, remembers that before she left the area in 1914 he seldom went out, but played music at home. Mary Elphick, Joe Marten's daughter, confirms this: 'When we were kids Dad used to get his concertina out. He used to keep on and on, going on, all the same tunes ... oh yes he was quite good.'

Will Marten: He used to play some of the old dance tunes, I'll tell you one - *Rustic Bridge*. *The Old Rustic Bridge* he used to play, but he used to keep on and on and on.

Besides the concertina, he could get a tune out of the melodeon, fiddle, whistle pipe and band fife, and he remained a friend of the Testers until his death.

On paying-out night of the *Green Man* Slate Club, Sally Tester put on steak and Christmas puddings for the tontine dinner in the bar and Lewis was kept up late to stepdance on the table.[10] By the age of eight he could play the tambourine like his uncle Tom and was proficient enough to go out to other pubs playing with Tom and Trayt. On one occasion they were piling out of the cart when someone, amused that Lewis was man enough to play music but too small to jump down off the tail unaided, gave him a hand and shouted out, 'Come here, you little scantiloper!' The name 'Scan' stuck for life.[11]

There were lots of melodeon players round about; melodeons could be bought for as little as four shillings, and Scan managed to get hold of one. The first tune he remembered trying was *The Sailor Cut Down in his Prime*, and with his one and only dance tune, *Soldier's Joy*, he went out busking at Christmastime with his younger brother, Will, on the tambourine.[12] Scan used to borrow Trayt's concertina when he was at work, and using his melodeon fingering, he was able to play a few tunes on one side of the concertina. After he had impressed everyone in the bar of the *Green Man*, his father saw the promise in him and bought him a concertina pitched the same as Trayt's.

17

MUSIC ON ASHDOWN FOREST

Although the family was now settled in Horsted Keynes, Trayt used to take Scan up to the pubs on Ashdown Forest when he was still very young. The *Foresters* at Fairwarp and the *William IV* at Nutley were cottage-sized beer-houses.[13] The *Foresters* was a rough pub; locals used to say that if there was a fight in the bar, instead of throwing everybody out, the landlord, William Osbourne, used to lock the door to keep them all in![14] They didn't take too kindly to strangers in Fairwarp and, in particular, they did not like young men from other villages taking an interest in their young women. From a Chelwood Gate perspective, 'there was always a feeling about Nutley, and Fairwarp was rougher still.[15] 'They'd look at you if you went over Fairwarp as much to say, "What the hell you want over here?" ... They used to go from here of a Sunday night for a pint of beer and punch up.'[16] Even into the 1930s the Danehill lads had to muster four or five strong to venture to a dance in Chelwood. Trayt, and later Scan, however, had credibility all round the area.

Fairwarp was a great area for fiddlers; some were old men when Scan was a boy and some he heard then were around eighty years old. Scan realised at the time that their music and dancing was not only very exciting, but reached back into the past. They were keen stepdancers, and this was where Scan picked up most of his stepdance tunes.

Scan: They used to know any amount of them, these old blokes did, and they was all fiddlers, you know. Nearly all of them was fiddlers. It wouldn't be nothing to see four or five fiddlers in a pub playing together. You never see a concertina; you might see a melodeon or something of that. I used to like to hear these old blokes up there; you know, they were blooming marvellous. There used to be one or two elderly blokes - jolly good! A lot of people didn't think much to them, but I knew ... they were blooming good! [RH]

William Walter (1851-1927) from Browns Brook was a Fairwarp fiddler from before Scan's time. He moved away in about 1880 to work as a carter on the Holbrook Estate, Cross-in-Hand, where he continued as an active musician.[17] Scan might well have come across him if he returned home to see friends and relatives. Browns Brook is a cluster of crofters' cottages on the forest a mile or so north of Fairwarp. Charlie Ridley, living there now, says 'everybody round about played something or other.' His father, Herman, was the leader of Ashdown Forest Temperance Band. Christopher Stephens, whose grandfather lived at Browns Brook, says that in recent years, as the old folk have died, piccolos and flutes have been found among their effects. His mother, Mabel (1895-1957), played the violin from music and his father, Nelson, played the cornet in the Temperance Band.[18]

Fairwarp fiddlers:
William Walter (left), whose death was reported in the Sussex Express, *25 February 1927, and Scan Tester, 26 May 1958.*

At Oldlands, just down the track towards Fairwarp, there was a family of fiddlers a few years older than Scan.

> **Scan:** There used to be a family at Fairwarp name of Gorringe, and one of them was blind. He was using a gun one day when the damn thing bursted - blinded him. He was a fiddler. He'd got two brothers played fiddle. This blind bloke, he was a good fiddler – weren't no mistake - and if I went into a pub anywhere he was, soon as ever he heard me speak, he'd say 'Hello, Scan, how you getting on?' He was always in a pub. Well, you know, they used to have a collection round for him then. [DN]

Blind Charlie (1875-1955) had actually stood in the way of a stray shot over a hedge when he was 16. With no question of compensation, he remained single, earning his living making mats and baskets. He played the melodeon as well as the fiddle, and several mandolins were found in his cottage after his death. Charlie's brother, Edward, played in the Ashdown Forest Temperance Band and another brother, Bill, was Scan's regular partner on the fiddle for many years before the Great War.[19]

> **Scan:** You know, in the pubs on a Saturday night they used to step for a gallon - a gallon of beer.[20] Three or four steps - you didn't want no more beer for the roomful. They used to come in just as they left off work, after they'd had a bit of tea and they'd all got hobnailed boots, nailed and pelted, and it was all brick floors! You could hear them! Yes, it was a good bit of sport. [DN]

Charlie Gorringe, fiddler, and his mother at Oldlands, Fairwarp; undated. The cottage had earth floors in two of its three rooms.
Right: detail.
(Courtesy Frank & Jean Gorringe)

It was worth watching. It was better than some what you'd pay to go and see to see these old blokes. 'Cause, you know, if you get a man between sixty and seventy, it makes you think when you're young yourself. It used to make me think when I was a young chap ... If the old ones do it, well, it's interesting to the young ones, I think. It used to be to me. They was jolly good, some of them old people, but you never see it now.[21] [R&DS]

The *Nutley Inn*, now known as the *Shelley Arms*, was another Ashdown Forest haunt frequented by Trayt and Scan; it attracted some of the same musicians and customers, but it was a quite different kind of pub.[22] It was an early-Georgian coaching inn, with large, high-ceilinged rooms and presumably a passing trade of travellers and boarders. James Cordeux, landlord from 1894 to August 1900, was a connecting link, as he had previously held the tenancy of the *Foresters* in Fairwarp in 1882.

HOPPING DOWN IN KENT

Hops for the brewing trade were widely grown in Kent and Sussex. Harvesting depended largely on female and child labour, with a few men pulling the poles, cutting the bines and collecting the full bins. Hop farmers employed the same seasonal workers year after year, providing transport and fairly primitive communal living quarters. Many families depended on the additional income, but hopping was seen as a holiday, and for Londoners from the East End and the south east it was a blessed relief from the stresses of slum life. The season began on 1 September and continued for three or four weeks.[23]

> **Scan:** I used to do a lot of stepdancing one time, and, course, when I was single we always used to go up the hop country there every year, and, course, we used to get our living, you see, for playing our musics and, ah, I've stepped against dozens of gypsies up the hop country ... My eldest brother was a jolly good stepdancer too. [AW]

> My eldest brother and me, we used to take our concertinas and go up the hop country, and we used to go in the pub with our concertinas of a night, and go

Hop-picking at Cranbrook, Kent; undated.

hop-picking during the day. Never used to draw no picking money, not before we came home. We used to earn our living in the pubs. We never picked up our hop-picking money until the forenoon of the day we were away. Oh, we had several pounds to bring home. Oh yes, that wasn't no bother at all. We used to go to a little place called Iden Green, and it was close to Benenden [near Cranbrook, Kent]. About a mile from there is a little place called the *Oak*. We used to go up there. They'd got a nice sized room and the landlord wanted us to go there of a Saturday night. The weekend we used to get the place full up with hoppers. My brother was a stepdancer and all and we would take turns. One would dance and the other would play. I've had some happy times up there. Yes, the *Oak*. We used to go there across the fields, well, footpaths. Ten minutes or quarter of an hour's walk. We usually used to go there every Saturday night whilst we were up there. [VS]

We used to sometimes have a month; mostly it was between three weeks and a month. It all depends how the hops were. You see, if they had cogates hops, well, they were small, but ordinary hops, as long as your finger, it didn't take you long to pick a bushel, but you had to pick six bushels for a shilling. We used to sit on the edge of the bins — one sit there facing me and I used to sit facing

him. We used to have the old bin there and all you had to do was snatch them off and let them fall in. You'd be surprised how quick we got a lot. Of course, we was used to it, you see, but, you know, little kiddies, they used to give them an umbrella and you'd be surprised how quick they'd get that full up. [VS]

You used to have three different lots; one farm was for Londoners, and another was for home-dwellers, and another for all round Sussex. But my brother, he used to pull poles for the home-dwellers always, so, of course, we used to stick in their set, and they used to pay him a guinea a week for pole-pullers, so he always had his money coming in. I used to have half a bin and then I used to help him pick his hops [hop poles?] up, because you had to pick them up clean, and then every chance he got he used to slip and help me pick in the bin, and then we used to share the money. Of course, he had his guinea; that was standing money; that kept us well away, that guinea did, both of us. [VS]

Yes, you could buy a pound of cake, currant cake, for fourpence. Of course, I was young, and, well, I lived on cake nearly. And some of the ladies, they come from round our country, round Nutley and Chelwood Common, so we never had any bother to get anything

21

cooked. We used to have a roly-poly suet pudding of a Sunday, and a pound and a quarter of beef steak each, fried, then we used to put the pudding in this gravy, mix it all together. Lovely! You couldn't get a better meal. We used to get potatoes. We used to go out in the potato fields and dig them up of a night. We'd always have plenty of potatoes. [VS]

They had huts, you know. I used to have a straw bed. They used to put some faggots down, and then put a thick layer of straw on top of it. Oh, you could sleep all right. [VS]

You see, all the people that went hop-picking then, they were used to it... Cor, you could see them sit there on the corner of the bin, and the old hops rolling over in. Some of them could pick hops you know! They could get a half bin whilst I was looking at it. And we used to do pretty well, because we went up there when we were pretty young. But it was more like a holiday, A lot of people went there for their holidays. There was no work attached to it; you was sitting down all day on the bin. This was years ago, before I was married. I was quite a young bloke then. Ah, that was the time to enjoy yourself! [VS]

SCAN'S BROTHERS, TRAYTON AND WILL

Trayt, according to Scan, was a minor black sheep in the family, a bit of a tearaway, who 'never worked'. Nevertheless he was their mother's favourite, always welcomed home after his wanderings. The sight of Lewes Prison once prompted Scan to comment to me, 'My brother did six months in there for assault', but he knew nothing more than that.

Their mother had taken a lad, Ted Fox, into the family, and he eventually worked his passage to Canada where, according to Daisy, he set up a mink farm, 'had the first combine harvester over there ... and became a millionaire'.[24] The *Sussex Express*, throughout 1910 and probably over a longer period, ran weekly display advertisements promoting Canada, backed by newsletters from an anonymous Canadian farmer. Advertising copy such as '160 acres Government land free for farming' and 'Canadian wheat realised this year 60/- an acre for an expenditure of 30/-' must have been very tempting.

Trayt seems to have faded out of Scan's music circle well before the Great War, and at some time he worked his way to Canada to join his foster-brother. He came home several times, and Daisy can just remember his occasional visits to her home. He was living at Burghurst Cottages, Horsted Keynes, in 1924, but had either died or moved on by 1925.

Bandsman W. Tester, Royal West Kent Regt.;
studio portrait, Malta, c. 1906-7
(Courtesy Paul Marten)

Opposite: Will Tester, photographed by
Daddy Francis of Nutley; c. 1908-15.
(Courtesy Daisy & Arch Sherlock)

Scan: Well, I suppose he was, I expect, sixty-odd when he died. He was like Will, his breath went ... He never played a lot a part of the time. See, he wasn't fit for playing and he never used to get about much latter part of the time.[25] [RH]

Will, baptised Willie and nicknamed Darky, came up close behind Scan, having been born a year later in Maresfield. He went through the same experiences, delivering fish and making bricks, and he heard the same music in the *Green Man* and at Nutley. Daisy thinks he probably went hop-picking with Scan and Trayt, but his daughters think perhaps his stories of the hop-fields were secondhand. As he was neither a cricketer nor a footballer it is unlikely he took part in the music-making associated with those activities. He worked as a baker in Maresfield until October 1905, when he went across to Maidstone and enlisted in the Royal West Kents, in which he served as a bandsman. After ten months in Malta, he bought himself out for £18 in April 1907 and returned home to marry May Baker in November 1907.[26] Having been 'tutored by the picked solo man of the world' [RH], he was a trained military band clarinettist with a year-and-a-half's experience, as well as being an ear-player on the concertina, melodeon and tambourine. Scan had a particular soft spot for him, and said many a time, 'My brother was a better concertina player than I was.'[27]

THE BOER WAR

Scan: I knew the blokes who went to the War. There was no conscription then; they were volunteers. Well, there was several of them volunteered to go. They wasn't called up like these others; they went on their own accord... I don't think there was anybody went from here what didn't come back. It wasn't like these other wars.[28] [RH]

When word went round that Sugar Woolgar was coming back from the Boer War, 'the whole village turned out'. He arrived at Horsted Keynes station drunk, and was pulled the mile or so into the village on a cart, with Scan heading the procession, playing all the way on the concertina. Later, three or four other Boer War 'heroes' received the same treatment. On the face of it this might have been more appropriately a job for Horsted Band than for a fourteen-year-old boy. At about this time, Scan played the side-drum and cornet by ear in the Horsted Band (see chapter 7).

Scan: I can remember this blacksmith bloke ... what helped start the band [Horsted Band]. When that [Ladysmith] was relieved, they set the blacksmith's anvils off. Well, they brought them outside this blacksmith's out here, and, course, we was boys. We run for our life, when he set them off. Cor, there was crowds of people out on the green. They knew what he was going to do, and he got both anvils out there and set them both off. I don't know how he done it but, I tell you, she was a tidy rattle, and they did that at lots of places.[29] [RH]

Well, I used to play with a chap; he was a mandolin player. He was a good musician, and he knew music well. He used to play and vamp along with us at Nutley. His name was Jack [Carr]. Anyway, he was in Ladysmith. You know, they surrounded Ladysmith, didn't they? Well, he was one of them in there, and he'd never say much about it, but I have heard him tell blokes a little sometimes, when they've asked him. [RH]

THE FIDDLE AND GYPSY MUSICIANS

Somewhere around 1904 - 1905 Scan decided to take up the fiddle. He said it came naturally to him, having played with so many fiddlers for so long, and two sessions in the woodshed were enough for him to get the hang of it.

> **Scan:** One night I went out in the woodlodge, took my fiddle out there, and they said, 'Where are you going, then?' I says, 'Going out playing!' They says, 'You can't play that damned thing!' I said, 'I'll bet you a shilling I can 'fore I come in.' Course, I'd been used to playing with a fiddle, you see, with my concertina. I knew just where to string up and all, and how to string up. I went out in the old woodshed by myself, and I played a tune or two afore I come in. It was rather rough music, but I got the tune out. I thought to myself, 'I know where the fingering is'. [I was] about eighteen, I should think. Seventeen or eighteen. I could use my fingers then. I could use my fingers very well fiddling, 'til, you know, my hands come bad. [RH]

Balanced against this claim that he was self-taught is the fact that he and Bill Gorringe separately told Mervyn Plunkett that Bill had taught him to play the fiddle. Had Bill formally passed on a complete method of bowing and dressing a tune, Scan might have been expected to have said as much, if only as an aside.[30] Late in life Scan could still play enough on the fiddle to show he had had an animated, dynamic style, characterised by a developed bowing technique. Since Trayt was a 'bloody knockout' on any instrument, he may well have played the fiddle; certainly two of Scan's other regular associates, Denner Head and Joe Marten, were fiddlers. Scan probably did not play the fiddle very much after the 1930s, and by the mid-1950s he could only manage to play for a minute or two. Rheumatism caused him creasing pain and equally severe frustration; his fingers went down accurately on the strings, but he was unable to get them up again.

> **Scan:** You see, my hands come bad years ago. You see, my fingers when I held them up all went numb. Used to be the marks of the strings in my fingers here, and I played hours like that till I got, you know, regular fed up with it and made my hands ache so that I got fed up with it. That's why I left off and I thought, perhaps, my hands would get better, but they didn't. Matter of fact they gradually got worse, 'cause I couldn't get my fingers down, you see. I can get them down now, but I can't get no pressure on them. But I often wished, you know, that I could have played. I'd just like to have played now, especially as being out round with first one then the other. I could have had a tune then. [RH]

Scan also played the mandolin, using the same tuning and fingering as the fiddle. The mandolin had some local popularity but Scan was not particularly taken with it.

Gypsies in the south of England; postcard post-marked 1906.

The Smith brothers at the Men's Club, Edenbridge, Kent; 17 February 1968.
(Photograph: David Nuttall)

Scan remembered the gypsies camped on Ashdown Forest as being poor; very few had caravans - just tents or bits of cloth hung over sticks - and many relied on music to supplement their income.

> **Scan:** That was nothing to see a gypsy kid come round the streets with a mouth-organ and tambourine.[31] You want to hear some of these gypsies on that. They practically used to rattle a tune more like I do, only they got this stick. You know, it don't half sound when you get a stick. You see, you got nothing to muffle it. With your hand you have, but with these sticks you ain't. [RH]

> **Fanny Lander:** We used to have lots of caravans round here one time ... By the *Red Lion* [at Chelwood Gate] on the right-hand side there used to be a patch called Gypsies' Corner ... Some of 'em used to move, but some of them used to be stationary up there ... Harris was one of them, and there used to be Leech. He used to go round the fairs ... selling winkles and cockles.

> **Bert Wood:** If they lost a kid, they'd bury 'em, and that was a sacred place for them.

> **Charlie Bates:** There was one up side where old Deegs used to have a nursery up Chelwood Gate. Well, there used to be a regular place up there where they used to stop, and they reckon ... they burnt the caravan and her in there, 'cause for years you could always see flowers there ... before my time, but they always said when a gypsy died they burnt the caravan and them in it ... Well, it was a gypsy law, wasn't it?

The fiddle was relatively common amongst the Ashdown gypsies and, if two or three of them got together, they would usually play *Brighton Camp* in unison in the key of G, the standard fiddle key for that tune; but if there were four or five, one might play the tune exactly the same, note for note, but in the key of C. The fingering is the same, but transposed one string below, and some of them by double-stopping could play in G and C at the same time. Late in life Scan was still able to play *Brighton Camp* accurately in this manner.

> **Scan:** You finger on two strings and, you know, that was a rare thing for the old gypsies to play ... You know, I've heard some of them gypsies damned good fiddlers. I've heard some of them play dance tunes, you know, but the majority of them used come round, they got three or four tunes they'd play and you never

hear them play nothing else. But *Brighton Camp*, well, that was the main tune, and they used to have their old finger right across on the other strings - two strings - and, course, you know, if anybody gets a clear tone, it's alright, ain' it? .... Course, I tell you, you got to shift your fingers over further. It's easy. Well, ... one night, I suppose, I just tried it. I found out I could do that easy enough. I used very often to get in a pub anywhere where there used to be laughing and talking and I used to play like that. I could play like that alright, but, course you see, if you was going to play a schottische or something like that, you'd find out that was a bit awkward, 'cause you got to shift your fingers quicker, ain' you? [RH]

One time of day before the 1914 War you very often see gypsies about with a fiddle or mouth-organ or mouth-organ and tambourine, and these fiddlers – I bet nine out of ten of them played *The Girl I Left Behind Me* like that.[32] Just that one; they didn't play no other tunes. They nearly always played a mouth-organ and tambourine or else a fiddle. That was pretty near all the two instruments ever I hear them. They was no good with a concertina or anything, you know. [RH]

If they come in anywhere and I was in [there], and they see me, they didn't want no telling who I was, you know. They knew! They wouldn't stop there long. They had a drink and stop there and hear me play a tune or so, and they very soon gone, 'cause they want get in another pub, somewhere where they can go round with the hat. They knew that wasn't going to work in where I was, you see! Course, I never bothered whether they went round for me or whether they didn't. I didn't play for that - not like that - but you know that's what they played for. They was always out for that. Course, if they was in a pub all the evening, they'd go round two or three times if they could. But I didn't want them to do that [for me]. [RH]

You see, many a time I put it in the blind box or something like that, and I've told the landlord, 'I want you to see where I put this money. This is the collection what they've had for me, and I want to put it in that box.' And he's give it out - told them. Well, they don't mind giving anything so much like that, but if they think you're scrounging, they wouldn't give nothing, and it was only pennies when they did give anything. I mean to say, 'taint like it was going to break anybody, was it? But a penny was a penny that time of day. [RH]

Without doubt Scan did busk in pubs, but much of the time his playing was for fun, and he and the people in the pubs had an unspoken understanding of where they stood. He would certainly have been embarrassed if his intentions were misunderstood and the code were broken. His point about the blind box refers probably to a much later date than 'before the 1914 War'.

Scan told the story of how he once paused outside a pub listening to the music, before deciding to venture in. The tambourine playing really took his fancy; it was strong and lively, carefully phrased and precise - everything Scan expected of a good musician. Wondering who it could be, he opened the door and found a woman and her two daughters playing in perfect unison! They were not people he knew, so they were either travellers or hoppers, or he was in strange territory himself. While the quality of the music stuck in his mind, the fact that they were women was equally remarkable. In one taped conversation about the old music he confirmed that, indeed, there used to be 'some women fiddlers'.[33] [RH]

GETTING ABOUT, CRICKET AND EARNING A LIVING

Scan, quite understandably, was sometimes hazy on dates, and he would try to pin them down with reference to important events such as the Boer War, the Great War or the date of his marriage. Trying to work out the time span of his regular commitments is particularly difficult, as they sometimes seem to overlap with each other. He was playing the tambourine with Trayt at the age of eight, in 1895, and he always gave the impression he was out pubbing when quite a young lad. He had left school and was earning his living at ten or eleven, and in those days there was no age restriction on frequenting pubs.

Apart from going to Brighton for his father's fish business and the annual trip to the Kent hop-fields, he confined his activities very largely to the villages and hamlets on the western side of Ashdown Forest, very often walking and later using a bike. He would go anywhere he thought there would be music and good company, travelling light and often sleeping out under a hedge. A trick he picked up from some of his gypsy pals on the Forest was put to regular use if he was late leaving a pub or a party; he would lie on the ground curled up inside his overcoat with none of his body exposed, then blow warm air inside the coat. It seems unlikely, but he always said that even when the coat was frozen stiff in the morning, he had remained warm and had slept well ready for work. If he felt no ill-effects at the time, he certainly paid for it with rheumatism later in life.

Scan's first job outside the family was for one of the big houses on the Forest, while he was lodging at Agnes Cross with his sister, Harriet, and her husband, Arch Blayber. Arch was the gamekeeper at Brook House for the Clarke family, who had made their fortune as coal factors. The sons were all cricket fanatics and Arch also acted as cricket coach. As Arch Sherlock said, 'That time of day they used to have to find a job for the good cricketers.'

Scan was taken on as an assistant groundsman, preparing the cricket pitch for the 'young gentlemen' who came to stay. The mid-week matches, with brass band in attendance, were for the toffs, but, if numbers were short, members of the ground staff were expected to complete the team. It was in this way that Scan played cricket regularly with a young Harold Macmillan. Around this time Scan earned a small supplementary income umpiring matches and repairing the ground for Fairwarp Cricket Club. Wicket keeping was hard on his hands, and it is debatable which contributed most to his pained hands later in life, rheumatism or cricket injuries. A cricketball smashed his cheek-bone in the late 1920s and he never went back to the game.

Above: Scan the cricketer; undated.

(Courtesy Daisy & Arch Sherlock)

Below: Extracts from Fairwarp Cricket Club accounts book. Scan earned 1s. 6d. for each match he umpired.

(Courtesy Frank & Jean Gorringe)

NUTLEY v. HORSTED KEYNES.

Played at Nutley on Saturday, re...ing in a win for the visitors. The game wa... in connection with the District League and the points were easily captured by Horsted Keynes.

NUTLEY.

First Innings.

A. Turner, c Frost, b F. Carr	0
E. Gillham, c Tester, b F. Carr	0
W. Tester, b W. Wilkins	12
T. Diplock, c Tester, b F. Carr	18
W. Keen, c Hume, b W. Wickens	7
T. Lawson, b F. Carr	0
W. Biles, c Baker, b Wickens	8
F. Mitchell, b Wickens	0
F. Taylor, c Wheeler, b Wickens	2
J. Taylor, b F. Carr	0
F. K. Mitchell, not out	12
Extras	4
Total	63

Second Innings.

A. Turner, b Baker	9
E. Gillham, c Foster, b Carr	6
W. Tester, c and b Carr	15
T. Diplock, c Lavender, b Carr	11
W. Keen, not out	9
F. Mitchell, b Tester	8
F. Taylor, c L. Tester, b Tester	1
J. Taylor, not out	0
F. K. Mitchell, b Baker	3
Extras	2
Total (for seven wickets)	61

HORSTED KEYNES.

R. Baker, b Biles	3
E. Newnham, b Biles	47
F. Tester, c Gillham, b Biles	9
F. Lavender, c Biles, b Keen	8
R. Green, c Tester, b Keen	2
F. Carr, not out	29
— Hume, b F. K. Mitchell	1
R. Foster, c Mitchell, b F. K. Mitchell	0
W. Wickens, b F. K. Mitchell	0
L. Tester, c Diplock, b Tester	6
— Wheeler, c Diplock, b F. Mitchell	1
Extras	10
Total	116

Above: Sussex Express, *16 July 1914.*

Sometimes Scan supplemented his living by wood-cutting and collecting bush faggots (the trimmings from stakes and poles) for firing in the brick-kilns, and in the summertime he cut litter on the Forest. They 'used to have waggon loads and waggon loads used to come off the forest. Men was up there days and days cutting bracken and the heather.'[34] With no set hours and no employer, he was free to go off sometimes for a week or so basking with one of his cricketing mates, Dennis - better known as Denner - Head. The two of them travelled around playing in pubs and sleeping in stables and lofts, presumably making as much, or more, busking as they would have done at their other activities.

Below: Fairwarp Cricket Club, winners of the Northern and Southern Cups, Nutley & District League, 1926.
Standing, left to right: Unidentified, Edward Gorringe, F. Gibbons, S. Walters, unidentified, J. Walters.
Sitting, left to right: A. Kenward, W. Weller, E. Marwich (capt.), W. Sutton (vice-capt.), W. Walters, Denner Head.
(Courtesy Audrey Castle & Peggy Head)

SCAN'S MUSIC PALS

Denner Head (1883-1969), originally from Collingford Farm, Danehill, lived for most of his life in Back Lane, Fairwarp, working as a woodman on the Forest before going into the coal business. He had his own lorry after the Great War, which he made available to Fairwarp Cricket Club for away matches, and he and Scan sat at the back of the lorry, leading the sing-song with their 'musics' on the way home.[35] Nobody now is able to describe his style or repertoire, though Arch Sherlock described him as 'great' on the fiddle and Phil Lucas confirms that this was his local reputation. His daughters say he was an ear-player and also played the tambourine, and Charlie Ridley remembers seeing him with a one-string fiddle; in fact, Denner tried to teach him when he was a kid. Like so many of his contemporaries he enjoyed a good fight, and he could give a song, usually *Golden Slippers*, if called upon.[36] He was regarded as a character - but so were most of his contemporaries - and he frequented the *Crocodile* in Danehill.[37] In his early days he played regularly in the *Foresters* and later on, in the 1940s, he played in the *Star* at Piltdown, where his brother, William, was the landlord.[38]

An old musician whom Denner Head knew from childhood was Mrs Stephenson. She would have been born in the 1850s and lived until she was about 90. Her father kept the *Oak*, a beerhouse in Danehill. After she married Edwin Stephenson from Nutley,

they kept a smallholding, Little Collingford, opposite the Heads' place at Collingford Farm. Remembered now as a 'real old farmer', she was also an old-style tambourine player, and Rose Avis, whose family moved into Collingford Farm after the Heads left, remembers her about 1919 playing at family parties with her daughter, Alice, a self-taught piano and concertina player.[39]

The Awcock Brothers from Danehill were yet another musical family, taking their interest from their mother, Mary Sherlock (born 1839), whose family were involved in the music in chapel.[40] Amos Awcock sang bass, tenor and alto in chapel, and probably never sang inside a pub in his life, but he yodelled for his own amusement in the woods and had a reputation for eccentricity.

> **Charlie Bates:** Amos used to play the fiddle and yodel. Yeh, he yodelled as well. Oh, he was marvellous yodelling.
> **Bert Woods:** Well, they used to reckon he used to come out onto the road of a night with a sheet over his head acting as a ghost.

His brothers, however, were much more down-to-earth, musically speaking. Arthur (born 1872), a gamekeeper, Alfred (born 1876), a gardener, and Albert (born 1883), a carpenter and builder, were all fiddlers. It seems likely that Alfred and Arthur did not play out very much, but Albert Awcock and

---

Unidentified cricket team with concertina and banjo.

Photograph acquired by Paul Davis from Mr. Webber, '10 miles from East Grinstead going to Gatwick'.

(Courtesy Steve Chambers)

Denner Head were great pals and played together in the pubs. Albert's daughter, Margaret Lucas, confirms he held the fiddle down on his chest, always tapped his foot when he played and could not read music. Her memory of his repertoire is rather sketchy, but she remembers *Nelly Bligh, Stars and Stripes*, some of the old minstrel songs and *If I Were a Blackbird*, and a night scarcely went by without his playing the fiddle at home. He also played the tambourine, a small one less than a foot across, currently in his daughter's possession.

Scan's stories of other musicians, characters with such marvellous names as Fishy Mason, Dido Wickham and Trombone Billy, should be dated, in all probability, from about the turn of the century to sometime during the Great War. Scan was young and eager then, getting around as much as he could, learning not only tunes and techniques from other musicians, but how to fit in with them. If there was a time he experimented and took musical risks, this was probably it.

Melodeon players were plentiful enough. Jack Gurr, better known in Horsted Keynes for his singing, played in the *Crown* and very occasionally in the parish room at a wedding or special event, but most of his music making was at home with the family. 'Father played all the old dance tunes' - polkas, schottisches, the *Maxina* and the *Veleta* - according to his son, Bert (born 1907). Jack's wife, Emma, could handle a melodeon as well, but as far as Bert knows they did not keep musical company with Scan. In his teens, Bert Wood (born 1890) of Danehill had a melodeon with the added refinement of a vibrato device:

> I had one that you just twist on the side and then it quivered ... I can remember buying it ... I give five bob for it - new'un. Yeh, five bob off a bloke coming round ... I think he got several like, and he's going round trying to sell 'em ... Oh, everybody played 'em ... everybody had a music of some sort. There's a kiddy over here had a tambourine, and we used to go over Horsted and play in pubs.

Bert Wood also recalled a 'tall ginger haired bloke' who 'used to get up on a wagon and play' the melodeon at the fair on the *Coach* club feast day.

> **Scan:** There was lots of them, and I often wonder where all they old musics went to. There wasn't so many double rows; there was more single, but I used to have a small one, a double-row one with the

stoppers on. Well, I used to have a big one one time - the last one I had - and I had that after I played a concertina a long time, but I got fed up with the old melodeon. I sold that and kept to my concertina. [RH]

> There used to be a chap; he was a lot older than me. He could play a concertina on one side, and we used to call him Bogie, and his name was Woolgar, Harry Woolgar, but we used to call him Bogie Woolgar, and he used to have this old cheap concertina every night wherever he went. He come up on the Green; he used to have it up there. We used to sit up there and make him play. [RH]

Punch Browning, a bricklayer by trade, was another Horsted Keynes concertina player, contemporary with Bogie Woolgar. Scan associated an untitled polka[41] with the former and *Jenny Lind, Old Joe, the Boat is Going Over* and *Not For Joe* with the latter. Bogie Woolgar was living in Barcombe when Scan spoke of him in 1959.

> **Scan:** I used to know an old bloke at Lindfield. He was a painter bloke, and if he dropped out of work in wintertime, he used to come out round playing. Fishy Mason his name was, and he was a little, short bloke about my height, and he always used to wear [an] overcoat and cut the lining and drop his old fiddle and his bow down in there, 'stead of carrying a bag or anything, see. That's how I used to carry it. You wouldn't hurt the bridge. I used to carry mine miles like it. Always did. I used to have a green baize bag as well, but hardly ever I took it. Never used to put it in a bag; I used to stick her down in my coat. [RH]

> I used to carry my little concertina; I used to have a green baize bag hanging over my shoulder, then put my overcoat on. I used to go in pubs and anywhere; nobody knew that I got [my] music, but some of them got a bit wide-o. They used to come round and knock me around the back. They said, 'I thought you'd got her!' Very often if I went in anywhere I didn't want them to know that I'd got it, because very like I wasn't going to stop. I bet a shilling some of them twigged me.[42] [RH]

Up in the Forest at Three Chimneys, a pair of cottages at Twyford in the parish of Forest Row, there was a nest of musical activity. Next to Scan's sister Jinny there lived the Ridleys. Three of the family were ear-players on the mandolin: Joe, a bricklayer, and his daughter, Maggie (born 1900), shared a twelve-string instrument, and his son, Fred Gurr, played the more usual eight-string version.[43] Maggie had taken violin lessons after hours at Twyford school from her teacher, Miss Newnham, which helped her to some extent with the mandolin. Shortly before the Great War, a young builder's labourer came to lodge with them. He had spent his childhood in a home in Forest Row and after some time at sea returned a proficient reading musician on the trombone.[44]

> **Scan:** [Joe Ridley] used to play a mandolin with him first when I heard him. This chap used to play with him; he used to lodge with him, and he used to play a flat-backed mandolin... This mandolin player used to vamp. He was a jolly good player... Course I knew him well, because he lived next door to my eldest sister. [RH]

Trombone Billy, as he was known to everyone, taught his landlord, Joe Ridley, to play the trombone from music, and Joe and his two sons, Fred and George Gurr (euphonium and trombone respectively), joined Forest Row Band. On Sundays a cornet player from Nutley used to cycle over for a spot of practice, and it was on Sundays too that Scan used to visit his sister, Jinny Thompsett.

> **Scan:** So one day he [Trombone Billy] says to me, he says, 'You're coming down the Green Man Saturday night.' He says, 'Bring your music.' So I took my concertina in there and I played along with them, and, you know, it didn't matter what you played for that trombone bloke, you know, he come in along with you. If he didn't know the tune, he'd come in for bass or alto or something. Yes, he'd have a part, and you wouldn't know from what he knew the tune, you know, but he was learning the tune all the time he was playing. [RH]

In the years immediately before the Great War, Forest Row Band went out every Saturday night in the warm weather, playing outside each pub in Forest Row in turn, encouraged by jugs of beer sent out by the landlords. Sunday night was another matter, as they could not interfere with the church service, so they took the crowd up to the *Ashdown Forest Hotel* on the Forest. The supporters sang as they rambled through the woods to Trombone Billy's solo renderings of all the popular songs.

Forest Row Brass Band, c. 1910.

(Courtesy Eric Byford)

Scan: I believe that bloke could play with anybody. He could play in any key and, course, he was an orphan boy, and I don't know where he was brought up, but he was a grown-up man when I first knew him, you see. I was a young bloke then, and he used to go out in the pubs by his-self playing. Didn't matter where it was to him, 'cause he was a jolly good player, mind you, and it wasn't hoarse. It was good music. [RH]

Scan partnered Trombone Billy in pubs and busking on Brighton beach. Their repertoire on the beach was exclusively song tunes, but Scan insisted that Trombone Billy was fluent enough on his old 'push-me-off-the-pavement' to play solo for stepdancing. He was in the army during the War and never returned.

Scan: There used to be a chap lived down at Leighton Road [Horsted Keynes]; he was a harp player and a banjo player, and he sent to this firm, where we used to send, and he got this mouth-organ for me... He got one with four sides; four different keys there was, like. It was alright - very useful. I don't know what become of it, but, course, I had it a long time and, you know, you was always tearing about somewhere of a night, and used to play along the roads, you know. [RH]

Although Scan heard others 'vamp' on the mouth-organ - playing the melody with a chorded, percussive accompaniment - he could never get the hang of vamping. In spite of playing the mouth organ very often, he stuck simply to the melody line.

Scan: This chap used to play I don't know what sort of harp it was - one of these flat harps, you know, used to finger with it. He was a very good player, and he could play a banjo very well too. He used to sit out on the Green here in the summertime up to twelve o'clock of a night, sit there singing, and he used to play the old banjo. [RH]

According to Bert Gurr the only person in the village who sang with a banjo was Alf Alexander. Scan told David Nuttall that at some time while he lived next to Horsted Keynes post office, from 1923 or 1924 to 1953, the postman played the dulcimer. Daisy and Arch Sherlock have no memory of this, so perhaps Scan was talking about Alf Alexander; the dulcimer might have been an autoharp or zither.[45]

Scan: I never played with a flute, just the piccolo and the whistle-pipe. There used to be a chap at Forest Row, Bert Richardson his name was. He was quite a young fellow, he wasn't old. He was captain of the football club, and when I used to play football for Forest Row,[46] the older ones what used to come and watch the game, they knew me, you see, and they said to me, they said, 'Why don't you bring your music then, Scan, with you?' And old Bert Richardson says, 'You bring it. I'll bring my whistle pipe.' He says, 'We'll have a tune.' So when we used to go to the outmatches, he used to play his whistle-pipe. He could play very well, too, and I wondered then, I thought myself, 'Well, he must have had a whistle-pipe in C for to play along with that C music.' [RH]

Scan, too, played the tin whistle at this time. Forty years or more later, he had the urge to play one again, thinking he could entertain himself. He was quite disgusted that after several attempts, he was unable to make a respectable sound on it.

There was a number of fife and drum bands round about in Scan's early days, including the Church Lads Brigade in Horsted Keynes, a school band at Fletching at the turn of the century and an unidentified band reported at the Diamond Jubilee celebrations in Newick.[47] It seems reasonable to expect evidence to have come to light of men and boys who could play dance tunes or song airs on a band fife, but perhaps the discipline of the fife and drum bands and the motivation of the participants, like those of the village bands, produced bandsmen rather than musicians.

DIDO WICKHAM AND DANCING AT NUTLEY INN

Scan: A chap [used to play with me], a piccolo player from Nutley. His name was Henry Wickham; we used to call him Dido. He was a real curly-headed bloke, and he could bloody well drink some beer, too. That's one of his main things; that was the worst part of it. And what he told me was, when I asked him where he got his music from, he said, 'Well, I was coming home from work one night, I met a fellow on the road, and he stopped me and said he hadn't got no money. He said, *Would you buy a piccolo off me?* I didn't know what a piccolo was. I said to him, *I don't know. How much do you want for it? Well,* he says, *I want half a crown for it, but,* he says, *You can't buy one in a shop for two guineas like it.'* [RH]

So he says, 'Course, I didn't think of buying it at all, but I said, *Let's have a look at it – what it looks like.'* He says, 'When I had a look at it I thought to myself, *I don't know nothing about it, but damned if that en't some good stuff.* 'Twas all made

of ivory.' Well, he says, *'I'll give him half a crown and chance it,'* and he said 'I hadn't got a lot more money then. I brought the thing home and it laid about in the drawer a long time.' [RHJ]

And this bloke [Jack Carr], he understood music well, and he was in the pub one night and old Dido was in there having a drink, and they got on talking about music like, and old Dido was always a bloke fond of music and his brother was a good musician; course, his brother had been a brass band bandmaster. So old Dido told him, 'I bought a music off a bloke on the road a week or two ago. He said it was a piccolo!' They got on talking so much this bloke said to old Dido, 'Next time you come up here put it in your pocket. I can tell you if it's any good or not.' So old Dido told me, 'I carried that for over a week in my pocket, and he never come up there. The very night I left it at home, he was come up there.' So he says, 'You will see it now, 'cause I'll go and get it, and when he opened it, he said, *Cor blimey, man, that's all ivory.'* Old Dido

Nutley Inn, *photographed by Daddy Francis.*
(Courtesy Gordon Turner & Phil Lucas)

says, 'Ivory?' He says, 'It'd cost you pounds, man, to buy an instrument like that. That's a professional's instrument.' Old Dido said, 'I thought, *Well, bugger me, I could make a bit on that. I never once thought about learning to play it.'* [RH]

He says to him, he says, 'Look, if you like to take the trouble to come down to my place, I'll learn you how to play that in a fortnight, and I'll guarantee you that.' Old Dido said, 'That's how I done it. I went down his place every night and on Saturday and Sunday night for a fortnight and I could play several tunes, time I finished.' He got the [sheet] music out, and he learnt him the music and how to finger it and all. Then he never touched music afterwards, not till sometime after ever we finished playing together. His brother got a brass band up in Nutley, and old Dido joined it, and he had a bass instrument, and I never did know what become of his piccolo. [RH]

Until 1911 or 1912 there was one brass band, the Ashdown Forest Temperance Band, which covered Nutley and Fairwarp, with a practice hut midway between the two villages. On the evening of an amicable decision to split into separate bands for each village, the bandsmen formed up outside the band-hut, and, according to Charlie Gorringe, the two halves marched off playing in opposite directions. Charlie Wickham became the bandmaster of Nutley Band and Ernie Best of Fairwarp Band.

Scan: You know, we used to play regular in the *Nutley Inn*, what's called the *Shelley Arms* now. We used to play there regular every Saturday night and, you know, sometimes we had old Dido's brother [Charlie Wickham], who used to blow a cornet, and there used to be a chap come up there and used to vamp on the old piano...There used to be Jack Carr; he used to vamp and play mandolin. He was a good bloke, he'd played in a string band in the Army; and then we used to have old Tommy's sister [Martha Stephenson] used to play a concertina as well, and I used to play the old fiddle, and another bloke, name of Bill Gorringe, used to play the fiddle along with me. And old Tommy Stephenson's father used to play a tambourine, and his tambourine was as far across as ... two foot, I expect, and he used to rosin her up and he used to rrrrrrrrrhhh! Yes! [RH]

Some nights there'd only be old Dido and me ... Dido and me played there night after night of a Saturday night by ourselves, and I've known him sit there playing to keep the party there 'til I got there of a Saturday night, when I've been out [at] football several mile out and

Ashdown Forest Temperance Brass Band, c. 1908.
(Courtesy Norman Edwards)

Press reports of activities by the Nutley and Fairwarp bands after the split.

(Sussex Express, 18 January 1914; 19 February 1914; 2 October 1914 and 19 March 1914.)

NUTLEY.

BAND SUPPER.—The members of the Nutley Band were entertained to supper at the Coffee Hall last Wednesday by the generosity of Mr. P. P. Lascelles, of Nutley Court. The company numbering about 26 sat down at 7.30 to an excellent repast served by Mr. Tribe. Mr. Lascelles presided, and after ample justice had been done to the bounteous spread, submitted the loyal toast, which was duly honoured.—Bandmaster Mr. C. Wickham then proposed the toast of " Our Host," in terms appreciative of the kindness of Mr. Lascelles in providing so excellent an entertainment that evening.—Mr. F. T. Ridley seconded and the toast was accorded musical honours and the recipient suitably responded.—The Vicar (the Rev. C. Neil) who was present, was next toasted, on the proposition of Mr. E. Kenward, supported by Mr. Lascelles.—In reply, the rev. gentleman expressed his pleasure at being present, and said he hoped that the band would meet with every success. The remainder of the evening was spent mid smoke and song, when amongst those who amused the company were Mr. P. P. Lascelles, Mr. Wickham, Mr. E. Kenward, Mr. N. Stevens, Mr. R. Stevenson, Mr. A. Moore, Mr. S. Streeter, Mr. A. Wickham, and others.

SOCIAL.—Another delightful parochial party took place on Friday evening when some 300 were present in the schools. These gatherings are deservedly popular and are well organised by the entertainment committee, of which the Vicar (the Rev. C. Neil) is chairman. The programme consisted of musical items that included glees by the glee party consisting of Mr. Neil, Mrs. Biles, Miss Biles, Mrs. C. Wickham, Miss Lascelles, Miss Gibbs, Mr. O. Shoobridge, Mr. T. Shoobridge, Mr. H. Appleby, and Mr. C. W. Sargeant, songs by Mr. H. Appleby and Mr. F. Taylor, and selections by the Nutley Band Handbell Ringers, who also contributed a quartette. Refreshments were served during the evening.

(Owen and Tom Shoebridge were Scan's cousins.)

FAIRWARP.

THE BRASS BAND.—The Parish Magazine says the band now practices on Monday and Friday (with the permission of Mr. M...) at Oldlands Rifle Range Room. There are vacancies for four or five new members. Application should be made to the Bandmaster, Mr. Jennings, at the practice room.—Under the careful and patient teaching of the Bandmaster, ably supported by the Committee, the new Hon. Secretary, Mr. C Wood, and the Assistant Secretary, Mr. F. Norman, backed up by the regular attendance and hard work of the members, the band should soon become musically and financially most efficient. The subscribers are heartily thanked for their generous support and are invited to continue the same. The retiring Hon. Secretary, Frank Ridley, Nutley, deserves not only many thanks, but some tangible recognition for his devoted services on behalf of the band, from its commencement.—The balance sheet for 1913 shows receipts, £13 11s. 5½d., and the expenditure leaves a balance in hand of £13 8s. 11½d.

NUTLEY.

AGENT FOR THIS PAPER. — Mrs. C. Whitewood, Grocer and Draper.

BANDMASTER'S BENEFIT.—During the time in which he has acted in the capacity the master of the local band, Mr. C. Wickham has become increasingly popular with his fellow-instrumentalists, and his impending departure from the district is a source of much regret to them. They determined that he should not go away without some tangible evidence of their esteem, and accordingly on Friday and Saturday turned out in the evening, and played selections in various places, the resultant collections going to form a "benefit" for the Bandmaster. Mr. Wickham is leaving to go into business on his own account, and takes with him the good wishes not only of the bandsmen, but the inhabitants as well.

---

never got back soon. You see, old Dido would sit there playing dance tunes and that for them to dance right up 'til I come back. When I got back, they'd say, 'Look, where the bloody hell have you been?' Sweat was pouring off his forehead like peas dropping down. Cor, he could play, you know. [RH]

You'd see him - he's right down like this here playing - and I'm blowed if he couldn't play, weren't no doubt about it, seeing he was right above all of us. And didn't that used to rattle in that room - that didn't half rattle. [H&HG]

I've heard ever so many piccolo players, and I've heard some good ones in bands and that, but I've never heard nobody could beat old Dido not with what he knew. See, he played by ear. You know, I don't think that ever he learnt a lot about music, but old Jack Carr said, 'He would have never learnt, if I hadn't have persevered.' He said, 'I knocked it into him.'[48] [RH]

Every Saturday night they used to come from Brighton. Two or three different parties put up for the weekend, you see, purpose come up there for round dancing ... and they had every dance there was. We never used to play no sets there ... and, course, that was a very good turn, 'cause there used to be sometimes five or six of us playing together there, and I have known seven play together ... We used to have a tidy band there. It used to sound very nice... Course, we never had this every week, [but] very often that lot used to get in there. They used to come along with their musics and, course, we all used to know all the same tunes. We had a good time! [RH]

No matter what the weather was, I used to go. Walk - ten miles that is - both ways. Sometimes I used to take my fiddle and sometimes I used to take concertina; it all depends - we had a brother and sister used to play with us - two concertinas - well, you see, that was enough concertinas. [H&HG]

Dancing at *Nutley Inn* originally took place informally in one of the bars, presumably the tap room, but at some point there was a move into the large reception room at the back of the pub for more formal Saturday night dances.[49] There was a collection, so in all probability the musicians, rather than the land-lord, ran the evening.[50]

Dido and Scan appear to have been the core musicians, but there is no evidence of who led the band, though most, if not all, of the other musicians were older than Scan. Nor is there evidence of how they developed their repertoire and learnt the new Edwardian round dances.[51] Jack Carr (born c. 1872), who had been in a string band in the Army, and Charlie Wickham (born c. 1873), a member of Ashdown Forest Temperance Band and then bandmaster of Nutley Band, were both musically literate; Dido (born c. 1875) was taught musical notation by Jack Carr, although rejected it as soon as he got the hang of his instrument. Jack Carr was at the Siege of Ladysmith; the question is whether he taught Dido before or after the Boer War. Scan acknowledged he learnt tunes from Dido.[52]

Scan's use of the word 'vamp' implies the pianist played by ear, and the rest of the band almost certainly were ear-players. Scan stated quite specifically that they played everything in G, which is further evidence of their playing by ear. If any of their material came from sheet music or gramophone records and was not in G, it was transposed to accommodate the concertinas and fiddles. Neither Will nor Trayt, in spite of his earlier association with the *Nutley Inn*, seem to have been part of this band. Tommy Stephenson was the gardener for Lady Castle-Stewart at Old Lodge, Nutley, on the Crow-borough Road, and his sister Martha lived just beyond his house on the same road.

The *Nutley Inn* band at is full extent comprised:	
Scan Tester	fiddle or concertina
Bill Gorringe	fiddle
Dido Wickham	piccolo
Charlie Wickham	cornet
Tommy Stephenson	concertina
Martha Stephenson	concertina
unidentified	piano
Jack Carr	mandolin
--- Stephenson	tambourine

SERVANTS' BALL AT THE *COACH AND HORSES*

The end-of-season servants' ball at the *Coach and Horses*, an alehouse with a large upstairs reception room at Danehill, was an important event in the social calendar of the working people in the district. Mrs Lander, oldest inhabitant of Chelwood Gate (born 1896), then Fanny Smith, danced 'waltzes, two-step and *Veleta*, *Haste to the Wedding*, the *Quadrilles* and the *Lancers*' at the ball in 1911 or 1912.

> **Fanny Lander:** I was about fifteen then, and there was a big room and, course, it was all full; everybody was there, and Scan was playing, and Bill [Will] and I think somebody else, but I can't remember that ... I only went the once; both my sisters and I went. We were all good dancers in those days ... You really got something out of the dancing in those days.

> **Scan:** You know, I used to play at the *Coach* ball. I played there for over 20 year, and I used to play from seven to two, and we never reckoned to play one tune twice. Me and old Dido Wickham, the piccolo player, and Tommy Stephenson, a concertina player. Only I used to play fiddle with them, you see, ... before 1914. Ah, but I played after that as well. Made the twenty years up. [RH]

> You know what I used to get? I used to have to play there Boxing Night from six to ten, and then the ball was what we used to call the Second Christmas Holiday - night after Boxing Night. That was from seven to two, and I used to have to play them two nights for fifteen bob the two nights. And I used to get my drink and a supper half way through and a supper when I done, if I liked. But I used to play there Boxing Night myself, and Dido and Tommy used to play in *Nutley Inn*, you see, that night - Boxing Night; then they used to come and help me Ball Night. Well, then we used to share the two lots of money, you see, so we didn't do bad, because sometimes they'd collect round very near a pound over there - them two - collecting round the room, and I earned fifteen bob over there, you see, so it was pretty well thirty-five bob between the three of us, so we didn't do too bad! [RII]

Will Marten, landlord of the *Coach and Horses* for over fifty years from 1876 to 1927, was Joe Marten's brother, and it seems more than likely that Joe and Trayt played in the early days, and brought Scan in when he was about ten years old.[53] Thus, if he played from 1897 to 1916, he would have 'made the twenty years up'. It is unlikely that the three musicians mentioned by Scan played together consistently throughout the twenty-year period, or that Scan always played the same instrument. His account probably describes the last few years.

The last time he played with Dido Wickham was during the Great War, and Scan linked their parting with his own move to Horam Road in 1917 or soon after. He could not place when they stopped holding the balls. 'I think they did have a ball about once after I played there.' [RH] On another occasion, he said, he handed over to his brother Will and a melodeon player. Will spent Christmas 1918 in Maretz in Germany, but he could possibly have played the 1917 booking.[54] Social changes already in process before the War, but then accelerated by it, reduced the number of servants considerably by 1918, and so, perhaps, the ball died through lack of support. Mrs Lander confirms the *Coach* ball did not survive the War.

MARRIED LIFE AT CHELWOOD COMMON

At 22 Scan married Fanny Turner, whose sister Amy was his brother Bens wife. Scan's mother-in-law, Granny Turner, was a baker with a general grocery shop at Chelwood Common, and Scan had done a variety of jobs for her before he married, including relining the bread-oven with bricks, delivering bread and picking up her lodgers from Forest Row station with a pony and trap. Scan and Fanny's daughter, Daisy, was born on 18 October 1910 in what is now Rose Cottage, Horsted Keynes, and shortly afterwards the family moved into a rented place at Chelwood Common.

> **Scan:** Daisy's mum was a good dancer. Yes, she was a fine dancer, and we used to go out to a lot of dances then, 'cause, you see, I only used to go out to a pub of a Saturday night, see, then, and if there was a dance on in the week we used to go. Daisy's granny used to have Daisy, while we went out to a dance. [RH]

> **Will Marten and Mary Elphick:** All round Chelwood Gate was lots of small holdings. They had fruit gardens and they had cows, pigs, and we've had haymaking - and the old forest was used

for cows - but nearly everybody had an orchard and possibly a cow or so ... I don't think this was a very poverty-stricken area ... not really ... Nearly every place had the pig pens ... When we were kids we never felt very poor or very rich, put it that way, but some of those who were in tied houses and that were pretty grotty really.[55]

Scan always had a shilling or two in his pocket, but was never that well off, and in order to keep a family he took a job with a building firm in Crowborough, walking a round trip of ten miles or more each day for a halfpenny an hour more than he had been getting locally. Yet shortly before he married, he had seen an opportunity for a bargain - a neighbour's piano was being repossessed - and more or less on the spur of the moment he paid £12 cash for it![56]

SERVANTS' PARTIES ON ASHDOWN FOREST

For several years after their move to Chelwood Common, Scan provided Saturday night entertainment for the servants below-stairs in some of the large houses on Ashdown Forest estates.

> **Scan:** This was just before the 1914 War, because it was while I was living at Chelwood, and I was most times in the summer working over at Horsted station for my father. Why I went up there to live was cheaper rent, and that was my first wife's home there, you see. That was when she was alive, and then the War started and, course, it quietened down then and I never went to these places no more after the War.[57] [RH]

I think the man that first got me to go to play anywhere like that was at a place called Chelwood Vetchery, and he was a head gardener there, and I used to go up there in the winter time, all the winter.[58] He used to save my job all the summer, so as I could go to work in the brickyard, and I'd come back there in the winter, when there wasn't so much work in the brickyard. Well, the gentlemen that had the place built was Sir Stuart Samuels. I expect you might have heard of him - he was a big pot and, course, it was a fine place. So when I was up there, the old head gardener came in *Nutley Inn* one Saturday night, and he heard the music going - course, we used to play in a long room at the back - and he come down there, and stood listening to us and having a drink. Well, I didn't know; I never see him, and didn't know nothing about it. So one day when I was working up there, he come round and was stood talking, and he said, 'Would you play to a servants' party in the house here for me. They want to have a dance and they want to invite the girls from the other houses round about to make a party,' and I said 'Yes, I will anytime, if you let me know a day or so beforehand.' He said, 'Alright.' [RH]

So it was he that started this going round. He got this party up there. You see, them houses was two or three mile, well, two mile off the main road. You look where they got to go back to of a night, if they go out of their evening-out or their afternoon-out, and then come back of a night. It was all dark you know; there wasn't no lamps there. If they couldn't get the coachman or one of the grooms to come out and fetch 'em, they'd got to walk. So they decided they'd have a night like that, so they invited these servants there. Course, they told them what they was going to do, and it gradually got round. I got three or four places to go to, you see. So I very near always got one of them places in a fortnight to go to, and, you see, you always come across the same girls and that there, because they come from the other houses to that party. They used to invite one another. [RH]

Usually I used to have to get there ten o'clock at night, but the worst part of it was, it was always four or five o'clock in the morning before the devils left off. Well, you see, I hadn't got time to go to bed when I got home. Many time I've come home, changed my clothes, and laid on top of the bed and had hour's sleep before I got up, and had my breakfast, and go to work. Well, that ten bob was all extra, you see. I very near always had that ten bob once a fortnight, and sometimes every week. But I have earned as much as three pound a night, and I used to go to Press Ridge Warren - that's at Wych Cross - and another place called Twyford. That was an old gentleman's place; only, that's right out

of the way, two mile or two mile and half off the main road. And then I used to go to Chelwood Vetchery and Pippingford. A gentleman named Captain Banbury was there when I went there, and he was a nice gentleman ... [RH]

Of course, you had plenty of grub. All the grub was made by the servants, you see. It was the cooks' doings. They'd got to do that to keep the servants, if they got good servants, and the cooks used to work all the grub like that. I used to have a damn great parcel, man! Well I've had a damn great parcel I couldn't get my arm round it for to bring home. I used to bike round these places, you see, and I used always to have got a bit of string with me and straps on my carrier, so I could strap it on. [RH]

I always had to take slippers with me, because in the servants' halls, you know, they used to get that blasted floor up; if you'd got a pair of thin soles on, and if you hadn't got rubber soles, soon as ever you stepped on the floor you was across the other side. And, course, they girls used to work on them floors, you know. They was lovely floors for dancing. There were plenty times we never had to buy much grub, only just a piece of meat. We never had to buy no bread or tarts and cakes or anything like that, 'cause we always had enough to last all the week, and it didn't matter which place I went, I always got a parcel. [RH]

DANCE TEACHER AND PROMOTER

Scan: You see, early on, well as long ago as I can remember, they didn't have dancing like they do now, you see, every each other week. They had only two dances a year, see, one in the autumn and one in the spring, but, course, they used to have a dance at Christmas-time, and they used to have New Year longnights ... but in a village hall or anything they only used to have two. Well, they was half-a-crown a time that time of day. Yes, I paid half-a-crown at that time a day to go to a dance, and where two gentlemen weren't allowed to dance together. Well, you don't want nothing [i.e., an organised ticket dance]... if you're dancing every night all the week in pubs, but this was, you know, what you would call a posh dance, see. About twice a year. That included refreshments. Well, there was always one or two in a village that time of day would organise anything, get anything up. You see ... two or three of them get together. Well, they worked together and get this dance up, find out how much it cost for anybody to play. I never played to many posh dances. I have played to one or two.... [RH]

When I left off playing [at the *Nutley Inn*?], old Bill Gorringe said to me, he says, 'Well, we may as well stick together.' He come to Horsted Keynes to live, and I come to Horsted to live, you see, so he said, 'We may as well mate up together as usual.'[59] I says, 'I don't mind.' So we used to go together us two playing and, you know, round about there, several miles round, if they had a party, if we couldn't come there, I bet you sooner ... they put it off so we could come, so as they could have a dance. [RH]

This must have been in the three or four years preceding the Great War. Bill Gorringe moved from Oldlands, Fairwarp to Valley Holme, Horsted Keynes, where, Arch Sherlock thinks, he worked as a coachman, but by 1913 or 1914 he had moved to Whiteman's Green Dairy, Cuckfield, where he was to remain for the rest of his life. Daisy Sherlock remembers going over to Cuckfield with the family to have tea with the Gorringes and the Gorringes coming to Horsted Keynes for return visits. This would have been during the 1920s. Scan and Bill remained friends, but appear to have stopped playing together.[60]

Scan: There wasn't no bands; nobody at all went out to play in old dances. I used to hire two rooms - one at Horsted [the Assembly Room above the butcher's shop] and one at Chelwood Common, and it used to cost me half-a-crown a night the room and light. They used to find light; it was only paraffin lamps like, and [I used] to charge sixpence a night from seven to ten. That was three hours. That was tuppence hour. That wasn't bad was it? We used to get several in there. [RH]

What Scan did not say, on this occasion, was that the sixpence included an hour's tuition, for Scan taught the round dances and set dances, and then there was general dancing for the last two hours.

Scan: I said to old Bill Gorringe, I said, 'Well look Bill, if you want to mate up with me,' I says, 'You can come in along with me, if you like, with these dances.' 'Well,' he says, 'I'd like to.' So old Bill started coming with me like, and we used to play to these dances, and that's where we used to play that *Indian Polka* tune.[61] [RH]

The *Alberts* are a set dance like the *Quadrilles* or *Lancers*, only the figures, there's five figures in the sets, see. The figures are some out of the *Quadrilles* and some out of the *Lancers*. Well, I had three months twice a week with a chap [Bill Gorringe?]: I had a set one end of the room and he had another set down the other end of the room ... All the winter I played for them ... Sometimes two fiddles, and a piano sometimes. [MP]

Busking on Brighton beach; undated. The band consists of cello, two violins and cornet, with
perhaps a piccolo or violin standing between the two female musicians.
They are playing from memory or by ear.

BUSKING ON BRIGHTON BEACH

Scan's busking at Brighton with Trombone Billy and later with two legitimate, musically literate concertina players spanned the Great War and, although perhaps unknown to him, was in a time-honoured tradition. Buskers did well from Brighton's earliest days as a pleasure resort, their main pitch being the beach and the promenade above it. The quality of entertainment provided by solo musicians, bands, minstrel troupes, animal acts, etc., was generally high and the performers took themselves seriously and did their best.[62]

The Brighton scene was still flourishing at the beginning of this century and Tom Bridger and Charlie West had a regular pitch. A pound bought them a licence for a year, and they restricted their busking to afternoons during the summer season. One of them played on the *Skylark* and Tom Bridger used to clean the windows of Woolworth's in the mornings. Then at night they would split up and play in separate pubs. Scan had known them for years, through his association with the fish market, and just before the 1914 War he started going out with them on those Saturdays when the mood took him.

> **Scan:** You see, the blokes what I used to play with, of course, they knew music; they played off of concertina music to learn the tunes. Well, then I used to learn them off of them, 'cause there was three of us, and I used to follow them two along. Well, after I'd heard it once, like, I knew it that time of day. They was jolly good players. Tom Bridger and Fred [Charlie?] West. He brought up a family of ten playing on the beach. They never used to do nothing only play on the

beach and in the pub. They played Anglos, only they always played B flats. I don't know why. [DN]

Johnny Doughty (1903-85) worked in Brighton fish market as a boy and he told Bob Fry he remembered the buskers with the little chap in the trilby hat following along behind. In an interview with Vic Smith, he recalled:

> There was two of them. One used to sit up in the bows of the Skylark, if she was on the beach and they were helping them up aboard, and one was playing the fiddle and the other was playing the squeeze-box.[63]

Scan eventually bought a 40-key B flat Lachenal from one of them for £5 in order to play with them. His C/G music would not have gone with their B flat/F instruments, unless, of course, they had tunes written in C and G. So what did he do before he bought their concertina? Did he borrow one of theirs or did he play the fiddle, and if so, how did he string the fiddle up to play in tune with them? Scan was eager to learn as much as he could from this different class of music. As a lad he had tried to learn to read music in Horsted Keynes Band without success, and now his second attempt was no better: 'I carried it in my pocket, 'til it rotted away!' [DN]

Buskers are not likely to split their takings with extra members unless they make a difference to the total collection. Scan confirmed it was worth his while to go down by train specially for the busking, and he could still get back in time for any evening commitment. He stopped going out with Tom Bridger and Charlie West in 1919: 'I was a bloody fool to stop.' [DN]

NOTES

1. Horsted Keynes school records for the period are not at the school, nor are they in either East or West Sussex Records Offices.

2. David Nuttall has found references to the marriage of William Tester and Sarah Orpah Shoebridge, and the births of Jane, Harriet and Alfred in the St. Catherine's House index; and he has a copy of Trayton's birth certificate. Lewis and Willie are recorder in the Danehill Baptism Register, but the other children are not. I have been unable to trace the family in the 1871 and 1881 Census returns.

   The *Parliamentary Register* lists a Trayton Tester, clearly not the Trayton Tester from Browns Brook (see note 25), as living with Scan's father in Forest Row in 1889

and 1891, and then at Martin's Fields in Nutley in 1891 and 1892, and at Ashgrove in Horsted Keynes in 1893. The 1893 entry records that he had previously lived at Chelwood Common, Burgess Hill and The Green in Horsted Keynes. It seems very unlikely that Scan's brother could have registered to vote five years under age and without a property qualification. It appears, therefore, that there was another Trayton Tester in Scan's father's household.

3. Deese: a 'Place where herrings are dried' (Cooper, *Glossary of Provincialisms...* (1853)).

4. Other fish retailers in the district included the Sedords from Cinder Hill and the Gurrs in Horsted Keynes.

5. Bob Fry.

'Old Lewis's [Scan's] father was a clay digger up at Station Field, digging clay at 15/- a week.' (Mrs. Coon, 'Memories of My Village: Horsted Keynes' [1956], Danehill Parish Historical Society Magazine, II, 12, (Jan. 1986), p. 8.)

Trayton Tester's birth certificate describes Will Tester as a brickmaker and journeyman in 1875. (David Nuttall)

6. Other pub games recalled by Arch Sherlock, Bert Wood and Charlie Bates, included shove ha'penny, Ring the Bull, marbles (on Good Friday) and quoits at the *Crown*, shove ha'penny and rings at the *Coach*, dominoes (six tables), darts and rings at the *Crocodile*, Toad in the Hole and Ring the Bull at the *Red Lion*.

7. His playing the cornet raises the question of whether he had any musical training and any degree of musical literacy. Scan's cornet playing did not come from Trayton.

8. Compare this account with the Isaac Cruikshank etching, *Triumphal Entry of 100,000 Crowns* (London, 1791). This shows the Foot Guards band, which includes a tambourine two feet across with bells on the inside strut (National Army Museum, London, ref. 7507-28).

9. Charlie Bates.

10. Members paid in to a slate club weekly and drew out at Christmas. In cases of need, members could draw in advance.

11. Scan told several stories about how he got his nickname; this is the one he told me. In the early 1920s he was called Tinkie.

12. Scan told Steve Pennells his partner was Ernie Baxter, but he could not have been, as Ernie was 13 years younger than Scan. Will told the same story to his grandson Paul Marten, in which he himself was the tambourine player.

13. The *Foresters* later became an alehouse. It has now lost its original character by being modernised. The original *William IV* building is now a dwelling house standing beside the present pub, built in 1928.

14. Charlie Gorringe.

Pub landlords have played a crucial role in traditional music: since they control the venue, they have the means to encourage or suppress pub music. Below, and in subsequent notes, are listed the known landlords of the relevant pubs to show turnover or consistency of the tenancies and to help date events from oral sources.

Foresters: 1882 James Cordeux; 1883 John Page; 1887 Thomas Weller; 1888-97 missing; 1898 William Osbourne; 1929 Herbert Rapley; 1932 Thomas Puttock; 1938 Fred Leake.

William IV: 1878 or earlier Thomas Weller; 1889 Jane Weller; 1902-07 missing; 1908 Eli Carter; 1913 Frank Blackman; 1923 William Stock; 1928 rebuilt. (Uckfield Petty Sessions Register of Licences, East Sussex Record Office.)

15. Mary Elphick.

16. Will Marten.

17. He was recorded as aged 20 in the 1871 census return. However, his obituary (*Sussex Express*, 25.2.1927) records his age as 65, whereas he was probably 75.

18. Evidence from Mabel Tester's grandfather, Job, provides an insight into how the hamlet of Browns Brook was squatted: 'I live in a plot of land I took in 25 years ago. I have never been to court to take a grant, but I pay 1/6 a year to Lord de la Warr.' (W. Raper, Litigation, Earl de la Warr [v] Residents of Ashdown Forest 1878-9, Book 4, p. 157, East Sussex R.O., Acc. no. 1954). William Walter's father also gave evidence.

19. Charlie Gorringe (Blind Charlie's nephew).

The evidence of Blind Charlie's father, Charles Gorringe, establishes the Gorringe family at Oldlands by 1865 (Raper, Litigation, Book 4, p. 16).

20. In the *Coach and Horses* beer was served in jugs of various sizes, but was drunk from half-pint glasses. Customers could offer friends a drop from their jug. At the Crocodile customers would offer a newly-arrived friend their glass, 'to drink down to your thumb.' The offer was returned when the friend bought his beer (Bert Wood).

21. Billy Bennington (b. 1900), of Barford, Norfolk, recalled stepdancers in hobnailed boots dancing on brick floors and then making up 'a foursome'. (*The Barford Angel* (East Anglian Life, unnumbered LP; 1980s)).

22. *Nutley Inn* landlords: 1887 Thomas Crouch; Oct. 1890 Alfred Hobden; June 1894 James Cordeux; Aug. 1900 Richard Cox; April 1908 Lewis Walters; Nov. 1919 George Newman (Uckfield P.S.L.R.).

23. Compare the song, *Hopping down in Kent*, recorded by Mike Yates in the 1970s (Mary Ann Haynes, Topic 12TS395; Louise Fuller, Topic 12TS285).

24. Ted Fox may have been a relative on Sally Tester's side of the family. After the Second World War he turned up unannounced, offered Charlie Bates a week's work to drive him round the district, and wanted to take Scan back to Canada.

25. Details of Trayton's death remain a mystery, and I can find no record at St. Catherine's House between 1924 and 1930.

There was another Trayton Tester (born at Browns Brook, 1.6.1866) living in the same locality at the same time. He was the son of Job and Jane Tester, the father of Mabel and grandfather of Christopher Stephens.

Scan told David Nuttall he used to send concertinas to Trayt in Canada.

26. Will's personal Army papers, including discharge document, in the possession of his grandson, Paul Marten.

27. Bob Fry.

28. War dead: 33 in Horsted Keynes in 1914-18, six in 1939-1945, and 48 in Danehill in 1914-18.

29. Scan told me in the late 1960s he had recently seen anvils set off. Gunpowder and wadding were stuffed into the hole on the side of the anvil and fired by a lighted fuse.

30. Some country fiddle players in Ireland, contemporaries of Scan, were taught to play the fiddle rather than left to pick it up unaided. For example, Jamesy Gannon, a carpenter of Achonry, Ballymote, Co. Sligo,

wrote tunes in *abc* notation for his pupils, and taught bow strokes, grace notes and triplets. Scan's repertoire and that of Gannon's pupil, Michael Gorman, contained some common material, including *Haste to the Wedding, Keel Row*, the *Veleta* and *Jenny Lind*, and Gorman played for the schottische, the barndance and the *Lancers*.

31. The mouth organ and tambourine were held together in one hand. Compare the manner in which the pipe and tabor is held and played.

    In the mid-1970s Mike Yates recorded duets by Jasper and Levy Smith on the mouth-organ and drum, sounding like a tambourine: *Cock o' the North*, a composite of *The Campbells are Coming* and *Garryowen, Flowers of Edinburgh, The Wind that Shakes the Barley* and *The Girl I Left Behind Me* (*The Travelling Songster: An Anthology from Gipsy Singers* (Topic 12TS304)).

32. *Brighton Camp* and *The Girl I Left Behind Me* are alternative titles for the same tune.

33. Scan definitely meant fiddlers and not violinists. There is some conflict in the evidence whether women went into pubs or not, and if so, when. For a discussion of the topic, see Ginette Dunn, *The Fellowship of Song. Popular Singing Traditions in East Suffolk* (1980), Ch. 2.

34. Will Marten.

35. A 'music' is local vernacular for any musical instrument.

36. 'There was always a fight outside a pub' (Bert Wood).

37. Landlords of the *Crocodile*, a beerhouse: opened 1899, Henry May from Horsted Keynes; 1935-41 Norman May (Uckfield P.S.L.R.).

    Bert Wood and Charlie Bates never heard music there and Scan never played there. The pub was held for 42 years by the same family, who determined it was a no-music house.

38. Mrs. H.C. Hardy fêted 300-400 children at Danehill to celebrate the Diamond Jubilee. 'Children's games and sports were generally indulged in. Among these was climbing the pole for a monster leg of mutton. The trophy was carried off by Willie Dier, Frank Baker and Denis Head being second and third.' (*Sussex Express*, 22.6.1897).

39. Mrs. Stephenson's son married Denner Head's sister, Mabel, and their daughter, Cicely, played the piano and piano-accordion in a pub, after she moved away from the district.

40. Raymond Leppard, internationally-famed composer, conductor and musician, is descended from these Sherlocks.

41. Scan's version of this tune appears on Topic 2-12T455/6, side 1, track 2.

42. Scan sent plans to Lachenal, the concertina maker, to have small concertinas made, one for him and one for his brother, to fit in their pockets. The maker sent him full-size instruments (David Nuttall).

43. Maggie, Fred and George had the same parents and were all born within wedlock; Maggie was surnamed Ridley and the other two were Gurr.

44. The children's home was run by Olivia Freshfield, unmarried daughter of the family at Wych Cross Place.

45. The dulcimer was known locally: Master Sales played a dulcimer solo at a penny reading in Mayfield in 1897 (*Sussex Express*, 12.2.1897).

46. Scan was a founder member of Danehill Football Club and later played for Horsted Keynes and Horam. 'L. Tester' played back for Danehill v. Fletching on Christmas Day, 1909 (*Sussex Express*, 31.12.1909).

47. Arch Sherlock remembered the band in Horsted Keynes.

    '[O]rder is only kept up with the greatest difficulty, the children generally being disobedient, rude and impertinent. To improve the order and make the school more popular, a Drum and Fife Band has been started to accompany the School Exercises and Drills.' (Fletching School Logbook 1881-94, entry for 20.10.1890; quoted in *Danehill P.H.S.M., III*, 6, (Feb. 1988), p. 13).

    A band from Newick was reported in *Sussex Express*, 26.6.1897.

48. Henry Mayhew interviewed a London street concertina player in the mid-nineteenth century: 'In the summer I sometimes go out with a mate of mine, who plays the piccolo. He's very clever indeed, and plays most extraordinary.' (*London Labour and the London Poor, III* (186V, p. 183).

49. The back room in which the band used to play burnt down in the mid-1980s. The outline of the walls remains.

50. There was no notice or advertisement for the *Nutley Inn* dances in the *Sussex Express* during the first half of 1905 or throughout 1910.

    Most of the dancers lived locally, but who made up the 'two or three different parties' who came from Brighton and stayed for the weekend? The fifteen miles or so, even by train to Uckfield and horse bus to Nutley, was not a particularly easy journey and was not within the normal resources of an average working man. The possibility is that they cycled, but 'every Saturday night' is perhaps an enthusiastic overstatement.

51. See chapter 5 for a discussion of round dancing.

52. Scan to Steve Pennells.

53. Scan was earning his living at 10. At a similar age, Michael Gorman was playing at all-night house dances with adult musicians (see note 30).

54. Daisy Sherlock thinks Will played with Scan at the servants' balls and Fanny Lander remembered him playing there.

55. Interwoven dialogue; one would start a sentence and the other would finish it.

56. Horace Jackson, Lewes, advertised new pianos from £6 - £14 (*Sussex Express*, -.11.1909).

57. Scan lived in Chelwood briefly before he married. He lived in Horsted Keynes for a short time in 1910.

58. 'Vetchery' was the spelling and pronunciation before the Great War. It is now spelt Vachery.

59. I have been unable to trace when Bill Gorringe moved from Fairwarp to Horsted Keynes. The *Parliamentary Registers* place him in Horsted Keynes in 1913 and Cuckfield in 1914.

60. Daisy Sherlock never heard Scan and Bill to-gether. This might be accounted for by Daisy's non-involvement in Scan's pub playing or by Scan giving up his other musical partners when Daisy was old enough to replace them. Daisy remembers going to tea at Tommy Stephenson's after Scan had stopped playing with him.

61. Scan described the *Indian Polka* as a round dance: chassé into the centre of the room for four bars, chassé out for four bars and schottische round for eight bars. There is a different American dance of the same name. The tune is *Louden's Bonnie Woods* or *Lord Moira*, composed by Duncan MacIntyre (*A Collection of Slow Airs, Reels and Strathspeys* (1795)).

62. Mayhew interviewed Whistling Billy, a London street musician, about busking at Brighton in the late 1850s: 'At Brighton Regatta I and my mate made 51.l0s. [£5 10s.] between us, and at Dover Regatta we made 81. [£8]... I used to go out with a mate who had a wooden leg. He was a beautiful dancer, for he made 'em all laugh. He's a very little chap, and only does the hornpipe, and he's uncommon active, and knocks his leg against the railings, and makes the people grin. He was very successful at Brighton, because he was pitied...' (Mayhew, *London Labour III*, p. 203).

63. *Musical Traditions, 7* (mid - 1987), p. 25.

Clematis Cottage, Horsted Keynes, Scan's home from the mid-1920's until 1953.

(Courtesy Daisy & Arch Sherlock)

Chapter 3:
Great War - 1957

The Great War seriously disrupted working and social life in the villages. Troops were camped and billeted in the area, horse artillery trained on Ashdown Forest and battalions of men marched almost daily through Danehill on their way to the coast for embarkation for France. Horses were bred and timber was cut for the war effort, but the most significant effect was the drain on the young, and not so young, male population. The casualties were high - five sons in one Danehill family - and those that came back after the war were never the same.

> **Charlie Bates:** During the War there was only about four men left in this village... who didn't go in the Army... Woodgate Farm was run all by women, 'cause as you go up the main road, there was a row of cottages and that was filled right up with Land Army girls... I can remember it now; there was a big corn stack there and many come there thrashing, and it was all girls bar this fellow what was driving the engine.

Scan failed his medical for military service and thus stayed at home when many of his contemporaries went to the war. Nevertheless, many aspects of his life were affected. His cricketing and football mates and the younger men who frequented the pubs and the formal dances were depleted. Fanny Tester's unexpected and premature death from pneumonia in 1917 broke the pattern of his life and called a halt to some of his musical activities, which were probably on the way out anyway. His father died in 1916 and the fish and brick businesses were not carried on by the next generation, the brick fields, or some of them at least, having been exhausted, and his mother gave up the *Green Man*. Scan could no longer fall back on seasonal work for his father, and he had a

Workers at an unidentified Sussex sawmill; undated. Scan is seated, far right.
(Courtesy Tony Wales)

Scan and Sarah, Hellingly, 5 April 1920.
Below: Daisy, Scan and Sarah, c. 1920.
(Courtesy Daisy & Arch Sherlock)

seven year-old daughter to bring up. Daisy went to live with her maternal grandmother, while Scan went into lodgings with Lias Baker, a local soft-fruit grower and pork butcher, for whom he had worked earlier as a drover, taking cattle to Haywards Heath market. Scan had been an estate sawyer years before and he now took a job as a sawyer for Box & Turner Ltd, timber merchants, first at Sheffield Park and then at Horam Road rail-way station, where he rented a caravan.[1]

Scan cycled to Chelwood at weekends to see Daisy and continued playing in his home district. Maggie Ridley has memories of the fortnightly sixpenny hops she attended at Twyford school in 1918 or 1919, where 'Scan played the concertina with a fiddle player'. They did the polka, 'very lively, kicking their legs up', and the one-step. William J. Bird, writing many years later about his first year as headmaster of Danehill School in 1919, remembered

> ...the dances in the school, where the
> lasses wore their best summer clothes
> and rather heavy shoes. There was no
> smart band in those days, but I
> remember being lulled to sleep by the
> wheezy tones which issued from the
> concertina. I remember the smell of the
> oil lamps and the sound of happy
> laughter from the dancers. The dances
> were really happy and joyful, and one
> wonders, by the doleful looks on the
> dance floor of today if the young folks
> are as happy at the dance as we used to
> be. I remember too, the hustle and
> bustle of getting desks back for the next
> day's school.[2]

While Scan was living at Horam Road he met Sarah Philadelphia Clark (born c. 1898), through her brother, who was the signalman at the level-crossing where Scan lived in a caravan. They married on Easter Monday, 5 April 1920, at Hellingly Church, staying on in Horam until 1923 or 1924. During that period, Daisy remembers, she and her father regularly cycled to Brighton on Saturdays to stay with Scan's sister Minnie, then on to Horsted Keynes on Sundays, and back to Horam on Sunday evenings. Thus, it would appear, Scan kept his Brighton and Horsted Keynes contacts alive.

The family moved to Horsted Keynes when Daisy was 13, as Scan felt the need 'to be near Will'. Initially they lodged with Scan's brother Fred at Salisbury Cottage, before moving into Clematis Cottage, on the Green by the post office.[3] Another brother, Bert, was third gardener at Sir Walter Scott's house, Tremans, and Scan was taken on as second gardener.

Will Tester's movements up until this time are not at all clear. His surviving daughters, Edie (born 1922) and Peggy (1929), have no first-hand knowledge of his early days or of his activities outside their home in the 1920s and 1930s. He re-enlisted in the West Kents in February 1916 and passed out in November in Chatham with a first-class signalling certificate and experience as a despatch rider. He served in France as a wireless operator and line layer in the Royal Engineers, and he was twice wounded and went down with pneumonia.[4] Back in France, he received a concertina from the family, but it was lost when he had to leave everything suddenly in the advance into Germany in 1918. There he bought a bandoneon from a German soldier who had lost a hand and could no longer play it. This bandoneon, with a fingering system not unlike that of the Anglo-German concertina, was to feature prominently in the Tester family music-making over the next few years. He returned home in November 1919 and lived on the Green, subsequently moving to Church House.[5] He had a number of jobs over the next few years - on the Harmsworth estate, in a fish delivery business with George Gurr, looking after the churchyard, cutting hair on Sunday mornings and working on the roads for the council.

Will's army pal, Jock Stewart, who had taught him the clarinet, occasionally went down to Horsted Keynes and played with the Tester brothers. He had a quick ear and picked up some of their tunes. Indeed, they might have learnt some of his.

> **Scan:** He used to live in London and ... I don't know how many years he served in the West Kents, but he got a jolly good pension. He served long time after his time, and he joined the Scotch Guards when he come out from there, and he used to play in the theatres. He'd go anywhere - wouldn't matter where it was - he'd go anywhere to play, and he'd take any instrument there was in a band from what he wouldn't earn the money, and, do you know, he was bad for a long time, and when he'd begun to get better, he went for his clarinets – to play his clarinets - and he couldn't blow 'em, and he was dead less than six months.... You got to tongue the reed, en't you, and he couldn't do it, you know. See, he played all his life... but it killed him all right... [RH]

> He was about the roughest man that you would see walk the street after he come out of the army. He didn't mind what he had on, anything done. He'd come down to our place from London; well, he used to wear a bowler hat and that. He come down very likely now, and very likely he'd come down Christmas. I bet you a shilling he hadn't had his hat touched with a brush or nothing ever since he wore it last time... We used to have a game with him sometimes and pack him up a weed in a paper to take home. He'd take it home for a plant and put it in a pot![6] [RH]

Will played the clarinet in duet with Scan's concertina at this time, always in the lower register to contrast with the concertina, just as later in the 'jazz band' they contrasted the bandoneon with the fiddle.[7] Daisy never heard her uncle Will play the clarinet, nor did she meet or hear Jock Stewart, though she

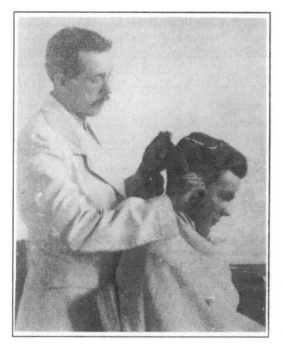

Will Tester, cutting hair in the Army, c.1916-19, and (right) in 1919. (Both courtesy Paul Marten)

knew of him. Will's daughters, remember Jock well enough - he used to bring his wife and children to stay - but they never heard Will play the clarinet. He did, however, get the concertina out at home and waltz round the room, playing a tune and saying to his wife, 'Come on, Mother, let's have a dance.'

Scan's daughter Daisy had started dancing lessons in 1915, when she was four-and-a-half. Emily Peak (née Warnett), born in 1886 the daughter of a local shoemaker, was a teacher at Danehill School and took a private evening class in one of the school-rooms.[8] All her pupils were girls and included Daisy's aunts Clara and Nellie, who were still children. Only adults' dances were taught - the polka, the waltz, the *Quadrilles, Lancers, Veleta* and *Boston Two-Step* - and Mrs Peak must have kept up with the latest, as Daisy learnt the *Maxina*, which came out in 1917, while she was still very young. Daisy had been picking out tunes on the black notes at home from the age of about five and, following her mother's death, the piano went with her to Granny Turner's. Her aunts Nellie and Kath (in her early 20s) were taking piano lessons, and her other two young aunts could play. Daisy picked up by ear from them and began playing duets on two pianos. Two pianos! It seems unlikely that very many working families would have owned pianos at that time, but Daisy's impression is that 'a lot of 'em had got pianos'.

THE FAMILY BAND – TESTERS' IMPERIAL

The village music and dance scene that Daisy entered in the early 1920s was quite different from that her father had been brought up with in the 1890s. She had played with Scan at home and knew much of his old repertoire, but she was precluded from pubbing because of her age. She has never really liked pubs, but when she was still only 13 the land-lord of the *Sloop*, William Awcock, moved the piano into the passage so she could play outside the bar while Scan played inside. At about the same time, they played about once a month for Lady Gertrude Decies, who organised fancy dress dances in a hay-loft at Danehill for the village people. Lady D.C., as she was popularly called, had come down in the world, and was making a living as 'Madame Sylvia' with a sweet shop and tea-room. The dances were a money-spinning side-line for her.

> **Scan:** I have played two places one night. Yes, Will and me played once or twice two places one night about a mile apart, and, well, that was really when I just started going out to play, like when Will and me started directly after the First War, and, course, then I gradually kept getting more and more ... It got like that they kept wanting us to go, so I

Ernie Carter's wedding party at Chelwood Village Hall, with Scan and his 'music' in pride of place; undated. (Courtesy Daisy & Arch Sherlock)

Tester's Imperial at home, c.1927-31. The local insurance agent, probably Richard Jameson, tried out his new camera on the band and 'it came out funny'. Sarah had sent for a year's supply of sheet music, although Daisy 'couldn't play by note'.

(Courtesy Daisy & Arch Sherlock)

got Daisy to come and play. Well, we got on alright the three of us. Well, it got like, that Will said to me one night, he says, when we was coming home from somewhere, he says, 'You know what you ought to do, Scan?' He says, 'You've got a damn good start now. You've got a hold. Everybody wants you,' he says. Why don't you have a set of drums?' Course, that put me in mind of it. I thought to myself, 'Well, I don't know. It wouldn't be a bad idea. We got plenty places to go to play now.' So I said to Daisy's mum, when we got home, I said, 'Well ... Will suggests we get a set of drums,' and she says, 'Well, I can't see why we couldn't.' She says, 'I'll be drummer!' Just like that. I said, 'Alright, we'll have one then.' So that's when I had my first set of drums... [in 1927 according to Daisy] [RH]

Daisy's mum was as good a round dancer as you'll find, and she got [an] idea about music, you know. It wasn't no good thinking you was going to learn her to play to time or anything. She already knew it and, you know, she

started on them drums - the very first night I would have gone out, if I'd have known it - the first night she ever had the drums, I could have trusted her, and she was good. [RH]

With the addition of drums, they had a 'jazz band', Testers' Imperial. Daisy remembers the dances they played: the schottische, polka, fox-trot, waltz, the *Gay Gordons, Boston Two-step, Veleta,* and the *Charleston.* The quickstep eventually took over from the one-step, followed later by the slow fox-trot.

Danehill Parish Magazine, 1922-24.

(Courtesy Phil Lucas)

Scan: Course, sometimes we used to play a schottische or a polka. We used to get asked for them sometimes with some of the older ones what was there. But they mostly consisted of one-steps, fox-trots and the *Esperance [Esperano?] Barn-dance* and the *Rosetta Two-step,* and such tunes as that, and the *Canadian Three-step.* [MP]

At some places there were strong preferences: the *Maxina* was danced only at Danehill reading room, and at the Sheffield Park reading room they were crazy about the set-dances, the *Quadrilles,* the *Lancers* and the *Alberts,* and very often they had five sets of dancers on the floor at a time. The Setford family were the enthusiasts behind this regular booking, and brothers-in-law George Setford and George Wilkins, in their thirties, shouted out the figures. At Chelwood Gate parish hut a whist-drive always preceded the dance, which then ran from ten o'clock 'til one or two in the morning. Ernie Carter, the master of ceremonies, occasionally took over at the piano to give Daisy a chance to dance.[9] Other regular venues were the parish room in Horsted Keynes, where as team captain Scan offered his services free for Horsted Keynes Cricket Club, and West Hoathly hall, next to the *Cat.* The dances were always taken seriously - no fooling about once the dancers were on the floor - but the crowds got up to all manner of tricks, like the time the Danehill lads had a few drinks in the *Crocodile* and brought a pony onto the dance floor.

Scan and Daisy picked up the latest dance-tunes from the wireless. They would rush back home after a dance had finished and tune in to the last ten minutes of the Savoy Orpheans or Jack Payne's BBC Dance Orchestra on a crystal set. If a tune took her fancy, Daisy would go straight to the piano and play it, then check it out next time it was played. If she was unable to get it, Scan would buy the record in Woolworth's in Haywards Heath, or his sister, Minnie, would get it in Brighton. There were four tunes on each record for sixpence; they would learn all four, play them at that night's dance and sell the record to someone at the dance the same evening. Some of the tunes Daisy and Arch were able to name were *Shepherd of the Hills, Pasadena, The Sheik of Araby, Margie, If You Knew Susie, K-K-K-Katie, Horsey Keep Your Tail Up* and *Tiptoe Through the Tulips.* They learnt *The Charleston* from 'a super dancer at Danehill; all the girls wanted to dance with him', and they used the original tune.[10]

Scan: Will used to come out sometimes with the old bandolium. It was lovely with us, you know. I played fiddle all the time; I never used to play nothing else that time of day. We used to have piano, violin and drums, and the bandolium when my brother used to come.[11] Easier for me. It used to be hard work for me to play [without him]. [MP]

Daisy recalls that Will seldom played with the band and certainly not when they went out with the drums. One job he attended regularly was at the Sheffield Park reading room; Daisy thinks that Scan and Will had worked out their own selections of tunes for the set-dances sometime previously, and as Scan preferred playing for round-dancing, he probably appreciated his brother's support with the set-dances favoured by the Sheffield Park crowd. Will was often unwell and was unable to keep up the pace, and the pace was tough.

Scan: We used always to be out three nights, and sometimes four we have been, and we used to go to work everyday, you know. [MP]

Daisy was working in service at Valley Holme, Horsted Keynes, and would get off at six in the evening. The dances would sometimes go on till two or half-past two; she would cycle home, then get to work for a seven o'clock start. Yet, as she says now, it never seemed to worry her.

The bandoneon was a rarity in Sussex, and only Scan and Will could play Will's instrument.[12]

> **Scan:** My brother sold it three or four times to blokes and he knew they'd never be able to play it, 'cause there wasn't only him and me could play it! He sold it three or four times, and bought it back for about half the money! [MP]

Will was certain he would be able to retrieve it in the same way if he raffled it, but this time he pushed his luck too far.

> **Scan:** Well, it was one Saturday night this raffle come off, but Will told me several weeks before he was going to raffle it. 'Well,' I said, 'I wouldn't mind having four or five tickets, but you know how it is, if I was to go and have four or five tickets, and happened to win it, they'd say it was wangled.' Anyway I said, 'I'll have a ticket, but I shan't come to the raffle.' Well, this Saturday night when it was raffled, they threw dice for it. Daisy and me was playing down the *Sloop* and Arch [Sherlock] went up to the raffle. Course, Arch knew us like 'fore ever he went out with Daisy or anything. Presently there was about nine or ten got out an old Ford car. Will was with them, and Arch come in the door carrying this music. Course, soon as I looked at it I knew what it was, so did Daisy and her mum. Daisy says, 'They got the old big music, Dad!' 'Well, I expect your Uncle Will's going to play.' Arch come round: 'Here you are, this is your prize.' 'My prize?' He says, 'Yes.' Arch threw for me and somebody else throwed, and they was tie, so they chucked up again, and damned if Arch didn't throw and beat this all. I said, 'Well, that's a bit of luck, ain' it?' Will said, 'Well, there they are; they all see it was fair. You won it fair enough.' [RH]

Testers' Imperial had a regular booking at the *Star Inn*, a small pub set back off the Piltdown - Nutley road, apparently in the middle of nowhere.[13] With very few locals around, James Rourke's dances attracted customers from Nutley, Fairwarp, Fletching, Maresfield and further afield.

Opposite: Scan and the bandoneon.

(Courtesy Scan Tester)

> **Daisy:** [It] used to be packed out. Half the time they couldn't all get on the floor … and it was a big room … with a stage and everything and a dressing room … and a lovely floor for dancing.

> **Scan:** I used to have a place at Piltdown. Well, there used to be a pub called the *Star* and this publican was an Irishman. He was ex-Irish policeman and his name was Rourke, and he had one of them big army huts out the back, and I went down there one Saturday with my concertina - Will and me did - and he said to me, 'Cor blimey', he says, 'You're the blokes I want!' He said, 'Would you come down here and play in that room for me?' I didn't know nothing about the room. Will knew him, you see; I didn't. He says, 'You're Will's brother, ain't you?' I says, 'Yes.' 'Well,' he says, 'He's told me about you.' I says, 'Oh, has he?' He says, 'I'll get a good piano up in there for you, if you'll bring your jazz band down here. He says, 'Why not come down here once a fortnight, Saturday nights from eight to twelve?' 'Well,' I said. 'Look, I'll tell you what; I'll come down and see you one night in the week. I'll bike down here to see you.' So I went down there and I agreed to go down. [RH]

A notice in the *Sussex Express* for 19 August 1927 confirms Scan's account:

> PILTDOWN: One of a series of the fortnightly dances to raise funds for a piano was held at the Star Hut on Saturday. A special orchestra was in attendance.

> **Arch Sherlock:** He was a character, he was, old Rourke … Well, he used to get so drunk, he couldn't serve behind the bar … Somebody said he was a police inspector, but I don't know … When he used to get towards the end of the evening, he used to give you drinks, never used to buy 'em.[14]

> **Scan:** You know, we used to go down there. We used to have, well sometimes, 120 and 130 [at a] shilling a time from eight to twelve, and he was an artful old bloke, he was. You know, he used to send to these big firms and he used to get stuff [soap samples, for example] for advertisements - to give away for

advertisements - and used to have spot prizes and all like that, and he used to give some of this stuff away for prizes - the best of it - and the other, perhaps, he'd give away in the room. You know, they buggers used to flock there every fortnight. They used to come from miles around. [RH]

Scan: There used to be a Brighton band; they come to Danehill to play to a posh dance up there. Some gentry, I don't know who it was now, got this dance up, so we went up there, and I knew the fiddler of this band from Brighton. The band was called the Excelsior Band, and he'd got a piano and he played the violin; he got a banjo player and drums.[15] He knew me, and so after we'd been in there a little while, he come down to me and stood talking to me just for a break in between the dances, and so he says to me, he says, 'Why haven't you brought your fiddle then?' I says, 'Oh, that wouldn't do to bring it up there,' I said, 'I shouldn't be nowhere with you people.' 'Oh,' he says, 'You would! I'll tell you what,' he says. 'I wondered if your wife would come up and give us a couple of tunes on the drums.' He says, 'I want to know whether [our drummer] thinks a woman can handle drums.' So she went up and I expect she was up there, well, biggest part of an hour playing, and he told me afterwards, he says, 'That cut his comb!' He said, 'He thought there wasn't nobody else could do them drums only him, but I knew there was.' He says, 'He ain't said no more about it, not to me! Not about his drumming.' No, she was pretty good. [RH]

And this banjo player from out this Brighton band, he was a jolly good player. You'll be sure he loved music. He used to get three or four blokes come up with him, and they used have a car and come up there [the *Star*], and he used to bring his old banjo up there. I can see him now; soon as ever he got in that room, he made straight for that stage. He used to come up there along with us, and I'm damned if he wasn't help, you know. He could play; there wasn't no mistake. 'Cor,' he says, 'I wish I lived up there [here]! You wouldn't have to go

out by yourself many times.' He says, 'I should be with you.' He was a regular lover of music he was. I don't know as ever I've seen him ever since we left. [RH]

Local jazz bands were doing very well, but Testers' Imperial had an edge on most of them. Scan thought it was because they kept better time for dancing, but in all probability there were other characteristics - qualities in the music and social compatibility - that appealed to the locals more.

Scan: We could have had two places of a night all the week, if we'd liked to have gone. Very often we had three places to choose from to go out one night in the week somewhere. [RH]

In the early days Scan, Daisy and Sarah used to cycle to the dances, until they got a motor-bike and side-car; later on, as they moved further afield, they would hire a taxi. Eventually, perhaps because of the Depression, the bottom fell out of band work.

Scan: You see, jazz bands had died out a lot before we left off... The money wasn't enough ... to keep on going. [RH]

The band's final resting place was the *Sloop*, a beer-house standing more or less alone by the River Ouse on the Horsted - Chailey road. In the mid-1920s William Cork had taken over the pub from William Awcock and continued the Saturday night dances. Two small rooms, with a pianola in one and a piano in the other, were opened into one on Saturday night, but even then the room was too small for the drums - they used just fiddle or concertina and piano - and the crowd stood three or four deep between the dances.[16] The band played from 7.30 until closing time at ten. As it was a pub, admission was free. There was no official arrangement for payment, but there was always someone who thought to take up a collection for the musicians.

Testers' Imperial packed up in 1931 as Daisy came of age and took a living-in job in service in Lindfield. If she had a long weekend off she might play at the *Sloop*, but Will stepped into her regular place and kept the session going for a while. Daisy married Arch Sherlock in October 1936 and moved to Danehill, where Beryl was born in November 1937. They rented Wheelwright's Cottage in Horsted Keynes, and then moved into a tied house at Cinder Hill just before the outbreak of war. Daisy occasionally had a tune with Scan, but her mother never touched the drums again after 1931.

Scan's commitment to the family band had not completely eliminated his old practice of pubbing. Bill Gorringe's nephew remembers Blind Charlie Gorringe playing with Scan 'for the crowd to dance around to' on Saturday nights in the late 1920s and early 1930s in the Forester and Charlie Bates attended dancing sessions in the *Coach and Horses* in 1926:

> I've seen old Tom Tucker and his missus up the *Coach* doing it [the polka] in the top room. Well, old Scan was playing then. The old polka ... 1,2,3,4,5 - the *Heel and Toe Polka* ... Well, old Tom Tucker learnt me it... They used to get up there at it. I mean, most of us, all boys, well youngsters, and old Tom and them up there like. It was hardly no women up there. It was dancing with each other ... when I was about seventeen - seventeen, eighteen. Well, we used to go to the pub at seventeen, but it was always 'eighteen', like. *Veleta, Schottische,* all them we used to do up there ... Yeh, dancing with fellas. It was no women up there.[17]

THE THIRTIES, FORTIES AND FIFTIES

Strangely, after the break-up of the family band, Scan seldom played in Horsted Keynes. He drank in the *British Legion,* and occasionally played there for a sing-song, but it was very rare indeed that he took his music into the *Green Man* or the *Crown.* He would usually do a turn at the tontine share-out, but most of his music-making in the village was at home with Daisy or at some special event, like a wedding or an anniversary. Neither was Will very active; the two brothers used to go out together sometimes to play somewhere. Will played the penny whistle at home, but he was unable to transfer his concertina skill to the piano accordion he had bought, and he saw the instrument as a useless liability. He was the boiler-man at St. Martin's jam factory at Cinder Hill during the war and supervised working parties of Italian prisoners-of-war on the land.

Scan reckoned he played at the *Stone Quarry,* Chelwood Gate, for forty years, on and off, which would have been from the early 1930s until the time he died. The pub was taken over in November 1930 by a local man, Alf Baxter, who probably encouraged Scan to start going there on Saturday nights.[18] Alf Baxter's brother, Ernie (1900-64), better known as Rabbity from his poaching exploits, played with him on the tambourine throughout the period, finding an appropriate beat for whatever Scan played, songs as well as dance tunes.[19]

Some of the other musicians who frequented the *Stone Quarry* were Jack Wheeler, who had his melodeon retuned in B flat in order to play with Scan and also played the triangle; Punch Browning, who must

Danehill School, c.1908-10.
Rabbity Baxter, back row, far right.
(Courtesy Phil Lucas)

Scan and Sarah at Daisy and Arch's wedding, October 1936.
(Courtesy Daisy & Arch Sherlock)

have been quite an old man at that time (concertina); Uncle Jack Smith (melodeon); and Bert Bennett (triangle). Will went there sometimes with a melodeon player from Nutley called Coleman, and well into the 1960s this man's brother, Leslie Coleman, also a melodeon player, would pick Scan up whenever he felt like it and they, according to Scan, 'played together for several years'.

There were other musicians around. Alec Hood, a Scotsman from Elgin, played the Highland bagpipes in the open air at Nutley in the 1930s,[20] and Bob Fry remembers a Great War veteran coming round every so often, busking on the Green at Horsted Keynes with a euphonium. His number, popular then in the late 1930s, was *Poor Little Angeline*. A neighbour of Scan's, Wilf Walder, could get a tune out of pretty well anything, including the violin; his father, Ernie, euphonium player in the old Horsted Band, was Scan's workmate, but apparently Scan and Wilf never played together.[21]

After the War some of the land girls organised a dramatic society in Horsted Keynes, and Scan, together with a trombone player and a double bass

player, took part in one of their shows. That was where he learnt *Buttons and Bows*, which dates it as having been in 1948 or soon after. Bob Fry worked with him at Broadhurst Manor around 1950, and the boss, 'Mr John' [Clarke], gave a harvest supper for his employees at the parish room; Scan certainly played at that, and at the Ashdown General Land Company's annual concert.[22] Scan and Sarah were always the first to put their names down for coach-trips out of the village to the seaside and stately homes, and it was then Scan came into his own, standing at the back of the coach, playing all the old popular songs on the way home.

Around 1950 Sarah Tester was taken seriously ill and Scan took three years off work to nurse her, during which time he played hardly at all. Sarah died in 1953 and Scan gave up Clematis Cottage to move in with Daisy, Arch and Beryl at Cinder Hill. At least now he could have a tune with Daisy, but he still did not go out playing that much. They took an annual family holiday at Lancing, on the coast, and until the late 1960s Scan looked forward to his sessions with the pianist (who doubled on the electric organ) in the *Three Horseshoes* on the sea-front.

NOTES

1. For a description of the sawyer's trade, see George Ewart Evans, *Where Beards Wag All* (1973), pp. 28-31.

2. William J. Bird, 'Danehill and Chelwood Gate in 1919: I Remember', *Danehill Parish Historical Society Magazine, III, 2*, (Oct. 1986), pp. 20-21.

3. I have no evidence of Scan's musical activity in the Horam Road area from 1920 - 1923/24. He played football for the local team, and he may therefore have played music after matches, which was the practice in his home area.

4. Will's personal Army papers (Paul Marten).

5. The *Parliamentary Register*, 1913, gives Will's address as 'Church cottages'.

6. 'All our bandsmen are Guardsmen. When the King holds an investigature [sic] or gives a dance we always have to find substitutes. You know they are not regular soldiers. They have a lot of free time. It is rather curious - an old tradition. They are paid by the officers and if there was a war they would not be classed as soldiers but as bandsmen. They get a slight allowance from the government. They can all play several instruments.' (Manager, Wimbledon Glider Rink, 28.2.1939 (Mass Observation, Sussex University Library, 5F XXXV5, p. 2)).

7. David Nuttall.

8. Assisted by her cousin, Mavis Lucas, Phil Lucas's sister

9. Ernie Carter was a bus conductor, formerly an estate gardener, and was Daisy Sherlock's next-door neighbour when she was a child.

10. Daisy Sherlock.

    The Charleston was composed in 1923 by black Harlem pianist, James P. Johnson.

11. Use of the bandoneon depended on whether it was in tune with the piano. Daisy says Scan never played the concertina in the jazz band.

12. I saw two second-hand bandoneons in Windo Martin's music shop in Duke Street, Brighton, in 1958.

13. The *Star Inn* is now a dwelling house, Grove's Farm.

14. James Rourke held the tenancy from 1924 to September 1928. His wife carried on until November, when William Head took over (Uckfield Petty Sessions Register of Licences).

    William Head's daughter and son, Rene (piano) and Bill (drums), and George Avis (violin) played fortnightly, week about with Testers' Imperial. (George Avis) These Heads were more of Denner Head's musical relatives.

15. The Excelsior Band played in Maresfield, Mayfield, Framfield and Hadlow Down in 1927, as frequently reported in the *Sussex Express*. One notice described them as 'from Crowborough.' Scan probably confused them with a Brighton band playing in the area.

16. Daisy Sherlock. This instrumentation does not conflict with the information in note 11. This was a duet, not the jazz band.

17. Note Scan's remark, when talking about a posh dance, 'where two gentlemen weren't allowed to dance together.'

18. The *Stone Quarry*, opened c.1870, was rebuilt just before the Great War and demolished in 1989. Chris Newnham took over the tenancy after Alf Baxter.

19. Rabbity Baxter kept a tambourine (identified as a Salvation Army model by Steve Chambers) belonging to Scan at the *Stone Quarry*. Shortly after Rabbity's death, Scan retrieved it and gave it to me. 'I had it in mind to give it to you, if anything happened to old Rabbity.' I don't remember ever meeting Rabbity and I never heard him play, but I learnt many years later he had been at our session in the *Crown* on 22.2.1958.

20. Alec/Alex Hood came to Nutley as a chauffeur, married Laura Wickham, moved into the original *William IV* building, then operating as a Cyclists' Touring Club hostel, and went into business as a market gardener. He practiced the bagpipes on the Forest or at the far end of his fields to be away from the houses, possibly into the 1940s (Christopher Stephens).

21. David Walden.

22. Scan worked mostly on building work for the Clarke family until long after his official retirement age.

Scan on holiday, mid-1930s.

(Courtesy Daisy & Arch Sherlock)

1 Victoria Cottages, Horsted Keynes,
where Scan lived at the end of his life.
(Photograph: Hamish Black)

Chapter 4:
1957 - 1972

I n 1955 Mervyn Plunkett, who was living in West Hoathly, recorded two local singers.[1] Pop Maynard had a degree of local fame for his success in the World Marbles Championship, held each Good Friday at Tinsley Green, but at 83 he was also a remarkable singer with a large repertoire of old songs. He frequented the *Cherry Tree* at Copthorne, and his frail form, dignified posture and slightly introverted delivery, even of a comic song, commanded attention whenever he got up to sing. George Spicer was quite different. In the prime of life at 49

and working as a cowman, his singing, mostly at the *Punch Bowl*, Selsfield, was much more extrovert and abrasive.[2] These two singers did not exist in isolation; they performed at appropriate times among their friends on their home ground, and there were many other singers about. The new teacher at West Hoathly school, Jean Hopkins, from East Grinstead, stayed with Doe and Mervyn Plunkett, and with their encouragement started singing songs from, and in the style of, her grandfather and great-uncle, Harry and Charlie Burgess.

Harry Holman (left) and Pop Maynard recording for the BBC in the Cherry Tree *at Copthorne on 4 February 1956.*
(Photograph: East Grinstead Courier)

I was living at home in Northfleet, Kent, and it was through Ken Stubbs, who worked nearby in Gravesend but lived in East Grinstead, that Mervyn and I met. Towards the end of 1955, Mervyn organised a do in the *Swan* at East Grinstead with Bob Copper, one of the now famous singing family from Rottingdean, as the guest, and I was invited to warm up the proceedings on the melodeon. Things took off from there. I began spending time in West Hoathly and Mervyn organised more pub sessions. In February 1956, Peter Kennedy recorded one of our sessions in the *Cherry Tree* for the BBC, and Pop, George Spicer, Jean and Mervyn appeared that June on the Sunday morning radio programme, *As I Roved Out*.

Pop Maynard had stepdanced and played the tambourine when he was younger, and there were still stepdancers in the *Cherry Tree*.[3] At the BBC recording session, one of the regulars from the nearby *Abergavenny Arms*, attracted to the *Cherry Tree* by the bar extension, picked up a tin tray and played it like a tambourine and sang 'From Wibbledon to Wob-bledon is eighteen miles' when Peter Kennedy and I played *Soldier's Joy*, but at that stage we had not come across any other musicians.

It was impossible to follow-up every lead and invitation to meet singers. Every pub session produced something new and Mervyn met and recorded many old singers, the most notable being Brick Harber, Jim Wilson and George Tompsett. At Cuckfield he came across Jack Norris, Peter Gander and Bill Hawks, who sang regularly in their local.[4]

At 59, Jack Norris was twenty-odd years younger than his mates.[5] A foreman joiner and coffin maker by trade, he was friendly and humorous and loved the old songs, and new ones as well. He was a remarkable musician, the melodeon player that appeals to me more than any other I have heard. He could play any song-tune that came into his mind on his double-row C/C sharp Hohner, and sing at the same time. It was as if the fingering came automatically as he opened his mouth. He was essentially a

Radio Times, *22 June 1956*

Opposite: Jack Norris, Halleigh's, Brook Street, Cuckfield; late 1950s.
Jack Norris and friends; late 1950s.
(Both courtesy Florence Norris)

58

On Saturday 24 August 1957, Mervyn assembled for the first time the West Hoathly Country Band of Music, or as Arch Sherlock was always to refer to it, the 'West Hoathly Scuffle Group'. I remember the evening at Bow Cottage, the Plunketts' home, as a heady, boozy do. Mervyn held the band together by thumping on my melodeon case. The music at times was marvellous, but sometimes it collapsed into total anarchy.

There was little trouble finding common ground - we all knew *The Girl I left Behind Me* and *Cock of the North* - and we took risks, the most successful of which was our schottische rendering of Jack Norris's song, *The Fox*. The greatest risk, however, was in inviting a neighbour we knew nothing about. Doë Plunkett taught Bill McMahon's children and had heard he was good on the spoons, but for all we knew, and slightly suspected, he was terrible! He turned out to be dynamite, and good fun as well.[9] Keys were the main difficulty: Scan had his B flat/F music and an out-of-tune C/G, I had my usual G/D melodeon and a slow-action C/F, and Jack was more used to playing in C sharp than C, but had a G mouth-organ, as did Snowy Howick from West Hoathly. Michael Plunkett, who played with me, then as now, in The Rakes, could manage G on his recorder, but had to tune his fiddle down a tone to get C with his D fingering.[10]

We were all encouraged, and some of us very excited, by our first efforts, and over the next few months the band grew in size and we began to be known in the district. The personnel was fairly fluid depending on who was available and how many Mervyn could pack into his car. At Rusper we met Bill Agate. During the War he had played for route marches in the Home Guard band on the mouth-organ and tambourine, playing both instruments together in the old style! My lasting visual memory of Bill is of his enormous hand, fingers like a pound of pork sausages, whacking away at a tiny tambourine. He had a tendency to push the beat, but his music had plenty of life and drive, in complete contrast to his slow speech and infirm frame. Jack Norris's mates from Cuckfield, Peter Gander (triangle) and Horace Gladman (mouth-organ and silent jew's harp), took part, and the third member of The Rakes, Paul Gross, joined us on the fiddle. In several pubs other people, who remained strangers to us, would occasionally join in on the mouth-organ or take a turn on the melodeon, and any number of make-shift percussion instruments, such as the tea-chest bass and the penny and beer glass, appeared. Although we played in the *Crown*, Horsted Keynes, and the *Stone Quarry*, Chelwood Gate, we gravitated to Copthorne, Balcombe, Cuckfield and Three Bridges, very largely away from Scan's home area.[11]

singer and his repertoire of old-fashioned dance tunes was very small. He had the commonly known *Cock O' The North* and *Keel Row*, and a schottische, *Another Cup of Coffee and a Little More Tea*, but his best number was another schottische, which Mervyn named the *Brook Street Polka*.[6] He was usually reluctant to play his one and only stepdance tune.[7]

One Saturday afternoon in July 1957, Don Jones, delivering greengrocery at the Plunketts' back door, heard me playing a few tunes in the kitchen. 'Who's that? My wife's father plays like that!' His father-in-law was Will Tester. The subsequent events were particularly significant for Mervyn and me, and resulted in a burst of energy and interest for Scan which carried him through to the end of his life. Mervyn followed the lead to Scan, rather than to Will, and called on him one evening soon after at Cinder Hill, quart bottles of beer under his arm and his tape recorder in the car.[8] Whatever was said that night established in Scan's mind our interest in his old repertoire, and the four pieces he recorded on that occasion were *In and out the Windows*, the *Monkey Hornpipe*, *Brighton Camp* and *The Man in the Moon*.

Left to right: Jim Wilson, Michael Plunkett, George Spicer, Paul Gross and Reg Hall, at the Princess Louise, Holborn, London; 7 March 1958.

(Photograph: Eddis Thomas)

In October 1957 Mervyn arranged a coach trip to London. We entered Pop Maynard, Jean Hopkins, George Spicer, Bill Hawkes and the full band in a competitive festival at Cecil Sharp House, headquarters of the English Folk Dance and Song Society. We shocked many of the people there and confused some of the adjudicators, who were used to genteel settings of folk songs. One of them, *The Times* music critic, criticised Pop Maynard for allegedly not knowing his words and for having a poor standing posture. Very few of the audience had ever heard a country singer before, and even fewer had ever heard country pub music. Some of them, it seemed, were excited by it. It was a great day out, marred by some pretty tense moments. The band let its hair down in a pub outside Redhill on the way home and Jack Norris wise-cracked the last leg of the coach journey - 'This must be Cuckfield; there are houses on both sides of the street.' Later that month there was a lively session in the *Cat*, West Hoathly; Alan Lomax was impressed by Mervyn's tape of the occasion and broadcast the band's rendering of Bill Agate's favourite, *I Wish They'd do it Now*, in his BBC programme, *Ballad Hunter*.

In the *Crown*, Horsted Keynes, in February 1958, some of the young lads, apparently resentful of our intrusion on their territory, set out to sabotage the evening. Mervyn's song, *Will the Weaver*, was the first casualty, abandoned after a few verses amid hostile comments: 'We've never had this sort of music round here before'. A middle-aged woman, one of the regular customers, quietly went over to the piano while the row was going on, struck up *Will the Weaver* in Mervyn's key and stayed with him until he finished the song. Will Tester, on his one and only outing with the West Hoathly Country Band of Music, took hold of Mervyn's tambourine and gave us a tantalising glimpse of the old Tester family magic. The next month Mervyn took the Tester brothers to a session in Glynde to meet up with Jean

Hopkin's family, the Burgesses. Art Winter, known to the Testers way back, was the resident melodeon player at the *Trevor Arms* and his gutsy old-fashioned pub music prompted Will to make what was to be his final flurry on the tambourine. A year later he was dead.

Mervyn was asked to make a contribution to *A Sussex Concert* in Cecil Sharp House in March 1958, and thus we had another outing to London. Jim Wilson from Three Bridges, George Tompsett from Cuckfield and Pop Maynard had never sung in a formal concert before, but they put their songs over as if they were in a pub, and Bill Hawks and Peter Gander's rough Cuckfield pub harmony in *Come All You Jolly Ploughboys* was in striking contrast to the gentle South Downs style of Bob and Ron Copper, who were also in the concert.

Our band that day included Scan, Bill Agate, Snowy Howick, Michael Plunkett and Paul Gross. Seamus Ennis, the Dublin piper, also appeared, and Scan was quite taken by his Irish music. He had never seen or heard of uilleann pipes before, and after some thought said he would have had no difficulty as a young man picking up Seamus's tunes, if he heard them enough times.

Later in the year we had a second crack at the EFDSS English Music Festival. Some of the rules had been ironed out and the conditions were much more relaxed and comfortable (although Cecil Sharp House is never that comfortable). Scan and I played a duet on tambourine and melodeon that was broadcast that night on the BBC Overseas Service, but the highlight of the day was the 'alternative festival', a party at my house in Croydon. It went on into the early hours with Harry Cox, Pop Maynard, Ernie Glew from Shoreham, Scan, Cyril Phillips and Fred Jordan, many of my Brixton relatives and plenty of other singers and musicians besides.[12]

The following afternoon, 11 October 1958, there was a grand concert of British music at the Royal Festival Hall. Pop Maynard sang a verse or two of *Rolling in the Dew* before Jeannie Robertson was brought on to finish the song![13] Pop was confused and upset and Jeannie was clearly embarrassed by such unimaginably crass stage direction. Scan, however, was given a respectable length of time. Left alone on the stage before an audience of over 2,000, he stepped towards the microphone and said, 'I'll play you *No. 3 stepdance* . . . Now I'll play *No. 5 Polka*, and finally, 'I'll play you a very old waltz tune', and went into *I Wonder Who's Kissing Her Now!*"[14]

At Christmas 1956 and New Year 1959, Mervyn captained a team of mummers, The West Hoathly Tipteerers.[15] For a couple of nights we went round various pubs and houses by arrangement. At the *Punch Bowl*, Selsfield, they had now idea we were coming. Mervyn burst into the public bar, heavily disguised, and declaimed, 'In comes I, Old Father Christmas', and George Spicer, standing at the bar, drinking with his mates, shouted out, 'It's old Plunkett!' At the *Vinals Cross*, Sharpthorne, we did the whole thing - surprise entrance, sword fight, the lot, and nobody took a blind bit of notice. Yet the same night, a youth club crowd turned the record player off and made us do it twice! We performed before the assembled family and servants in one big house and the butler served bottles of brown ale in his pantry - and half of us good socialists! Scan came out with us the second year. I remember waiting outside the *Green Man* in Horsted Keynes, freezing cold in the pitch dark, waiting our turn to make an entrance. I was in Marks & Spencer pyjamas as the Little Turkish Knight, and Scan, as the Little Turkish Knight's Mother, was in an old fur coat, looking like a cross between Arthur Askey and Bud Flanagan. We were both the worse for drink and I had no idea where we were. 'Do you know this pub, Scan?' 'I blooming well ought to, I used to live here!'

It would have been impossible to keep so many of us together for long. Some of the old chaps were in their late seventies and eighties, and sadly many were not to be around for much longer. Brick Harber and Peter Gander died within four months of each other in 1960. Pop Maynard sang a faltering *Shooting Goachen's Cocks Up* at his ninetieth birthday party at the *Cherry Tree* in January 1962, and before the year was out he had gone. And so they all went. Most of the organising energy and inspiration had come from Mervyn and, when he moved to Cambridgeshire in 1959 and then to Scotland in 1960, it became difficult for him to keep up his activities in Sussex, although he was still around, on and off, for the next five or six years. He had come across Cyril Phillips, who was then farming 360 acres at Firle, and was invited with Scan to a supper Cyril put on for his employees and friends. Cyril, whilst being a perfectly genuine countryman, had a rustic stage-countryman act with a load of comic songs. Being a farmer, he got on quite well with the Young Farmers and members of the Pony Club, and he arranged several engagements for us to play for dancing at harvest homes and hunt suppers. My mother's brother-in-law, Bob Keightley from Brixton, and Steve Pennells from Carshalton, Surrey, both fiddle players, Hilda Gibson, a friend of Scan's from Twickenham, who played the concertina, and Bob Davenport, a singer from County Durham then living in London, sometimes came out with us.[16]

Reg and Scan, music festival.
Cecil Sharp House, Camden Town, London;
10 October 1958.

(Photograph: Eddis Thomas)

The sessions organised by Ken Stubbs from 1960 onwards, after Mervyn had left the area, were always in pubs where there were local singers, although normally there was only singing at tontine share-out time. Ken had been associated with our West Hoathly music-making from the very beginning and he knew Pop Maynard very well, having spent time digging his garden and taking down his songs.[17] Naturally enough, his first sessions were with Pop and Harry Holman, the potman in the *Cherry Tree* at Copthorne. It was Pop who put Ken on to Jim Wilson, his friend from years back, when Ken had asked about the song *Barbara Allen*. Jim, a retired railwayman, used to drink in the *Plough* at Three Bridges, and he would quip and wisecrack with his mates all round the bar, procrastinating until he had built up enough interest and anticipation to burst into *The Keyhole in the Door* or *Never Go A-rushing*. The *Half Moon* at Balcombe was convenient for Bill Agate and a couple of singers, Corn Botting and Jack Arnoll. At the *Cherry Tree* in Rusper, Harry Manvelle played music-hall songs and between-the-Wars stuff in a rough, lively style on the melodeon and sang about his 'cock-a-doodle-do'.

Ken's postcard invitations went out to the faithful, and scan, dependent on others for transport, turned up nearly every month. He appeared to know the tunes of all the old country songs, even those sung by strangers, and often he would join in with the concertina behind Pop and the others in songs more usually sung unaccompanied. At the *Stone Quarry*, Chelwood Gate, Ken heard an old man sing *While Gamekeepers Lie Sleeping* identically to the performance he had just recorded from Tom Willett on a caravan-site miles away in Middlesex. The singer, it transpired, was Noah Willett, Tom's brother![18]

In January 1965 I took Scan to the *Fox* at Islington Green in north London. Thursday evening was club night in the upstairs room; there was a small admission charge at the door, a few regular singers and musicians, and a master of ceremonies kept the pace going. Each week a different guest was invited and went home better-off by a few pounds. Scan went down so well he was invited back on eleven more occasions, sometimes with Cyril Phillips, and once or twice with Daisy and Arch. Our band was made up of Scan's London mates - Steve Pennells, Bob

Keightley, David Nuttall, Bob Davenport, Michael Plunkett and Paul Gross - and Scan was usually encouraged to give a song or two. On his eightieth birthday we gave him a big party, and when the club at the *Fox* closed down in March 1968, some others, the Tappers, Rod Stradling and Tony Engle among them, continued to invite him for another couple of years to the *King's Head*, just along the road.

Melody Maker, *September, 1965.*

THE FOX, Islington Green, N.1. New Lost City Ramblers, Bill Clifton, Bob Davenport and The Rakes. Next week: **THE WATERSON FAMILY, JACK ELLIOTT,** from Birtley. **SCAN TESTER.** Residents. Members 6s. 6d., Guests 7s. 6d. Come Early!!

Opposite, top: At the Fox, *Islington; 1965.*
Bottom: Steve Pennells and Scan, the Fox; *1965.*
(Photographs: Douglas Baton. Courtesy David Nuttall)

Below: At the Keele Festival, July 1965.
(Photograph: Brian Shuel)

The event that Scan seemed to enjoy most of all was the Keele Festival, in Staffordshire, in July 1965. It was a three-day affair, Friday night, Saturday and Sunday. We lived-in, full board, on the college campus, with good food, good company and music and dancing everywhere. Scan, Steve Pennells (fiddle), Bob Davenport (singer and triangle) and I went together and played for the Friday night dance, and then played as and when we liked in the bar and at a couple of more formal concerts.[19] Michael Gorman (fiddle), Felix Doran (uilleann pipes) and Margaret Barry (banjo), three of the finest Irish musicians around at the time, were on the concerts with us, and a tape exists of Scan playing the tambourine with them. Although there was very little call for Scan to play in Horsted Keynes at that time, there was great local interest in his trip to Keele, and there was a waiting list of people in the village to borrow the souvenir album printed later in the year.

There were a few more concerts and festivals in which we were involved together: Guildford, in October 1965, where Jack Elliott, a retired miner from County Durham, sat in with the band on the ukelele-banjo; Devonport, in December 1965; and a return to Keele, this time with The Rakes, in July 1966. Cyril Phillips had given up farming and, with time on his hands, he was able to partner Scan fairly often. After Jack Norris died, Cyril had his melodeon and learnt to accompany himself on some of his own songs. They went to Ted and Ivy Poole's club in Swindon, Wiltshire, and the next day a

Scan and Cyril Philips; 1967. (Courtesy Daisy & Arch Sherlock)

Below: Melody Maker, 10 July 1967.

special session was laid on for them at the *Eagle* at Bampton in Oxfordshire. They were guests at the Cecil Sharp House festival a couple of more times, and at the Sidmouth Festival in Devon.

Cyril and Scan stayed at my house when they came to London, and after the 1963 festival we ended up playing at a wedding party, or, more correctly, a day-after-the-wedding party, at the *Constitution* in Camden Town. There was still plenty of food and drink left, and the guests who had come over from Ireland were still around, so the parents of the bride were delighted when we turned up with Jimmy Power (fiddle) and Johnny Gorman (concert flute), two well-known local musicians, and Scan's singing of *The Lakes of Coalflin* pleased the Irish crowd.

After the 1966 festival I took them to my regular Saturday night pub job at the *Grave Maurice* in Poplar in the East End. The crowd, all locals, were mainly Irish, and the band, led by Jimmy Power, played Irish dance music, but was always called on to accompany two Cockney singers on *Ragtime Cowboy Joe* and *I Left My Heart in San Francisco*. Scan and Cyril went down well, as they did the following morning at our other regular Irish session in the *Favourite*, off the Holloway Road in north London.

Mervyn Plunkett's meeting Walter and Daisy Bulwer at their home in Shipdham, Norfolk, in 1958 led to us both visiting them several times over the next few year, the LP English Country Music resulted from one such trip.[20] Walter (born 1888), a retired tailor and barber who still kept his hand in, had a range of interests, the greatest perhaps being the fiddle and

SCAN TESTER

ON and around his eightieth birthday, many folk fans are gathering in various places to do honour to Scan Tester, that fine traditional performer on the concertina. But nowhere will tribute be paid more meaningfully than among his own folk—as it was last Sunday at the New Inn, Hurstpierrepoint.

Scan was himself in great form—a short man with twinkling eyes, who walks firmly and quite briskly, contradicting every one of his eighty years. His singing voice (for which he is hardly known at all) is quite remarkable.

Among those who shared his birthday cake and presented him with a handsome carved-wood plate were Dick Richardson, a fine trad-style singer; Ray Chandler, who picks banjo in an original virtuoso manner that is as English as Barney McKenna is Irish; Roger Watson, a grand singer/songwriter from Nottingham. Harry Monsdeli and Derek Lockwood steered the event cheerfully. And a host of youngsters — fifteen to nineteen-year-olds—came gladly to sing for this man four times their age.

The most touching moment of all came when the Chanctonbury Ring Morris Men danced a spectacular leapfrog specially for Scan. As they passed his " flower - power " birthday chair at the start of the dance, each in turn made a graceful bow to Scan, echoing the good wishes of the scores of singers present—and indeed of the whole folk scene for a fine old man.

—ERIC WINTER

piano duets he played with his wife. He had been taught the fiddle, with some violin technique, by his father as a small child, but soon after that, while still very young, he began to play by ear and to invent and improvise second parts, which later he also managed on the viola, cello and double bass. Much of his experience matched Scan's: he had played in all sixteen of the Shipdham pubs, and before the Great War had played at servants' balls and on the piccolo, clarinet and slide trombone in the village bands. Between the wars he had been a member of a string orchestra organised at the church and well into the post-war years he had led his own dance band of cornet, fiddle and piano, first on mandolin and later from behind a set of drums; he claimed he had played at a hundred weddings. Although he shared many musical values with Wallace Chisholm (see chapter 9), he leaned heavily towards Scan's way of thinking and doing things, and he would have been in his element in the *Nutley Inn* band.

It was Daisy Bulwer who suggested I should take 'Stan' - they could never get his name - to see them for a get-together. Scan was always game for anything. 'If you're ever going anywhere, I'll always mate you', he often said to me, and we made the trip to Shipdham in July 1966. The three of them established social and musical rapport very easily, and they all recognised the uniqueness of their encounter. Initially I helped them - perhaps directed them would be more honest - into common ground, and there was complete compatibility in their renderings of the old country potboilers, *Jenny Lind, Brighton Camp* and the *Heel and Toe Polka*, for example, and not surprisingly the more recent but old popular songs. Music hall singalongs, *Tipperary* and the like, sounded both spontaneous and well-practiced. They even strung their Harry Lauder songs in the same order as each other!

Gradually they moved into more challenging territory, trying to recall the complexities, the introductions and bridge passages, the key changes and the various strains of *Hiawatha (A Summer Idyll), Stars and Stripes, Washington Post* and *Boston Two-Step* and similar composed pieces.[21] Clearly they had once experienced a demand for this sort of material. Walter could remember the melody lines from the printed scores, but his fiddle harmonies were certainly not as written, and Scan had demolished some of the chromatic structure and plastered over the cracks. Given more time together they would have almost certainly compromised on working arrangements of a good number of march and old-time dance compositions. Strangely they did not stray beyond the First World War, except for Scan's foray. into the Swinging Sixties with his then current favourite, taken from a singing group he fancied, The Seekers.

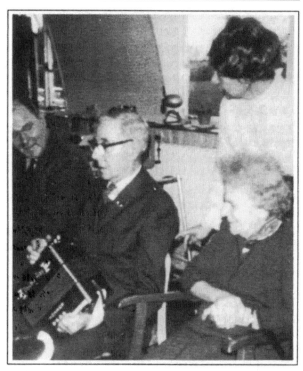

Jack Norris playing for an old people's do at Cuckfield; late 1960s – early 1970s.

(Courtesy Florence Norris)

From about 1966 Ken Stubbs's pub sessions settled down to a regular pattern of two or three a month, alternating between the *Cherry Tree* at Copthorne and the *Crown* at Edenbridge.[22] Cyril Phillips, George Spicer, Steve Pennells, Alan Waller (fiddle) and I from the old gang used to go occasionally, and there were a few other local singers like Louise Saunders (later Fuller), and Toby Hayward, a mandolin player from South Godstone in Surrey, who shared much of Scan's later repertoire.[23] Transport was difficult and Scan was dependent on others to pick him up and see him home.

These sessions were more formal than most of us were used to. Ken acted as master of ceremonies and encouraged everyone to give a song or play a tune. Several younger musicians, some sympathetic and sensitive, others competent in their own way but musically incompatible with Scan, used to join in. At these dos and at various folk song clubs - the *Lewes Arms* in Lewes and the *Central Club*, Peacehaven, for example - Scan's music was admired and welcomed, but he was usually called on to do a turn rather than to play for the entire evening. As a result his working repertoire was reduced to a couple of dozen old faithfuls. The skills he had acquired in a lifetime of pubbing - pacing an evening, building an atmosphere, exploiting an endless repertoire, playing the crowd, side-stepping hostility, etc. - were never put to use, but it probably suited him well enough. At that time of life he enjoyed the attention and conviviality, and he could afford to coast.

Around this time, David Nuttall, from Merton Park in Surrey, a banjo player in his early twenties and briefly the fourth member of The Rakes, began playing the concertina. He went to the *Stone Quarry* fairly often from about 1967 to play with Scan and Bill Avis. 'Cor, you don't want to catch that last train home tonight. You can stay with us'; so David used to put up for the night with Charlie Wheeler, a tambourine player whose uncle, Jack Wheeler, had been Scan's mate on the melodeon years before.

> **Scan:** I always go there every Saturday night, unless I've got something on special like. I do stay away sometimes, when I've got a job and that I can earn a few bob at, like, because I don't earn much up there, but they treat me good and the old landlord's a good bloke and I like it; that's why I go up there. I've got pals come up there. [R&DS]
>
> I always get a good crowd up there, and I don't mind as long as I get a good crowd to play to. I don't like sitting playing to myself. [VS]

Bill Avis (died 1986) from Maresfield was Scan's regular partner at that time. The crowd wanted a sing-song with the old pub favourites, and Bill could oblige on the piano-accordion. He and Scan were good pals, but there were differences in their rhythmic approach and Bill's style, typical of 1940s piano-accordion players, lacked Scan's sense of urgency and pulse. 'You know, I've tried to liven him up. I keep telling him, but it's no use.' [RH]

Denner Head frequented the Stone Quarry *in the 1960s when Scan was playing there.*
(Courtesy Audrey Castle & Peggy Head)

Below: Toby Hayward at the Men's Club, Edenbridge, Kent; 17 February 1968.
(Photograph; David Nuttall)

David Nuttall: Scan would start things off with a few of his dance tunes, which Bill didn't play, after which it was mostly songs for the test of the evening; I was simply expected to join in - and they had a few years start on me! 'Reg brought this kiddy along who was dead keen to learn,' I overheard Scan telling Denner Head one night. 'Play in or you won't learn 'em,' was Scan's advice to me. Well, I learnt them.

One Sunday while Scan and I were taking a walk round by the church in Horsted Keynes, sharing twenty Senior Service, payment from the night before, 'These blokes, David,' he said, 'These blokes think I can play concertina, but I can't play anymore, not how I used to, like. Mind you keep it up now; it'll be an interest for you when you retire.

On one visit to Horsted Keynes we all went to a pub in Crawley to sit in with a band in a pub there led by a piano-accordion player ... Bill [Avis] wisely played the washboard ... Scan was in with every number. I particularly remember them doing a break-neck *Who's Sorry Now*. Scan was with them all the way.

Like so many of his neighbours, Scan was an enthusiastic and expert gardener, with a plot of land behind the parish hall, and two gardens at Victoria Cottages which he divided with Arch Sherlock. He always prided himself on his skill and the quality of his produce, and in his eighties he was still active.

Scan: Well, I've got a bit of an allotment up the village, and I go up there and spar about. Thaws all I do. I don't work for nobody; I don't want the money. I go up there; there's plenty wants doing, but I don't do it all in one day. I've got a chair up there, and I just have a go, and then I think to myself, 'Well, I'm going to have a smoke now.' I sit down in the sun. Yes, I never worry. I think, 'Well, there's another day left, and if I don't finish it, someone else will.' I never worry about it. [VS]

It's surprising what you can grow, but I want manure now, and that's expensive stuff. I wouldn't mind buying a couple of loads, if it was any good, but that last load I had, I didn't know I had it. Well, it's only wet hay. You can't farm like that. If you go on taking stuff out the ground, you want to put something back, whatever gardening it is. What I do, I've got an old bin made of eight foot

The Stone Quarry, *Chelwood Gate; 1971.*

(Photograph: Hamish Black)

lengths of galvanised, and I chuck everything in there. Every little while I get my fork out, and I turn one end in, and, do you know, that's damn good stuff when you get it out and dig it in. [VS]

Each winter towards the end of Scan's life, the cold and the damp wore him down a little more; the rheumatism in his finger joints got worse and playing the concertina was very painful. He seldom went out in the wintertime, but as the warm weather broke through, he sprang back to life, and his neighbour and friend, Bob Fry, would take him to various music evenings.

> **Bob Fry:** Towards the end, you see, when I used to take old Scan out - in fact, the very last one we did, just before old Scan died - he'd begun to fail a bit and he hadn't been too well. There was a do on at the Coppers', and Scan had been a bit rough, and I rang through, actually, and told them. Course, Daisy was a bit worried and she said, 'I don't know whether Dad will be able to go' ... I went to see her in the afternoon before he was due down there, and I said, 'Well ... what you reckon?' and she said, 'Well, Dad said he'd like to go.' She never minded if he went with me, and we went down there and we had a terrific evening, absolutely terrific. Scan was really on form ... It was really amazing, because he really hadn't been at all too good, but as the evening sort of wore on, it began to give him a lift you know, and it wasn't, well, only a week or two after that he died. That was his last public do.[24]

Scan died at home after a very brief illness on 7 May 1972 and was buried five days later in Horsted Keynes churchyard.[25]

> Cor, there was several there. They come from miles around. Yes, there was a tidy crowd alright.[26]

NOTES

1. Mervyn Plunkett (1920-86) tape recorded many singers and musicians in Sussex, Norfolk, Dorset, Cornwall, Oxfordshire and Hampshire. He and I jointly produced four issues of Ethnic: *A Quarterly Survey of English Folk Music, Dance and Drama* in 1959 and an EP, *4 Sussex Singers* (Collector Records JEB7) in 1961, featuring George Spicer, Pop Maynard, Jean Hopkins and Jim Wilson. Plans are in hand to deposit his papers and recordings in a public archive and to issue the recordings on cassette. His obituary appeared in *Folk Music Journal*, V, 4 (1988), pp. 538-540.

2. LPs by these singers were issued in the mid-1970s: George Maynard, *Ye Subjects of England* (Topic 12T286); George Spicer, *Blackberry Fold* (Topic 12T235).

3. 'Best music there is - fiddle and tambourine.' (Pop Maynard to me, 1956.)

4. The Cuckfield *Parliamentary Register*, 1915, lists Bill Gorringe, Peter Gander and Bill Hawks as living at Whiteman's Green.

5. William George 'Jack' Norris was born in November 1898 at Chiltington, West Sussex, and moved to Cuckfield with his parents as a child. His father was a steamroller driver and played the melodeon at home. Jack was an aircraft mechanic in the Royal Flying Corps in the Great War. He worked for 33 years for Stephen Knight, builders and undertakers, in Cuckfield. He was in demand to provide music at weddings and in pubs. He died in January 1972. (Florence Norris)

6. The first part of *Another Cup of Coffee* is the second part of the *Original Schottische Polka*, which appears in the manuscript book of Michael Turner, the nineteenth-century fiddler from Warnham, Sussex (Anne Lough-ran and Vic Cammon, *A Sussex Tune Book* (1982), tune no. 34.).

   Jack Norris to me: 'It takes a good melodeon player to play *The Girl I Left Behind Me.'*

7. This stepdance tune was played by Scan (Topic 12T455/6, side 4, track 2) and Bill Gorringe (side 2, track 2c).

8. Mervyn was accompanied by his friend Dougie Moncrieff. In later years Arch Sherlock remembered the second person as Peter Kennedy. In fact, Peter Kennedy called on Scan much later.

9. Bill McMahon was born in Liverpool in 1920, landed in Normandy on D-Day and after the War moved to West Hoathly. 'Round the house! Mind those chaise, please!,' which he shouted before every performance, harked back to the Irish country kitchen dances of his father's early days. Bill's ambition at the time was to play the spoons with a trad jazz band. He could also stepdance.

10. The Rakes, a London-based barndance band, was formed in 1956 and is still active.

11. The informal leadership drifted between Mervyn, Scan and me. In retrospect I can see that from Scan's point of view, he played in our band. Apart from a few sessions in the Stone Quarry, we never played much on Scan's territory and I thus never met any of his old music-making partners, except Bill Gorringe.

Opposite: At Dave Wall's Club in Edenbridge, Kent; early 1970s.

(Photograph Ian Mason)

12. Harry Cox (born 1885), retired farmworker, singer and fiddle/ melodeon/ tinwhistle player from Norfolk; Ernie Glew, singer from Shoreham, Sussex; Fred Jordan, farmworker and singer from Shropshire.

13. Singer from Aberdeenshire.

14. *I Wonder Who's Kissing Her Now* was published in 1923, and was popular again in the 1950s. Testers' Imperial used it for the last waltz (David Nuttall).

15. The text and description of the play came from Harry Burgess, Firle, Sussex.

16. Bob Keightley (1914-89), market trader. His school violin teacher refused to continue teaching him when she caught him playing *Hold That Tiger* by ear. Though never a pub pianist, he had a remarkable London pub piano style and he sang some little-known London comic songs, two of which are featured in *The Bolden Lad* (Arts Council film, directed by John Tchalenko, 1980). Bob and lived in the same house from 1958 to 1967, and thus Bob got to know Scan.

17. Ken Stubbs: 'Te Life and Songs of George Maynard', *Folk Music Journal*, IX, 4, (1963), pp. 180-196.

18. The LP *The Roving Journeymen – The Willett Family* was recorded in 1962 (Topic 12T84).

19. Scan gives a colourful account of our arrival and the dance in an interview with Rod and Danny Stradling, published in *Folk Roots*, 31, (Jan. 1986), p. 12.

20. Topic 12T296.

21. There were at least two early 78 rpm records of *Hiawatha* issued in Britain, which could have been influential in popularising the tune among country musicians: Vess L. Ossman (USA), G&T.GC6387 (1903); Band of H.M. Coldstream Guards (UK) (1910), reissued on World Records SHB41. Mike Yates recorded a version under the title *The Pony March* from Jasper Smith (southern England) in the mid-1970s (Topic 12TS304).

22. Ken Stubbs ran sessions in a number of Sussex pubs until about 1978.

23. Toby Hayward played in a dance band before the Second World War. Ken Stubbs and I recorded him in the early 1960s at his home in a non-stop medley of 75 popular songs and tunes.

24. Interview with Bob Fry by Sean Goddard, 12.11.1985.

25. His obituary in *New Musical Express* ran to six-and-a-half column inches.

26. Scan quoted out of context.

Part II:

Context and Comment

Club outing from the Eclipse, Montgomery Street, Hove, Sussex, in 1913. The party includes
a concertina player, with a good quality 30-key Anglo, and a trombonist. Scan's teaming with
Trombone Billy at about the same time period was evidently not unique.
(Courtesy Graeme Kirkham)

Introduction

Scan's accessibility and longevity as an active musician provide an opportunity to document and discuss the music and dance activity of a small rural area over an eighty-year period. There were two distinct threads of musical tradition within the working population of that community: the first essentially aural, with skills, techniques, repertoires and attitudes deeply rooted in country working people's language, lore and life, and the second, a modification of the elite culture of the gentry, musical literacy allied to the values of genteel respectability. Some musicians were self-taught and played by ear, while others were trained and were musically literate. Some sang in church in one style, and in the pub in another. The two elements of tradition lived side by side, sometimes within the same person. The overlapping was as complex as the social structure itself. There was another significant dimension, namely, the relationship between the upper and lower strata of society, in that the music and dance culture of both allowed for originality, invention and self-expression, and there was room for cross-over of values, sometimes in the form of parody.

Scan was a central figure in his home community, but he was far from being the only musician. There were many others, at various levels, who served the needs of local working people. His area was bounded by his limited mobility but there is ample evidence of music and dance activity in neighbouring villages and towns, as indeed there is for the rest of Sussex, England and Britain as a whole. Influences from other areas must have penetrated Scan's part of the Sussex Weald, which may have been isolated, but was certainly not insular. Scan, deeply bedded in the aural tradition, had the dancing scene tied up around Horsted Keynes, while Wallace Chisholm, music teacher and band master, held a similar position a few miles away in the town of Uckfield (see chapter 9). They were polar extremes of a continuum; their co-existence, representing among other things differences between town and country, offers a clue to understanding the nature and causes of cultural diversity and regional style within the British Isles.

Scan is described, outside his own community and time, as a 'traditional' musician, and certainly his repertoire and style and the uses he made of his music ally him to others in Great Britain and Ireland who are similarly labelled. The strength and vitality of traditional music owes something to the way its practitioners side-step, parry and confront assaults from the outside, and in so doing absorb, re-model and adapt material to fulfil changing social demands. 'Traditional music' is a descriptive term and to attempt to define it here, in an attempt to place cultural and aesthetic values upon Scan and his associates, could easily deteriorate into a quest for purity. Labelling, in this instance, is more likely to cloud issues than illuminate them.

Some of the evidence assembled here will illustrate the close proximity, geographically and socially, of the 'other' culture, the music and dancing of the country middle class and gentry, and its overspill into sections of the poorer, working community. Newspaper reports give an idea of some of the musical and social events in neighbouring areas and further afield in Sussex. Seldom in the form of advertisement, but written as news items after the event, they were sent in by local correspondents, perhaps the postmaster or a shopkeeper, whose aspirations and values were directed up rather than down the social scale. The blandness and stodginess of these accounts were further compounded by sub-editing into a conventional style. Interestingly, Horsted Keynes, Danehill, Nutley and Fairwarp were particularly poorly reported in the Sussex Express. This may have been due to the absence or indolence of local correspondents, but it might also be concluded that the musical activities of Scan and his associates were dominant in his area, and being too far down the social scale did not warrant reporting.

Scan's was essentially a man's world. Friendly Societies, village bands, cricket and football clubs, slate clubs and smoking concerts - institutions associated with music-making - were exclusively male. But some women were involved in public music-making, and women became increasingly more so as the

Daisy & Arch Sherlock at Victoria Cottages; 1971.

(Photograph: Hamish Black)

period progressed. What then of that male preserve, the taproom in the public house? As the pub was a major outlet for music, we need to know for certain if women had any presence there at all.

> **Bert Wood:** Oh, they wouldn't have 'em in pubs at one time... They used to stand outside. You take the drinks out to 'em... It caused trouble, soon as a woman got in there.

He was talking about the *Crocodile*, Danehill, in particular and pubs in general. His son-in-law, Charlie Bates, says things changed after the Second World War, but not after the First. How is this to be reconciled with Scan's story of women tambourine players and evidence elsewhere of women broomdancers and stepdancers? How could the waltz, the schottische, the polka, the *Waltz Vienna* and the *Heel and Toe Polka* have sustained their existence for so long as pub dances, if women were not around? Were women only in the pubs at very specific times and on special occasions, such as wedding parties? Scan's mother actually worked full-time in the *Green Man*, although the licence was held by Scan's father, and for considerable lengths of time the licensees of the *Sheffield Arms*, *Nutley Inn*, the *Prince of Wales* at Cackle Street and *William IV* were women.[1]

In Scan's family, the father sang, three sons played instruments and another was a singer, while the fifth son was by reputation too shy to do anything. But what of the mother and two daughters? Are we to believe they never sang, or stepped or knocked a tune out of a music? Their contemporary, Emma Gurr, played the melodeon at home, while her husband, Jack, occasionally played in the *Crown*.

Interior of Sheffield Park Reading Room; 1987. Tester's Imperial had a regular booking there.

(Photograph: Reg Hall)

74

Was this a representative pattern? Did women make music and sing largely in the privacy of their homes, while the men had a more public outlet? Martha Stephenson's presence in the dance band in the back room at the *Nutley Inn* appears to have been an unusual phenomenon, yet Scan made no comment about it.

Slightly higher up the social scale, the daughters of shopkeepers and tradesmen learned the piano and some were playing publicly at village events by the turn of the century. At a dance in the schoolroom in Fletching in 1909, for example, 'Miss Langridge presided at the piano', but the genteel report in the local newspaper missed the point, that the dancing from 7.30 p.m. to 1.30 p.m. meant a six-hour slog for the musician.[2] Daisy Sherlock, an ear-player, belonged musically in her father's camp. Her public image, however, was no different from that of other girls and young women who, having received piano lessons, were available to take part in the post-First World War boom in village hall dancing.[3] Women fulfilled part of the expanding demand for musicians, although their role was generally confined to playing the violin and the piano. Speaking proudly of the exceptional role his wife had adopted, Scan could say, 'You never see a woman drummer.' [RH] The Great War did, of course, soften attitudes and changed public house behaviour, and not long after the War, Testers' Imperial were playing for mixed dancing at the *Sloop* - not in a private room but in the bar.

There is no doubt music and dancing provided Scan with strong personal satisfactions, not just in achievement but within local society. From early childhood music placed him among the men, and he was privy to their conversation and values. This edge on his peers carried him into adolescence as 'one of the boys'; music admitted him to a diversity of small social systems, and in old age kept him in young company. Music and dancing were fun and the musician was at the centre of it all, popular and sought after. Scan gave of his best, very often with no question of financial gain, but behind it all were economic possibilities and realities. The collection made for him in a pub, his own enterprise as a

dancing teacher and dance promoter, the week's supply of food he took home from the servants' parties, the packet of fags from a pub landlord, all supplemented his wages from other sources, and the formation of the family band kept the economic possibilities within the family. Scan never owned property, but in other ways he shared many economic values with the last of the Wealden peasantry.

To make sense of Scan's musical activities it is helpful to categorise them into five sections:

1. **Pubbing: 1895 - 1924.**

    Saturday nights, tontine shareouts, weddings, etc.
    Old songs, stepdances, the *Reel*, the *Broom Dance* and couple and round dances.

2. **Organised dances: 1897 - 1924.**

    Nutley Inn, servants' balls, servants' parties and his own dance promotions.
    Couple, round and set dances.

3. **Testers' Imperial: 1924 - 1931.**

    Semi-pro family band, public dances.
    Modern ballroom, couple, round and set dances.

4. **Coasting: 1931 - 1972.**

    Outings, the *Stone Quarry*, domestic.
    Current popular tunes and old favourites.

5. **Revival: 1957 - 1972.**

    Folk clubs, festivals, concerts, etc.
    Exposure beyond his own community.
    Recourse to his old repertoires in new social circumstances and settings.

These classifications are not discrete or mutually exclusive, and there are at least two important additional strands, namely, the village band and busking on Brighton beach. The events of sections 4 and 5 have been covered, but analysis of sections 1, 2 and 3 requires further examination of dance repertoire, tune repertoire, instruments and style.

NOTES

1. The following are examples of women who were licensees: Susannah Coomber, Sheffield Arms, 1872-86; Ellanah Marchant, *Nutley Inn*, 1878-82; Ellen Marchant, *Prince of Wales*, 1886-94; Jane Waller, *Nutley Inn*, 1889-1901 or later (Uckfield Petty Sessions Register of Licences).

2. *Sussex Express*, 19.11.1909.

    See also *Sussex Express*, 1.1.1914, where the musician at a Boxing Night dance at Framfield was Miss D. Berry.

3. The following arc examples of female musicians at public dances: Miss Buxton, banjolele, A. Bolton, drums, and R. Green, piano, in the church room, Whatlington (*Sussex Express*, 7.2.1930); Miss White, piano, and A. Bolton, jazz [drums] at the same venue (*Sussex Express*, 2.5.1930); E. Huss, Miss E. Tester and Mr. Rusich in Brightlington (*Sussex Express*, 7.3.1930); and Mrs. Anderson's Band from Wadhurst in Mayfield (*Sussex Express*, 14.3.1930a).

'Stepdancing, Tap Room', by Charles J. Staniland, published in The Graphic, 22 October 1887.

The venue is the King's Head, Hoverton, Wroxham, Norfolk, and the fiddler is the landlord, Mr. Jimpson. Note the 'Ring the Bull' game.

Chapter 5:
Dances and dance tunes

Country stepdancing has been widespread through the southern half of England and in Ireland. There has been a range of styles, but the common characteristics - the relaxed posture, the low centre of gravity, the loose swinging arms, the rhythmic beating and scuffing of the feet on the floor and the glazed facial expression - unite the diversity into one recognisable phenomenon.[1] At its simplest, yet often most effective, the steps are little more than rhythmic battering and shuffling, picked up by watching others or invented by the dancer. Scan, like many others, learned precise steps and phrases from older stepdancers. Others, particularly in Ireland, learnt in childhood from itinerant dancing teachers, paying a small price for each step, and they were taught to dance sequences of steps, first leading with one foot and repeating the phrase with the other. It was good fun for the dancer and the onlooker alike, and a spirit of daring and informal, and sometimes formal, competition entered the proceedings.

In the *Foresters* at Fairwarp, in Scan's young days, they did the *Reel* (or *Four Hand Reel*, to give its generic name), which combined the centuries-old hey, a soft-shoe walking and weaving figure, with step-dancing.

> **Scan:** Course, they used to come in the pubs, you see, with their heavy boots on - the old pelted boots and all - and yorks and all on, and you see 'em out in the room that time of day doing the old stepdances, and they used to, if there was enough of 'em, they'd form a figure eight or form a four angles, you know, cross angles, and, you know, there was a lot of different ways they used to dance.[2] [AW]

There used to be what we called a reel. It was ordinary four corners, four of them, and they used to step, and then the second part they change over and go in and form the figure eight. And really, they was old people that done it, mind you. They young ones, they used to join in. Get two in a set, see, so as to learn 'em. [MP]

They did the *Broom Dance*, cocking their legs up in time to the music as they passed a broom from one hand to the other under each leg in turn for eight bar phrases, followed by a walking figure. It was sometimes danced by four people at a time, when the walking figure became a hey. Scan's accounts of the *Reel* and the *Broom Dance* give little precise detail; both dances have had wide currency in southern England at least, and, I suspect, in the case of the *Broom Dance*, in southern Ireland too, and presumably embraced some measure of local and personal variation.[3]

By the time I met Scan he was too old to stepdance. He would get in the mood with the music and try a few steps before losing his balance and giving up in disgust. There was still stepdancing to be seen in country pubs in the 1950s and, of course, it survives in pockets even now and surfaces particularly when travellers get together. However, the heyday of stepdancing in Scan's area was long past, and several local people well into their seventies claim never to have seen it. My guess is that Scan had little or no call to play his stepdance tunes from just after the Great War until he met Mervyn Plunkett in 1957.

> **Scan:** You know, when you get older, the times are different and you don't get in the company where there is any stepping. [AW]

Scan's stepdance tunes, in all probability, originated in the second half of the eighteenth century. According to George S. Emmerson, 'The earlier hornpipe [i.e. before the mid-eighteenth century] was a peculiar syncopated limping gait to a tune in triple time - three /two, six /four or twelve/eight.'[4] While hornpipe dancing existed in both village communities and on the stage, he wonders whether Thomas Arne's *New Hornpipe*, performed by Mrs Vernon at Covent Garden in 1760, 'was the first of the new genre of common-time hornpipe'. Both country and stage hornpipes were high dances, performed high off the ground in soft-soled shoes. The metamorphosis to the close-to-the-ground stepdancing indigenous to southern England and Ireland during this and the last century occurred when working men began to wear heavy leather soles and domestic buildings used timber or brick flooring. Soil floors, common even in Scan's day, or soil covered flag stones would give little sound back to a stepdancer. Emmerson says stepdancers in the last century preferred wooden surfaces, like a table or a door taken off its hinges, or dancing in hob-nailed boots on brick floors.

Without being specific, Scan gave the impression, by calling a certain type of tune in his repertoire 'step-dance tunes', that stepping was done exclusively in fast common time. Evidence from elsewhere indicates the use of other rhythms and, of course, Scan's own broom dance tune is in 6/8.[5] Scan had few names for his stepdance tunes and late in life resorted to numbering some of them.

> **Scan:** Well there it is. I've never heard the names, you see … You see we just played for our own amusements. Course, lot of these tunes the old people didn't … know the names, you see … The majority of 'em was fiddlers, you know. [AWG]

Scan claimed he knew 'any amount' of stepdance tunes, but in later years his recall ran only to those appearing on the Topic records and a version of *Waltzing Matilda*.[6] Among these tunes, *Soldier's Joy* is standard and has been common through Britain, Ireland and America; one of his untitled stepdances appears elsewhere as the *Cliff Hornpipe* and is known within Irish traditional music; and the *Monkey Hornpipe*, which takes its name from a pub dance, shares the last four bars of each part with the *Sailors' Hornpipe*. Scan's *No. 1 Stepdance* has phrases and a structure like some other tunes, but *No. 2* strikes me as being unlike anything I have heard elsewhere.[7]

Another of Scan's untitled stepdances seems to be *the* southern English hornpipe, often apparently the only stepdance tune known to some musicians.[8] Scan's *Reel* seems to be standard in southern England as the tune for the *Four Hand Reel*, although it too is used for stepdancing.[9] Could these have been prototype country hornpipes, originating with, and circulated by, country fiddlers, the first of the new common-time hornpipes? Neither appears to have a proper name among country musicians. If, in fact, they were prototypes, they needed no specific titles.

The former was published around 1781, untitled, but associated with a stage dancer, Robert Aldridge, who was active in London and Edinburgh. It was later named after John Bill Ricketts, an Englishman engaged in circus promotion in the United States in the 1790s.[10] The title *Rickett's Hornpipe* is American, so not surprisingly it is unknown among English country musicians. Irish musicians, among whom the titles, *Rickett's Hornpipe* and *Manchester Hornpipe* are known, may have learnt it directly or indirectly from print. The question remains: where did Aldridge get it from? Does the country version pre-date its stage use? The Italianate structure of the *Reel*, based on tonic, subdominant, and dominant chords, sets it aside from other country hornpipes, and perhaps ensured its integrity. Could the word 'breakdown', which we understand now, among other meanings, as an alternative to hornpipe, and which appears in several country titles, have been its original title or the original description of the genre?

Advertisements for sheet music and dance instructions for Pop Goes the Weasel *and* La Tempête.

Note that both Coulon and Jullien were offering their own versions of La Tempête.

(Illustrated London News, *19 March 1853*)

COUNTRY DANCES

Scan had many tunes in 6/8 and 2/4 time, dating from the eighteenth century, which have persisted in popular usage until the present day. Many have had varied careers. They have been used for country dances (using the term in its technical sense), for songs and jingles, and been played by country musicians for stepdancing.[11] Later, some were adopted for the polka and quadrilles. Whether they *originated* as published compositions will probably never be known. Many were published and circulated among literate ballroom and theatre musicians, and co-existed in the repertoire of brass, military and fife and drum bands in villages and towns and in the Army. Among the tunes Scan played, *Seventeenth of March* or *St. Patrick's Day* was published in 1748, *Garryowen* in 1800, *Bonny Dundee* in 1854 and *The Irish Washerwoman* in 1789.[12] The regimental march of the Royal West Kents, which Will Tester must have played hundreds of times in the West Kents' band, was a medley of two such tunes, *A Hundred Pipers* and *Bonnets so Blue*.[13] O'Neill claims *The Girl I Left Behind Me*, probably the most widely known of old country tunes in southern England, as Irish, dating from the early part of the eighteenth century:

> [B]andmasters, at the request of the officers and soldiers, began to use the melody as a parting tune, and by the end of the [eighteenth] century it was accounted disrespectful to the ladies of the regiment to march away without playing 'The Girl I Left Behind Me'.[14]

Some measure of the currency of this material can be taken from the repertoire of 'Old Sarah' (born 1786), who learnt the hurdy-gurdy in 1806 to busk on the streets of London. Of the first eight tunes she learnt, excluding the National Anthem, Scan knew at least five: *Garryowen, St. Patrick's Day, The Girl I Left Behind Me, Haste to the Wedding* and the minstrel song *Oh, Susannah!* In the late 1850s she reported:

> The first tune I ever played was 'God save the King', the Queen as is now; then 'Harlequin Hamlet' [*Garryowen*], that took me a long time to get off; it was three weeks before they put me on a new one. I then learnt 'Moll Brook'; then I did the 'Turnpike-gate' and 'Patrick's day in the morning': all of them I learnt in the Union. I got a poor man to teach me the 'New-rigged ship'. I soon learnt it, because it was an easy tune. Two-and-forty years ago I played 'The Gal I left behind me'. A woman learnt it me; she played my cymbal [hurdy gurdy] and I

listened, and so got it. 'Oh, Susannah!' I learnt myself by hearing it on the horgan ... I always try and listen to a new tune when I am in the street, and get it off if I can: its my bread... 'Hasten to the Wedding' is my favourite; I played it years ago, and play it still. I like 'Where have you been all night?' It's a Scotch tune... At some places they like polkas, but at one house I plays at in Kensington they always ask me for 'Haste to the Wedding'.[15]

I heard Scan play *Pop Goes the Weasel, Rakes of Mallow, Cock o' the North, Keel Row, Old Mrs Cuddledee* and *No Luck about the House* among these old tunes, and almost certainly he would have played many more late in life, if only he could have triggered his recall. In common with Old Sarah, however, he placed a special value on *Haste to the Wedding*:

> That's one you want to strike up when you get out somewhere and you get a nice lot. Then they want to know! Most people like them old jigs, you know. I used to know several Irish and Scotch jigs, but they're all gone. [VS]

Thomas Wilson's *Companion to the Ballroom*, published in 1816, gives the notation of a large number of country dances available to elite society. An evening's dancing at a private function or at a subscription ball in public assembly rooms would have involved a repertoire of many different dances, all variations on well-known dance figures. Some of these dances were known and performed lower down the social scale, and Scan's dance repertoire before the Great War included one 'country dance' of this kind. Fanny Lander remembered the *Galop*, or *Haste to the Wedding*, danced to Scan's music at the *Coach and Horses* servants' ball:

> You lined up, men lined up and women lined up, and you took hold of her, and you went through an archway. I think that was *Haste to the Wedding*. It was really lovely in those days. You really got something out of dancing in those days.

Scan taught the *Galop* in 1959, after a thirty-five year lapse, at a social evening in Gravesend. He demonstrated with the minimum of verbal instruction and moved with a gliding, lilting walk and an occasional slip step. He described the musician's task as keeping the music going until each couple, no matter how many were in the set, had danced in first position and had galoped to the bottom of the set.[16]

Scan: When you danced one of them *Galops*, you danced a lot, you see... If you get a roomful, the devils lasted so long. [MP]

There was another *Galop* that appeared on local dance programmes among the gentry in the late nineteenth century, but that was a couple dance, also known as the *Galopade*, which dated from 1829.[17] Scan's dance may well have been a hybrid, combining the galop movement from the *Galopade* with the country dance formation. For dances of later origin, such as the waltz and quadrilles, Scan played medleys of tunes, but as far as the *Galop* was concerned, he followed the old country dance convention of one dance, one tune.

There has been no study or adequate explanation of the social relationship between the country dancing of elite society on the one hand and the country dancing of country working people on the other. Clearly, there was some common ground. Circulation among the elite can be explained by the existence of professional dancing teachers and professional musicians available to sell their services. The 'season' required its participants to acquire social skills, dancing being one of them, which were then practised in public for the duration of the season. The dances were therefore taught and rehearsed. No such explanation fits further down the social scale, where economic resources were not available and leisure opportunities were much less frequent. The

dances may possibly have been picked up by house servants, or may have been learnt by literate country fiddlers from instruction books, and they were practised at dancing booths at fairs and weddings.

Two mid-nineteenth century descriptions of country dancing by country working people mention just one dance each. Mayhew's informant, 'Whistling Billy', a London street musician, who played in the West Country in the late 1850s for local and migrant Irish harvesters, had this to say:

> My country dance was to the tune 'Oh don't you tease me, pretty little dear.' Any fiddler knows that air. It's always played in the country for country dances. First they dance to each other, and it's hands across, and then down the middle, and then it's back again and turn. That's the country dance, sir.[18]

Thomas Hardy had his Christmas party-makers in a Dorset cottage dance to the same tune under another title, *The Triumph*.[19] On the face of it, both groups appear to have known only one country dance and the custodianship seems to have rested with the musicians. If this was a general rule, and this is by no means proven, Scan's single country dance fitted the convention. He, too, played *Pretty Little Dear*, but for him it was simply another polka tune.[20]

Scan and Reg playing for The Galop *at a social evening in the Art School, Gravesend, Kent; 27 February 1958.*

QUADRILLES, LANCERS AND ALBERTS

The Quadrille is a dance of four or five figures for four couples in square formation. It was introduced into British high society from France, at Almack's in London, in 1816, with a 'spin-off' version, the *Lancers*, making its debut at a society ball in Dublin the following year. The music publishing houses supplied a constant stream of variations on the theme, thereby satisfying the elite public's demand for fashionable novelty. Charles d'Albert's *Albert Quadrilles*, based on existing figures, was one such variation and matched the two original sets in popularity and staying power.[21] The difficult steps, which led to Cruikshank's characterisation of quadrilles as a grotesque romp, required too much learning and eventually atrophied to simple walking.[22] The music was in the light classical mode of the time: some pieces were composed especially, but some were adapted, on the cheap, from popular operatic arias and national airs.[23]

Quadrilles were slow to filter down the social scale in southern England. In the middle of the last century, there was a revival of interest in quadrille dancing among the elite, and by the early 1880s it had become a minor national movement at the lower end of the urban middle class and the upper working class. The Volunteers (the forerunner of the Territorial Army, formed in the 1860s), offered a mantle of respectability for shopkeepers, artisans and small contractors, providing organisation, locations and ready-made bands. Professional dancing teachers found extra custom for their classes and rewarded their pupils with 'long nights' and end-of-season quadrille parties.[24] Elsewhere, in Ireland and the West Indies, for example, these set dances were

taken into the repertoires of rural working people and moved further from their upper-class ballroom origins. They were modified and adapted to existing vernacular styles, taking on characters of their own.[25]

In small Sussex towns there were quadrille bands - for example, Chisholm's at Uckfield, Finch's at Haywards Heath and Anderson's at Forest Row - and quadrille classes and long nights were held in the villages.[26] Scan almost certainly did not attend the quadrille class held in Fletching National Schools in 1905, but he did see the sets danced at Horsted Keynes feast days, and they were established as part of the repertoire at the Coach ball, in all probability by the time he started playing there.[27]

The string band of the Royal Engineers, which played at the Inhabitants' Ball in Lewes in 1897, used exclusively light classical material, as might be expected at such a select function.[28] A view of the repertoire, instrumentation and orchestrations used by a small town working musician, contemporary to Scan, would have been possible if only Wallace Chisholm's personal collection of sheet music had not been dispersed after his death (see chapter 9). Recordings of regimental marches made in 1915-7, however, include material in 6/8 time that is probably a fair approximation of the quadrille music played by Volunteer and village bands.[29]

There are commercial recordings of vernacular musicians from Scotland, where quadrilles entered the popular field very late and thus survived much later into this century. Peter and Dan Wyper, from near Hamilton, were straight-laced melodeon players with, I suspect, a smattering of literacy, and they were in the music business as retailers. Peter Wyper

Typical local press advertisements of the 1880s, from the Bermondsey and Rotherhithe Advertiser and Southward Recorder; 22 October 1881.

recorded *Lion Quadrilles* in 1910 and *Blackthorn Stick Quadrilles* in 1912, and Dan Wyper recorded the *Pibroch Quadrilles* in 1921, both using traditional tunes, i.e., jigs, polkas and reels. However, at about the same time Dan Wyper recorded *The Original Lancers* using the original published melody line with simplified piano vamp, which eliminated the excesses of the composer's harmony. William Hannah's *Thistle Lancers* and *Lothian Quadrilles*, recorded in 1924 with button accordion, fiddle and piano, are closer to the vernacular style, utilizing what seems to be written quadrille material, modified to the taste and techniques of people used to traditional music. *Patience Quadrilles*, recorded in 1930 by a Glasgow neighbourhood band run by a cycle dealer, Bob Smith, reverts to the classic practice of using selections from operetta. However, the drive and attack of the semi-legitimate violin playing and the loud, wild drumming are anything but Sullivanesque.[30]

> **Scan:** Course, I used to play the *Quadrilles* and the *Lancers* and the *Alberts*… Course, they was a little later dance, but they're very old dances, you know. The *Alberts* were the prettiest of the lot. [MP]

> Me and my brothers … we used to play all the old set dances, *Lancers*, *Quadrilles* and the *Alberts*. Oh, we used to play the whole issue, and at that time of day there was always certain ones in the room were real set dancers, and you had to play a certain amount to keep them coming. Cor, I used to like playing that time of day, because nearly everybody was a round dancer, and as soon as ever you started, you'd get a floor full up. I used to like playing them better than I did any, but a lot of round dancers didn't know the sets, so you used to have to be careful or you could make it bad that way. [VS]

> We had to be careful what we played, so as not to upset anyone.[31]

Scan's tune repertoire for these set dances is now lost, except for one figure of the *Lancers* recorded by Peter Kennedy. Daisy says they used mostly songs and march tunes, and she remembered specifically *I Love a Lassie* for the chain figure. The first figure of the Lancers was danced to the tune which the mid-nineteenth century fiddler Thomas Shoosmith, of Arlington, Sussex, noted in his manuscript book as *John of Paris*, which was also the regimental march of the Rifle Brigade.[32]

While the waltz can be danced by just two people to a tune on the wireless, quadrilles require much more formal organisation. Once community demand began to wane, set dancing was on the way out. Newspaper evidence indicates that all the other local quadrille classes ceased to function before the Great War, so Scan's dancing classes with Bill Gorringe catered for a new, albeit rather old-fashioned, clientele, some of whom demanded the set dances right up to the time Testers' Imperial disbanded in 1931.

THE WALTZ, POLKA AND SCHOTTISCHE

Round dancing was the creation of the same class of dancing teachers and balletmasters, tuned in to continental high fashion, who introduced the quadrille to nineteenth-century society. The waltz, first seen in England in 1812, introduced new concepts. Partners embraced each other and danced as couples around the ballroom, independently of other couples, and this independence allowed a degree of personal choice in the movements and steps. The polka and schottische followed a generation later, in 1844 and 1848 respectively.[33] The process by which they became known further down the social scale is not known for certain, but there was a considerable time delay in their dissemination. A generalised account of dancing in private rooms in London pubs, published in 1861, gives some indication of the differences in style between the social classes, and the tardiness among the poor in catching on to the fashion of those better off.

> 'Twopenny-hops' are much resorted to by the costermongers, men and women, boys and girls. At these dances decorum is sometimes, but not often, violated… There is nothing of the leisurely style of dancing - half a glide and half a skip - but vigorous, laborious capering…. The music is always a fiddle, sometimes in the addition of a harp and a cornopean… The other dances [apart from stepdancing] are jigs, 'flash jigs' - hornpipes in fetters - a dance rendered popular by the success of the acted 'Jack Sheppard' - polkas, and country-dances, the last mentioned being generally demanded by the women. Waltzes are as yet unknown to them.[34]

Those making their living in the dance business invented dances, some in new, exotic rhythms, but all based on the format established by the waltz, the polka and the schottische. Some new dances barely saw the end of a season; others had more appeal and remained in fashion for several years. The *Varsovi-*

enne and the *Heel and Toe Polka*, in common with their parent round dances, have survived as vernacular dances modified by country working people in places throughout Britain and Ireland until modern times. The last nineteenth-century round dance to concern us pointed a new direction for our imported dances: the *Military Schottische*, better known as the *Barn Dance*, was introduced in 1888 from the United States rather than the Continent.[35]

Scan had a large selection of tunes for round dancing and claimed he could go on all night without repeating any of them. The sources of this material have never, to my knowledge, been discussed in print. In fact, within the folk dance movements in England, Scotland and Ireland, with the notable exception of Peter Kennedy's field collecting in the 1950s, the material has been ignored and largely despised. Some exploration, however tentative, is long overdue.

Nineteenth-century printed social dance music falls, broadly speaking, into two categories. First, there are compositions following the current academic rules and fashion, melodies complicated, even dramatised, by the use of chromatics and modulations, and prettified by trills, the rhythmic stress being that of academic rather than vernacular music. The second group are essentially diatonic, except perhaps for chromatic grace notes and chromatic lead-in notes; harmonic structures are simple and the general construction of the pieces is nearer that of traditional music. Some of these tunes may have been in the public domain before being filched by publishing house hacks, but who can now tell? A polarised typology such as this is a useful tool for analysis, but oversimplification carries with it dangers, and it should be understood there are gradations between these two extremes.

Jullien's *Original Polka* (1844), in all probability, set criteria for subsequent polka music composition. Easy to master for even a moderately proficient amateur pianist, its construction has the hallmarks of schooled composition, and it lies midway between the suggested polar extremes. Pitched in the key of G, the first sixteen bars are based on alternating G and D chords, but start on D rather than G and resolve on a G chord. The second twelve bars are pitched in D, but written with a G key signature, and are built on a three-chord structure of D, A and G. Although the themes are diatonic, they could not be mistaken for traditional tunes. The reversed order of the chords in the first part and the change of key in the second part, coupled with frills, dynamic variation from *pp* to *ff*, a leap of a seventh from F sharp to E in the seventh bar and three equally timed Gs in the eighth bar, stamp the piece with a marked period feel. The heavily accentuated first beat in each bar is

rhythmic caricature; it is so foreign to vernacular music, it could never have been sustained within popular culture.

The testimony of an adolescent, earning his living playing the concertina on Thames excursion boats, provides evidence of an ear-player picking up material from literate professional musicians around 1852-1853. The tune he singles out, Charles d'Albert's *Sultan Polka*, subsequently became a standard country pub dance favourite. Or is this perhaps an example of a composer cashing in on an already popular tune?

> I'm nearly fifteen now; but I can remember when I was seven, being particularly taken with music. I had an uncle who was captain of a steamer that run to Richmond, and I was always on board with him; and they used to have a band on board... I used to go and listen to them. I learn all their tunes by heart. They mostly played dances, and very seldom any sentimental songs, unless anybody asked them... When ... the musicians put the harp down in the cabin, I'd get playing on it... I learnt myself several tunes, such as the 'Sultan Polka'. I must have been eight years old then. I didn't play it with both hands: I couldn't do the bass.[36]

The lad goes on to talk of the present (1861 or a little earlier), and singles out the *Varsovienne* as being a popular request by the ladies.

Another of Mayhew's informants, an Italian organ grinder, describes the popularity of various types of music among the social classes. His organ rolls would probably have been cut from printed scores, but here again is evidence of the exposure of Scan's type of material on the streets of the capital.

> There is two 'Liverpool Hornpipe'. I know one these twenty years. Then come 'The Ratcatcher's Daughter'; he is a English song. It's get a little old; but when it's first come out the poor people do like it, but the gentlemens they like more the opera, you know. After that is what you call 'Minnie', another English song. He is middling popular. He is not one of the new tune, but they do like it. The next one is a Scotch contre-danse. It is good tunes, but I don't know the name of it. The next one is, I think, a polka; but I think he's made from part of 'Scotische'. There is two or three tunes belongs to the 'Scotische'. The next one

LA POLKA.—In consequence of the numerous applications made to MRS. JAMES RAE for instruction in this Fashionable DANCE, in its most recherché and perfect style (as danced in the élite of society in Paris), Mrs. RAE has decided upon devoting MONDAY and FRIDAY EVENINGS for the practice of it To commence NEXT MONDAY, the 22nd instant, at her residence, 50, Berners-street, Oxford-street, where terms and particulars may be ascertained.—The Soirées Dansantes on Wednesday Evening, as usual.

20 April

Published this day, price 1s.,
HOW TO DANCE THE POLKA !—All the Quadrilles, German Waltzes, Highland Reels, &c. &c., according to the Method of M. COULON. With a History of the origin of the inimitable LA POLKA. *.* Sent to any part of the country by post, free, on receiving a remittance of 1s. 4d.

4 May

LA POLKA.—MRS. JAMES RAE, the First to introduce La Polka personally from Paris, begs to announce that REUNIONS are held at her Residence, 50 A, Berners-street, Oxford-street, on Monday and Friday evenings, for the exclusive practice of this interesting dance, as taught in Paris, in its most pure style, by M. CORALLI, fils, and as danced by his pupils in the élite of Parisian society.

4 May

LA POLKA.—Mrs. JAMES RAE has the honour to announce that she has REMOVED from No. 50, Berners-street, to No. 16, Manchester-square. In addition to private instruction, her Polka Réunions, for the exclusive practice of the " Drawing-room Polka," " Polka Cotillon," and " Valse à Deux Temps," are held, under distinguished patronage, at her new residence, on Mondays and Fridays, where terms and particulars can be ascertained. Her Academy, hitherto held at the Hanover-square Rooms, is now continued in Manchester-square, on Mondays and Thursdays.

8 June

GRAND POLKA BALL.—Mrs. JAMES RAE has the honour to announce that her GRAND FANCY and FULL DRESS POLKA BALL will take place at the HANOVER-SQUARE ROOMS, under the most distinguished patronage, on THURSDAY, the 27th of JUNE. Tickets, and all particulars, to be had only of Mrs. JAMES RAE, 16, Manchester-square, where the names of the Ladies Patronesses can be ascertained.

8 June

THE REDOWA POLKA, Danced by Mdlle. Cerito and M. St. Leon, at her Majesty's Theatre.—Just published, the charming Music of this favourite Polka, arranged for the Pianoforte, solo, price 2s.; duet, 2s. 6d.—" The newest and prettiest of Polkas."—Athenæum, June 1.—" The music of the Redowa Polka is immeasurably the most graceful and characteristic. Certain it is that the Redowa is infinitely the prettiest of Polkas."—Times, May 24.—London: CHAPPELL, 59, New Bond-Street

15 June

JULLIEN'S ORIGINAL POLKA.—The ninth edition of JULLIEN'S original POLKA is now published.—The immense success of this celebrated dance having induced many unprincipled persons to sell to the public spurious imitations, M. Jullien has published the original Polka at his own office, 3, Maddox-street, Bond-street; and, in order to secure the public against the possibility of purchasing the false copies published under so many disguised forms, he has attached his signature to each copy of his original Polka. None can therefore be relied on which have not his autograph. Correct copies of Jullien's original Polka to be had only of the respectable music-sellers in the kingdom, by asking for Jullien's original Polka, signed by the author.

22 June

DANCING TAUGHT in the most fashionable style, by Mr. WILLIS, 41, Brewer-street, Golden-square. Private Lessons at all hours to Ladies and Gentlemen of any age, wishing privacy and expedition. An Evening Academy on Mondays and Fridays. Lessons in the Polka and Valse à Deux Temps every day.—A card of terms may be had on application. The room may be engaged for private parties.

22 June

LA POLKA.—THE LADIES' GAZETTE OF FASHION for July (Price 1s., post-free 1s. 6d.) contains Music of Polka Dance and Important Novelties given in no other work : 50 beautifully coloured Costumes, Patterns of Morning, Evening, Promenade, and Sea-side Dresses; Hats, Bonnets, Caps, and Fashionable Millinery; with Descriptions, Tales, Poetry, &c. The Ladies' Gazette contains the Paris Fashions before any other work.—G. BERGER, Holywell-street, Strand.

6 July

POLKA MATINEES, 16, Manchester-square.—Mrs. JAMES RAE has the honour of announcing to her Patrons and Friends, that she has REMOVED from 50 A, Berners-street, to 16, MANCHESTER SQUARE. Mrs. Rae's Réunions for the exclusive practice of the Polka and Valse being sanctioned and honoured with the greatest success, will be continued every FRIDAY MORNING, from Two to Five o'Clock. Mrs. James Rae's Academy for Dancing and Exercises (so many years established under the most distinguished patronage), and hitherto held at the Hanover-square Rooms, will in future be continued at her Residence, where terms and particulars may be ascertained.—Private Lessons daily; also Families Attended at Home.

6 July

The polka comes to London, 1844

Reports of the polka craze among elite London society in 1844 illustrate the promotional methods employed withing the music and dance business and professional rivalry between composers, publishers and dance teachers. Endorsement of originality and authenticity enhanced saleability in this field of high fashion, and each of the leading figures set out their case.

The *Illustrated London News* made some claim to being the first in the field, with its publication of Jacques Offenbach's music for the *Polka Dance*, and news of the polka being the rage in Paris (23 March).

Mrs James Rae began teaching *La Polka* on 22 April, claiming to have introduced the dance to London elite society. This was a first step in a campaign of escalating self-promotion which proceeded through the year.

JULLIEN'S ORIGINAL POLKA.—Monsieur JULLIEN has the honour to announce that he has just published the seventh edition of his Original Polka, with description by E. Coulon, splendidly illustrated by Brandard. The immense success of this celebrated Polka having induced unprincipled persons to publish spurious imitations, Mons. Jullien has published the original Polka at his own Office, 3, Maddox-street, New Bond-street; and in order to secure the public against the possibility of purchasing incorrect copies, he has attached his signature to each copy; none can therefore be relied on which have not his autograph. Current copies of Mons. Jullien's Original Polka to be had only at the respectable Music Sellers in the kingdom. Also, No. 2, the Royal Polka; No. 3, the Drawing room Polka; No. 4, the Rage of Vienna Polka; No. 5, the Imperial Polka; No. 6, the Douro Polka; No. 7, the Ducal Polka; all by Jullien, The Pollington Polka by Kœnig, and the Opera Polka by Puzzi. The numerous base plagiaries of Mons. Jullien's Original Polka having on all their Title pages the following words—"The celebrated Polka, performed at every Theatre in London, the Nobility's Balls, &c."—M. Jullien feels compelled to inform the public that none of those pretended Polkas have been performed at Theatres, and that the above-mentioned Polkas, by Jullien, are the only Polkas that Mons. Jullien and Herr Kœnig have played nightly at the Soirées where they have had the honour to conduct, viz.:—the Duke of Wellington, the Duke of Beaufort, and the Duke of Leinster's Balls, the Countess of Jersey and the French Ambassador's Soirées, Countess of Mansfield's Fête, and at the Balls, Soirées, and Parties, given by the Marquis of Clanricarde, Marchioness de Salis, Countess Wilton, Countess Powis, Countess Norbury, Earl Sefton, Earl of Dartmouth, Lord Foley, Lord Kilmaine, Lady Bateman, Lady Balfour, Lady Demville, Lady E. Fielding, Lady Charlotte Guest, Lady Johnstone, Lady Bowyer Smith, Hon. Mrs. Carleton, Hon. Mrs. Damer, Hon. Mrs. Law, Hon Mrs. Meade, Mrs. Ames, Mrs. Arabin, Mrs. Edward Buller, Mrs. Tyrwhitt Drake, Mrs. Buller Elphinstone, Miss Elwes, Mrs. Charles Grenfell, Mrs. Hatfield, Mrs. Hogg, Mrs. Charles Mills, Mrs. Powel, Mrs. Ravenshaw, Mrs. Sebastian Smith, Mrs. Staniforth, Mrs. Symonds, Mrs. Wyndham, H. Fellowes, Esq., and all the leading Balls of the haut ton; also, the Royal Academy Ball, the Caledonian Ball, the Polish Fancy Ball, the Oxford Grand Commemoration Festival, &c., &c. &c.; in which Mons. JULLIEN and Herr KŒNIG have had the honour to conduct the above-mentioned POLKA, and where they have never played, or have been asked to play, the spurious imitations published under so many assumed forms and disguised titles.

3 August

16, MANCHESTER-SQUARE.

MRS. JAMES RAE begs to announce that she has LEFT TOWN for TONBRIDGE WELLS, to fulfil her country engagements, and introduce the POLKA to her numerous pupils in Kent. Mrs. Rae will remain for the first Six Weeks at the Sussex Hotel, Tonbridge Wells, and then proceed to Maidstone and Rochester. Mrs. Rae will be in London every Tuesday and Friday, for the purpose of continuing her Lessons, at her residence, 16, Manchester-square, and also receiving any new Pupils. The Academy will be resumed as usual the first week in December.

7 September

Mitchell's Illustrated and Improved Work on the Ball Room.—Now ready, price 1s.

POLKA LESSON BOOK, or Ball-room Guide.—In addition to a complete Course de Polka, with beautiful representations and correct instructions how to execute the various figures, so that a lady or gentleman may readily become a proficient, this work forms a perfect compendium of the etiquette of dancing with the figures of all the Quadrilles, Gallopades, Mazurkas, Polonaises, Polkas, and all those dances more particularly adapted at Court. May be had, by order, of any bookseller, or of the publisher, C. MITCHELL, Red Lion court, Fleet-street; who will send the work (postfree) on receipt of 1s., or postage stamps of equal value.

21 September

THE INNISKELLING POLKA FOR THE PIANOFORTE.—Just Published, Price 2s., as performed by the Bands of the Coldstream Guards and Enniskillen Dragoons.—May be had at Mc CARROLL's Music Library, 171, North-street, Brighton, and all respectable Music-sellers.

21 September

SIX POLKAS for 1s.; with plain Instructions for Dancing them, in No. 45 of THE PIANISTA. Tenth Edition.—No. 46 contains Two Complete Sets of Polka Quadrilles, composed by Musard, for 1s.—Either Number sent free for sixteen stamps addressed to the Editor 23, Paternoster-row.—Supplements to 45 and 46, PIANISTA, each 2s., or by post, free, thirty stamps, contain Thirty-one Songs sung by Mr Wilson, forming Two of his Scottish Entertainments, complete.

MUSSWOODS: TURNER 12, Poultry.

2 November

NEW MUSIC. — ANNEN POLKA (Strauss). — Notice is hereby given that the above Polka is our exclusive copyright, and we hereby caution and warn all persons publishing and selling the same, other than our edition, will be prosecuted forthwith. To those who fancy the melody is a national air we beg to refer them to the declaration made by the author himself:—' I testify and declare that my Anna Polka Op. 137 consists of original themes invented by myself.—Vienna, the 5th of October, 1844. Signed Johan Strauss, in the presence of Tob. Haslinger."—R. COCKS and Co., 3 Princes street, Hanover-square, London, publishers by Royal license, to her Most Gracious Majesty the Queen, and sole proprietors of all the latest and most fashionable compositions of Strauss, Lanner Labitzky, Musard, Santon, and Camille Schubert.

2 November

WELSH QUADRILLES.—The very popular set, now playing, will be found in the "PIANO," December, price 1s., or 1s. 4d., post-free. Also Tolleque's favourite Planet Waltzes, the set of six; the celebrated Weisbaden Polka, and the Ems Polka, by C. Hunter, now played at Vienna; Three beautiful Irish Polkas—the ipua ry Polka, the Waterford Polka, and the Kilkenny Polka; and Mr. Allen's very voi e Song—"In the Grove near the River," as sung by him with great applause, pet o f Music for 1s., cheapest work published, 12 pages in every number. Published DUNCOMB, 10, Middle-row, Holborn.

30 November

The claims of Jullien – composer of the *Original Polka* – gained additional support when Mlle. Carlotta Grisi and M. Perrot danced the polka to his 'original' score at Her Majesty's Theatre (27 April).

Then, setting one of its advertisers against another, the News printed a 'true description' of La Polka, procured by Mrs Rae from M. Corelli, a dancing instructor to the nobility of Paris, the week after it had printed an advertisement for M. Coulon's instruction book (11 May). By December, Coulon's book had reached its fifth edition and the price had been reduced from 1s. to 8d (7 December).

By the end of the year, new polkas and polka hybrids poured off the printing presses and the market was big enough for everybody, including plagiarists and forgers. Jullien's success was assured, with or without his protests.

(All advertisements and references, *Illustrated London News*, 1844.)

85

Title page of Jullien's Original Polka, *1844*
(Courtesy David Nuttall)

is, I think, a valtz of Vienna. I don't know which one, but I say to the organ-man, 'I want a valtz of Vienna'; and he say, 'Which one? because there is plenty of valtz of Vienna'. Of course, there is nine of them. After the opera music, the valtz and the polka is the best music in the organ.....

It won't do to have all opera music in my organ. You must have some opera tunes for the gentlemen, and some for the poor people, and they like the dancing tune. Dere is some for the gentlemens, and some for the poor peoples. [37]

A number of Scan's round dance tunes can be attributed to mid and late nineteenth-century printed sources, and all of them, it would seem, fall within my second category of composed tunes, at the extreme limit of the polarity. *The Heel and Toe Polka* is none other than *Sultan's Polka* by Charles d'Albert, which ran to countless editions and remains in print today. In current popular tradition it is also the tune for the children's jingle:

> *One, two, three, four, five,*
> *Once I caught a fish alive.*
> *Why did you let it go?*
> *Because it bit my finger so.*[38]

The *Varsovienne* was written by Francisco Alonzo for the dance invented by Desire, a Spanish dancing teacher in Paris, and was introduced in London around 1853.[39] Subsequently there were many other variations on the original composition and as early as 1861 Mayhew reported a version of the corrupted title, *Waltz Vienna*.[40]

Jenny Lind, the 'Swedish Nightingale', took London society by storm in 1847, after her English debut as an operatic soprano at Her Majesty's Theatre. Anton Wallerstein's composition, *Polka de Jenny Lind*, appeared in London, having probably been published previously on the Continent, to celebrate her success and to exploit the outbreak of 'Jenny Lind fever'. Phineas T. Barnum's promotion of her in the United States in 1850, may well account for the tune's popularity in America.[41] Wallerstein, in keeping with the convention of composers at that time, wrote three parts to his polka. Musicians in the oral tradition, a hundred years later, and as far apart as Sussex and Chicago, Norfolk and Donegal, play versions of Jenny Lind Polka compatible with each other, but, following their own conventions, use only the first two parts of Wallerstein's piece.[42]

Rosalie, the Prairie Flower, by G.F. Wurzel, dates from 1855; Scan's version and those of other country musicians are amazingly close to the original.[43] Another of Scan's untitled polkas - in fact, *Bric a Brac Polka* by Charles Coote, Jr. - introduces several structural differences from the original composition.[44] The key change into the second part has been eliminated, presumably to accommodate the single-row melodeon, and the last four bars of each part, although related melodically to the original, are quite different, and have been reconstructed to follow local melodic conventions. The third part and a bridge passage have been left out altogether. The minstrel song, *Buffalo Girls*, as Scan played it, contains a subtle variation from the printed melody in the first part and a total invention for the second.[45]

Advertisements for a variety of D' Albert compositions, including the 15th edition of his 'celebrated Sultan's Polka, which has exceeded all other polkas in popularity', and two sets of quadrilles based on 'national airs'.

Illustrated London News, 12 January 1856

(The 58th edition of the Sultan's Polka *was announced in the* Illustrated London News *for 18 December 1875.)*

D'ALBERT'S ALBUM for 1856.—Just Published, price 14s.—Elegantly bound in Watered Silk and with a variety of Illustrations by Brandard. The great popularity of M. D'Albert's former Albums has induced still greater care in the production of the present, and the publisher feels assured that the Album for 1856 will be found the most elegant and attractive Musical Present ever produced. It contains a number of entirely new Valses, new Polkas, new Quadrilles, &c., &c., composed expressly by M. D'Albert. Sent free of postage.—CHAPPELL, 50, New Bond-street.

D'ALBERT'S CIRCASSIAN POLKA. Just published, splendidly illustrated, price 3s. A rival and companion to D'Albert's celebrated Sultan's Polka, which has exceeded all other polkas in popularity. Sent free of postage. CHAPPELL, 50, New Bond-street.

D'ALBERT'S BONNIE DUNDEE QUADRILLE, beautifully illustrated. Price 4s. M. D'Albert's last and best set of quadrilles on Scotch airs, just published. CHAPPELL, 50, New Bond-street.

D'ALBERT'S SULTAN'S POLKA.—The 15th Edition of this favourite polka: also the KING PIPPIN POLKA, 18th Edition. Price 3s. each, beautifully illustrated; full orchestra, 5s.; postage free. CHAPPELL, 50, New Bond-street.

D'ALBERT'S ENGLAND. A Quadrille on English Airs. "The most celebrated and most sparkling of all M. D'Albert's popular Quadrilles on National Airs."—Musical Review. Solo or duet, 1s.; full orchestra, 5s. CHAPPELL, 50, New Bond-street.

Not for Joseph was composed by a music-hall performer, Arthur Lloyd (1839-1904). The chorus - 'Oh dear no, oh dear no, not for Joseph, not for Joe' - was taken up as a political jibe and directed at Joseph Chamberlain.[46] One of Scan's untitled waltzes couples a theme from an Italian song, *Il Baccio*, by Arditis, with another that appears on American old-time fiddle recordings.[47]

George Grossmith's 1886 song hit, *See Me Dance the Polka*, has been improved, not only by a subtle shift in the melody but also by an additional part composed by Bill Gorringe, and *Down the Road*, by Frederick Gilbert, popularised by Gus Elen in the music halls in the 1890s, has similarly had a second part added to it.

> **Scan:** There's two parts to a tune, and if there was a tune I learnt and I … didn't have the other part, well, I made a part up to it. [MP]

In the case of another of Scan's schottisches, the second part as played by Scan and Bill Gorringe is in the major key, as opposed to the minor key part in the original. David Nuttall identifies this tune as *Rainbow Schottische*, by Henry Kleber, and *Winter's Night Schottische*, arranged by Charles Coote, identical melodies dating from around 1856.[48]

One of Scan's waltzes was known as *Sweet Smiling Faces* by Harry Cox of Catfield, Norfolk.[49] Two other old waltzes Scan learnt from Trayton: *Nutley Waltz*, which Scan associated with dancing at *Nutley Inn*, and *The Man in the Moon*, for which a broadside text has been found.[50] The schottische recorded by Bill Gorringe is a relative of the country dance tune, *The Steamboat*.[51] One of Scan's favourite polkas was also played by Walter Bulwer. It shares one eight-bar part with *On the Green*, a multi-themed piece the Norfolk hammer dulcimer player Billy Bennington learnt from a village band, which in all probability learnt from a written score.[52]

Some of the tunes Scan used for round dancing presumably had little currency beyond a small network of musicians. Others circulated far and wide, even across national borders and oceans, apparently with little assistance from commercial media. If there was a degree of insularity within Scan's early environment, and if his repertoire of round dance tunes now strikes us as unique, he and his mates were, in fact, in the mainstream of a popular culture that existed among rural working people throughout the British Isles, and he shared tunes with musicians he could never have met. (See Appendix A.)

THE VELETA AND SEQUENCE DANCING

The combination in 1900 of the best-selling *Merry Widow Waltz*, and Arthur Morris's dance invention, the *Veleta*, brought about another fashion in ballroom dancing.[53] Based on the existing form of round dancing, the *Veleta* spawned a generation of derivatives: the *Military Two-step* (James Finnigan, 1906), the *Boston Two-step* (Tom Walton, 1908), *La Rinka* (W.F. Hurndall, 1909), the *Progressive Barn Dance* (C.J. Daniels), the *Esperano Barn Dance* (T. Almond) and many more.[54] Scan and his friends accepted them as similar to the old round dances; Scan, in fact, called them round dances, although professional dancing teachers favoured the term 'sequence dances'.

> **Scan:** I played the *Cake Walk* and the *La Rinka*. Of course, the *La Rinka* was a skating dance, and I used to play them one time of day, but they didn't last long; they went out of date. [MP]

Indeed, many lasted no time at all, but a half dozen or so passed into popular tradition and are still danced. The highly mannered posturing demanded by the Old Time Dance Committee of the official Board of Ballroom Dancing and projected on the television show, *Come Dancing*, has fortunately not affected the more natural style to be seen at socials and wedding parties, when middle-aged working people get together. Scottish accordeon players, from the Wyper Brothers in Edwardian times to William Hannah in the 1920s and Jimmy Shand in the 1930s, recorded music for these couple dances. The records by Jimmy Shand and his Band issued between 1947 and the late 1950s, including *La Rinka*, the *Barn Dance*, *La Va*, *Eva Three-Step*, *Gay Gordons*, *St. Bernard's Waltz*, *Military Two-Step* and many polkas and waltzes, are evidence enough of a market for these 'old-fashioned' dances.

The two decades either side of the turn of the century produced a great number of music hall and Tin Pan Alley songs, which became lasting, universally popular favourites. *Daisy Bell*, *Old Bull and Bush*, *Dear Old Pals*, *The Honeysuckle and the Bee*, *In the Shade of the Old Apple Tree*, *After the Ball*, *Comrades*, *Just Like the Ivy*, *Man who Broke the Bank at Monte Carlo*, and *Two Little Girls in Blue*, come easily to mind, and there were dozens more. Sheet music, gramophone records and personal appearances of Florrie Forde, Harry Lauder, Harry Champion and others at the variety theatres spread the songs around, and Scan had many of them, which he fitted into his dance and sing-song repertoires. He heard the gramophone early in this century, although he did not buy one until the 1920s, and he went to the variety theatre in Brighton. His interest was in tunes, rather than performances and throughout his life he had no particular favourite professional musician or singer. In spite of the many records of his own kind of material available nationally by Peter and Dan Wyper, he told me he had never heard of them, nor had he heard of Alexander Prince, a prolific recording artist on the duet concertina. Fairground organs were more to his taste.

> **Best Woods:** There used to be fairs come round. He'd be out there listening, and the organ's going round, and he'd have it ... Yeh, he'd have it on there next day. Yes, stand out there listening to it.

Over the Waves, a Mexican waltz of 1891, was one particular tune Scan learnt from a fairground organ:

> **Scan:** I got on the roundabout and I sat there till I learnt to play the bloody thing! [DN]

Yes, it was only a penny a ride then, mind you. That was before the War, and I sit on there till I learnt it, and I don't know how many rides I had, but not many, because I heard it - heard this regimental band playing it at Crowborough sports - and I'd sort of got hold of bits and pieces and, you know, that all come to me when I got on that blinking roundabout, listening to the organ playing it. [DN]

There's nobody likes music better than I do ... For example, when we used to have the clubs and fairs, those organs. I've always said, 'I wouldn't mind having one in my front garden.' Because it's marvellous things they are ... Well, he's a clever man that makes them. [AW]

NOTES

1. 'The Norfolk men are great at stepdancing. It is curious to watch the impassiveness of their faces and the utter stolidity of the upper part of the body and arms, and contrast them with the marvellous rapid patter and stamp of the feet on the floor.' (Charles J. Staniland, 'Norfolk Nooks', *The Graphic*, 22.10.1887, p. 457).

2. 'Yorks' are strings tied round trouser legs, just below the knee, to keep the dust out of your eyes.' (Jack Norris).

3. 'Women definitely did it even in the days of long skirts; it was a matter of feminine pride that women could outlast the men when in competition.' (Humphreys Family, 'A Broom Dance From Devon', *English Dance & Song*, XVIII, 6, (1954), p. 205).

   'A dear old Symondsbury woman in full black skirt and tight bodice did a spirited broom dance.' (M. E. Mayne, 'An Old Dorset Musician', *E. D. & S.*, XV, 1, (1951), p. 152).

   There are photographs of two mid-Suffolk women performing the Broom Dance in John Howson's, *Many A Good Horseman: A Survey of Traditional Music Making in Mid Suffolk* (1985), p. 33, 46.

   For examples of sound recordings of Scan's tune for the *Broom Dance*, see Appendix A.

4. George S. Emmerson, 'The Hornpipe', *Folk Music Journal*, II, 1, 11970), pp. 12-34.

5. Irish country stepdancing is commonly in hornpipe, reel and jig-time and less commonly in hop-jig-time. A sound recording of Irish stepdancing in waltz-time is the McNulty Family (Mayo/New York), *The Stone Outside Dan Murphy's Door – Waltz Clog*, Rex U234 (1937). Dick Hewitt (Norfolk) can apparently step in any rhythm.

6. **Scan:** 'That used to be a real old pub song, didn't it, at one time.' [DN]

   Waltzing Matilda was published in 1917 (i.e., after the Gallipoli campaign). Does Scan's stepdance tune pre-date its publication, or did Scan base it on the song air at a time after he had stopped playing for step-dancing?

7. The earliest known printed version of *Soldier's Joy* is in McClashan, *Collection of Scots Measures* (c.1781).

   Scan's untitled version of the *Cliff Hornpipe* is on Topic 2-12T455/6, side 4, track 7.

   Charlie Wills, Ryall, Dorset, told me the *Monkey Hornpipe* was danced to the *Keel Row* by two men facing each other, squatting and holding both hands with each other. They kicked each leg out in turn in time to the music until one gave up.

   Scan's *No.1 Stepdance* and the *London Clog* are different hornpipes, sharing some common characteristics. Stephen Baldwin's *Liverpool Hornpipe* lies between them and makes the connection.

   For examples of sound recordings of these tunes, see Appendix A.

8. Scan's untitled version of this hornpipe is on Topic 2-12T455/ 6, side 4, track 8; Bill Gorringe's version is on side 2, track 6c.

9. For an account of Bert Pidgeon, melodeon, Alfie Tuck, tambourine, and a set of old-timers performing the *Four-Hand Reel* at the Women's Institute Symondsbury, Devon, see Mayne, 'An Old Dorset Musician', p. 140.

   For examples of sound recordings of Scan's tune for the Reel, see Appendix A.

10. '[D]anced by Aldridge' (McGlashan, *Collection of Scots Measures*). Information on John Bill Ricketts is contained in Emmerson, 'The Hornpipe'.

For examples of sound recordings, see Appendix A.

One title for the tune, *Pigeon on the Gate*, used in Suffolk, belongs to an Irish reel. The syntactical structure of the name (noun/preposition/article/noun) is used for Irish reels and jigs, and very rarely for hornpipes.

11. A country dance can be described simply as a line of men facing a line of women. Usually there are four eight-bar figures, the fourth being a progression, where the top couple finishes at the bottom of the set, and thus every couple eventual dances in the top place, or every other couple moves down one place and the remaining couples move up one place.

12. These are the earliest known references to the following tunes:

St. Patrick's Day: Rutherford, *Two Hundred Country Dances* (see Francis O'Neill: *Irish Folk Music* (1910), p. 234).

Garryowen appeared in a pantomime, *Harlequin Amulet* (O'Neill, p. 234).

Bonny Dundee: Moffat gives the date and credits the composition to Charlotte Sainton-Dolby (*Minstrels of Scotland* (1896), p. 242).

Irish Washerwoman. Thompson, *24 Country Dances for 1789.*

The *Irish Washerwoman* represents two musical traditions in its composition. The first part, which harks back to Dargason or Sedany (John Playford, *The English Dancing Master* (1650-51)), is in what in Irish and Scottish music I term 'ethnic' style, i.e., based on a two-chord structure. The second is Italianate, employing a more complicated chord progression.

For examples of sound recordings of the *Irish Washerwoman* and Scan's *17th of March*, see Appendix A.

13. Scan played *A Hundred Pipers.* I do not know if he knew *Bonnets So Blue.*

14. O'Neill, *Irish Folk Music*, pp. 178-9.

W. Chappell noted of *The Girl I Left Behind Me:* 'This air has long been in use on the English stage as the Morris Dance, and introduced in all village festivities and processions. It is also played when a man of war weighs anchor; and by each regiment on leaving the town in which they have been quartered: indeed, no air has been, for the last fifty years, more universally popular.' (Chappell, *A Collection of National English Airs* (1838)).

The following are examples of country and country dance tunes used as regimental marches:

Kinnegad Slashers, Gloucestershire Regt.

With Jockey To The Fair, King's Own Yorkshire Light Infantry.

Speed The Plough, Suffolk Regt.

Huntsman's Chorus, King's Own Royal Rifle Corps. (The above from National Army Museum, London, ref. 6501-38.)

Corn Rigs, King's Own Royal Lancashire Regt.

Ap Shenkin, Welsh Regt.

Old Towler, King's Shropshire Light Infantry. (Regal G7304, G7310 and G7310 respectively by Regimental Band of H.M. Welsh Guards (c.1916-17)).

Dashing White Sergeant, The Berkshire Regt. (Winner 3078, Band of H.M. 1st Life Guards (1917)).

15. Henry Mayhew, *London Labour and the London Poor, III* (1861), pp. 159-160.

'Come, Haste to the Wedding… is more frequently to be heard upon the chimes of country churches than any other, and usually played when a wedding is about to take place. In 1767, it was introduced into a pantomime called *The Elopement*, performed at Drury Lane Theatre, and we have not yet seen any older copy.' (Chappell, *National English Airs*, p. 129).

For examples of sound recordings, see Appendix A.

16. I remember Scan's *Galop* as follows:

Longways for as many as will.

8 bars: Join hands in lines and dance with a springy walk forward and back twice.

8 bars (or more, depending on the number of couples): Partners join both hands across the set, galop up the set, following the top couple who casts left, galoping down the set to the bottom and up the set to their original positions.

8 bars: The two lines stand in position while the top couple galops between them to the bottom of the set.

I am unable to remember whether there was a fourth part! Fanny Lander mentioned an arches figure.

17. Philip J.S. Richardson, *The Social Dances of the Nineteenth Century in England* (1960), p. 69.

The Galop was on the programme at the Batchelors' annual ball, Lewes, in 1914. *Sussex Express*, 8.8.1914).

18. Mayhew, *III*, p. 202.

19. Thomas Hardy, *Under The Greenwood Tree* (1896), chapters 7 & 8.

The Triumph appears in Preston, *24 Country Dances for the Year 1793.*

The country dance, *Sir Roger de Coverley*, was still commonly danced at genteel private gatherings until comparatively recently. Rev. J. Ward Petley talked on 'Old Sussex Customs' at the Women's Institute meeting at the *Star* hut, Piltdown 'Afterwards members joined in dancing Sir Roger de Coverley.' (*Sussex Express*, 21.3.1930).

20. For recorded examples of Scan's tune *Pretty Little Dear*, see Appendix A.

21. Richardson, *Social Dances*, pp. 58, 70-74.

Charles Louis Napoleon d'Albert was born near Hamburg in 1809 and came to London in 1816. He is described as a French dancing-master and composer. He spent time with the ballet in Paris and became the ballet master at the King's Theatre in London [in the 1840s]. (Stanley Sadie, ed., *The New Grove Dictionary of Music and Musicians, I* (1980).

22. G. Cruikshank, *Elegancies of Quadrille Dancing*, engraving (1817) (Reg Hall Collection).

23. The nearest we are likely to get to the original sound of the music is the Smithsonian Institute's recorded recreation, using original scores and authentic period instruments. This, of course, was not a functioning dance orchestra, and the performances sadly lack dance quality. Jullien's famous orchestra of the 1850s might, perhaps, have interpreted the notation with a little more lilt. (Smithsonian Social Orchestra And Quadrille Band (Washington, D.C), *19th-Century American Ballroom Music: Waltzes, Marches, Polkas and Other Dances, 1840-60*, Nonesuch H-71313 (1974).

24. Perseverance Cricket Club, annual ball, *Bridge House Hotel*: 'Mr. Goll's quadrille band was in attendence and played upwards of 24 pieces of music, comprising quadrilles, polkas, lancers, caledonians, redowas, schottisches, alberts, valses and galops.' (*Bermondsey and Rotherhithe Advertiser*, 5.3.1881).

25. Larry Lynch, in his recent book on Irish set dances, states: 'Throughout the nineteenth... century rural people danced sets in their houses and at public gatherings'. This is based on a misinterpretation of secondary source material. I am in process of piecing together the evidence and in anticipation of completing the research, I suggest the introduction of quadrille dancing in rural Ireland dates from the last quarter of the 19th century. (Lynch, *Set Dances of Ireland: Tradition and Evolution* (1989), p. 2).

26. Some further *Sussex Express* references to quadrille dancing in Sussex:

Burwash quadrille class (6.3.189ZI.

Winding up Burwash quadrille class (6.4.1897).

Battle quadrille class long night (7.1.1905).

Rotherfield quadrille class end of season dance (7.1.1905).

Haywards Heath quadrille class end of season dance (4.3.1905).

Heathfield and Waldron quadrille class (28.4.1911).

Harry Martin, West Hoathly Tipteerers, told me that the *Lancers* was danced to melodeon and piano in East Grinstead during the Great War.

27. *Sussex Express*, 11.3.1905.

Dancing classes were still being held there in 1910 (*Sussex Express*, 11.2.1910).

28. *Sussex Express*, -.2.1897.

29. Band of H.M. Irish Guards, *Regimental Marches of King' s Royal Rifles, Royal Irish Rifles, East Lancashire Regt., East Surrey Regt., Royal West Surrey Regt.*, Winner 2805 (1915).

Regimental Band of H.M. Welsh Guards: *The Buffs, Royal Sussex Regt., Queen's Own Royal West Kent Regt.*, Regal G7308; *Royal Irish Rifles, East Surrey Regt.*, Regal C7310 (c.1916-17).

30. *Lion Quadrilles*, Columbia-Rena 1436-8, (4th Figure is also on Topic 12T376); *Blackthorn Quadrilles*, Columbia-Rena 1946-8; *Pibroch Quadrilles*, Regal G7681-2; *Original Lancers*, Regal G7686-7; *Thistle Quadrilles*, Parlophone E3150-1; *Lothian Quadrilles*, Parlophone E3147-8; *Patience Quadrilles*, Beltona 1512-3.

Other examples: Fred Cameron (Elgin), *Scottish Quadrilles*, Zonophone 309-311 (1909); Bob Smith, *Ideal Lancers*, Beltona 1691-2 (1931) (5th Figure is also on Topic 12T320); Bob Smith, *Highland Quadrilles*, Beltona 2337- 9 (1934).

31. Interview with Scan Tester, *Mid Sussex Times*, 2.9.1971.

32. Anne Loughran and Vic Gammon, *A Sussex Tune Book* (1982), tune no. 67.

Recorded examples of the tune Scan used for the 1st figure of the *Lancers* include:

Band of H.M. Irish Guards, Winner 2722 (1914).

Regimental Band of HM. Welsh Guards, Regal G7310 (c. 1916-7).

Fred Pidgeon (Devon), *Circassian Circle*, Folktracks FSA087 (1954).

33. Whereas the polka took elite society by storm, the schottische appears to have caused no such stir, at least as evidenced in the contemporary press. The earliest reference I have found is a classified advertisement offering lessons in *La Schottische* (*Illustrated London News*, 21.10.1848).

34. Henry Mayhew and Peter Quennell, *Mayhew's London* (n.d), p. 42.

35. Richardson, *Social Dances*, p. 113.

36. Mayhew, *III*, p. 182.

37. Mayhew, *III* , p. 176.

38. For examples of sound recordings of the *Heel end Toe Polka*, see Appendix A.

39. Richardson, *Social Dances*, pp. 97-8.

An early band recording of the original tune is: Musique de la Garde Republicaine (France), *La Varsoviana, Danse de Salon de Alonzo*, Lutetia F3081 (undated).

40. For examples of sound recordings of Scan's *Waltz Vienna*, see Appendix A.

41. Sadie, ed., *New Grove, X*, pp. 865-866.

42. Wallerstein was born in Dresden in 1813. He was a professional musician, who began composing in 1830, and specialised in composition from 1841. (Sadie, ed., *New Grove, XX*, p. 179).

43. Song sheet, with piano accompaniment (David Nuttall Collection); broadside (Steve Roud Collection).

Recorded examples of this tune:

Billy Ballantine/Jimmy Hunter (Northumberland), *Schottische*, Topic 12T283 (1954).

Dan Wyper, *Selection of Schottisches*, Rena 1345 (1910).

44. Scan's version of this tune appears on Topic 2-12T455/6, side 4, track 2.

I have seen a copy of the sheet music for the *Bric a Brac Polka* with the acquisition date of 1885 in handwriting. I worked from a manuscript copy from John Howson.

45. *Buffalo Girls* was first published in 1839 (Alan Jabbour, accompanying notes for the LP *American Fiddle Tunes* (Library of Congress L62).

46. Peter Gammond, *Your Own, Your Very Own!*, pp. 24-25 (David Nuttall).

47. Scan's version of this tune appears on Topic 2-12T455/6, side 4, track 3.

    For examples of sound recordings, see Appendix A.

48. Scan's version of this tune appears on Topic 2-12T455/6, side 1, track 7, and Bill Gorringe's on side 2, track 6d.

    For examples of sound recordings, see Appendix A.

49. Scan's version of this tune appears on Topic 2-12T455/6, side 3, track 8.

50. The first part of Scan's *Nutley Waltz* is the first part of *L'Amour Endomi Waltz*, c. 1810, by Leor. du Terrail, one of the 46 pseudonyms of Charles Arthur Rawlings (David Nuttall).

    A broadside text of *Man In The Moon* is in the possession of Steve Roud.

51. Bill Gorringe's version of this tune is on Topic 2-12T45S/6, side 2, track 6e.

    The Steamboat is printed in Maud Karpeles, *Twelve Traditional Dances* (1931), p. 27.

52. Walter Bulwer (Norfolk), untitled (1962), Topic 12T240; Billy Bennington (Norfolk), *On the Green* (1972), Topic 12TS229.

53. David Nuttall identifies the tune Scan used for the *Veleta* as the *Inspiration Veleta* by Everitt. Examples of country recordings of the same piece are:

    Percy Brown (Norfolk), *Waltz for the Veleta* (1972), Topic 12T229.

    Michael Gorman (Co. Sligo), *Veleta Waltz* (1952), Folktracks FSA 077.

54. 'I believe that details are available of some six hundred sequence dances... Only the best of them reach the ballroom, and of those which do, very few survive for long.' (Victor Silvester, *Old Time Dancing* (1949), p. 40.

    Silvester (1949) and Michael Gwynne give instructtions for some of the dances in Scan's repertoire, and give dates and composer credits (Gwynne, *Old Time and Sequence Dancing* (1950)).

One of the two concertinas Scan owned at the end of his life, a 30-key C/G, made by C. Jeffries, c. 1900.
Now in the possession of Will Duke of Barcombe, Sussex.
(Photograph: Graeme Kirkham).

Chapter 6:
Fiddle, concertina, melodeon and tambourine

I n spite of its introduction at the very pinnacle of English society - at the court of Henry VIII - the violin met with resistance among the elite. Its brilliance of tone, greater volume and carrying quality, found little favour with lovers of the established viol. Discussing gentlemen players of the viol before the Restoration, Anthony Wood wrote, 'They esteem a violin to be an instrument only belonging to a common fiddler.'[1] Violins were initially imported, and were therefore expensive, but within sixty to eighty years of their first appearance in England there were apparently enough fiddles in the hands of working men for the phrase 'a common fiddler' to have meaning. John Playford, author of dance manuals for the elite, wrote of the treble violin in his *Introduction to the Skill of Music* (1660) as a 'cheerful and spritely instrument much practised of late.'

By the middle of the seventeenth century the violin was established as the dominant instrument in mainstream art music and the dance music of the elite, the instrument of the professional, trained musician. In its other guise, as the fiddle, it was the most popular dance instrument at the lower end of the social scale. Trained professional musicians presumably modified their viol techniques for use on the violin, but had there ever been a popular tradition of viol playing? 'Common fiddlers', I suggest, invented and developed their own playing technique and evolved a new repertoire, partly by the adaptation of existing material and partly by the creation of new genres, within a generation or two.

Early evidence of 'common fiddlers' in Scan's locality is found in the personal account book of Giles Moore, rector of Horsted Keynes, 1656-1679, which provides not only the names of two fiddlers in the village, Cain(e) and Old Joseph, but some clues about their activities.[2] Moore records payments to a fiddler or fiddlers at eighteen weddings, although he officiated at many others without making similar payments. The questions arise: what were the status and function of the fiddlers at the weddings and why did the rector pay them? Keith Thomas's general comment, that the Puritans 'objected to the

bagpipes and fiddlers who accompanied the bridal couple to church,' suggests that the Horsted Keynes fiddlers might have processed to the church with the couple and the rector's payments were tips, just as he doled out to the 'howling boys'.[3] However, on 25 April 1664, Moore recorded 'Giv'n at H Pellings feast to the Fiddler 6d his son 4d', which at face value would establish the fiddlers as secular performers employed for the festivities following the wedding ceremony. A third possibility, supported by what is known about Sussex church bands, but unsupported by the fact that the payments were recorded in Moore's personal accounts and not those of the church, is that the fiddle music was used in the church service. What seems clear is that, as a leading member of the local gentry, he patronised the village musicians.

There is no reason to doubt the direct line of descent from Cain and Old Joseph to Scan, the Gorringes, Denner Head and the Awcocks, but equally we must not assume it. What changes in style and fashion, social function and status could have occurred in 250 years?

A fiddler closer to Scan in time and not too far away geographically was Michael Turner (1796-1885), shoemaker, parish clerk and sexton at Warnham in Sussex.[4] He was seen towards the end of his life as a local character, perhaps a link with a disappearing past, and a brief biography was published, for sale on a picture card:

> He was in great request at Village Fetes
> all the neighbourhood round, and at the
> big houses, to play the music at their
> dances; and between times he would
> perform a first-rate jig playing his fiddle
> the while, or sing a capital comic song.[5]

As leader of the church choir, consisting of fiddle, clarinet and cello, he claimed he could 'play the tune on his viol, sing the 'seconds' himself and beat time with his head for the rest'. He was musically literate, to some degree at least, as he left two manuscript

John Hope, aged 97, of Beaconsfield Terrace, Cross-in-Hand.
(Sussex Express, 19 August 1927)

books dated 1845-9 and 1852, containing tunes for quadrilles, polkas, waltzes, country dances and psalms. Some, if not all, of these pieces were copied from print and included expression markings in the notation.

Turner was respectable and respected, relatively poor but at the upper end of the working community. His biographer was from further up the social scale and may not have been privy to all of Turner's activities. Did Turner ever play in pubs? He played for his own jig dancing, so did he also play for stepdancing? Clearly he was employed by the gentry to play at their private balls, yet he also played at village fetes - a foot in two camps. Christopher Stephens of Fairwarp remembers his father talking of the 'old days' when Mr Cap Hemsley (fiddle) and Old Frog Spat from Five Ashes went to the big houses to play, booked by the gentry, Christopher thinks, to add local colour for their house guests. Did Turner allow himself to be patronised or was he a real craftsman employed because of his practical skill as a dance musician? Did he have two working repertoires, one by ear and memory for the village working people and the other from print for the gentry? Did he follow the expression marks on the sheet music, or did he play with a flat tone and even volume?

The manuscript books indicate a heyday during his early middle age, half way through the nineteenth century, with an up-to-date repertoire of recently published pieces (*Le Tempête*, *Jenny Lind Polka* and the *Original Schottische Polka*, for example), but what did he play as a young man, and did his repertoire progress with changing fashions later in his life? His biographer makes no comment about whether he had any musical partners, except for mention of the church choir. It is difficult to visualise him making secular music without contact or association with other secular musicians. Did he play in a dance band of any sort?

In 1927 a newspaper reporter chanced upon a fiddler with elements in his experience common to Michael Turner, who might well have met or known Scan and the Fairwarp musicians. John Hope, a carpenter, moved to Cross-in-Hand, near Heathfield, around 1887 from nearby Hadlow Down, where he had been born in 1829. Aged ninety-seven when he was interviewed, he first of all sang to the reporter What is the Life of a Man to his own fiddle accompaniment, and then talked of his early days playing for dancing at Blackboys and Hadlow Down:

> Though he has never belonged to an orchestra, Mr Hope used to be in great demand at the country balls, where he had to play on an old fiddle, owned by

his father a hundred years ago ..... Asked to name his favourite tunes, he named "The Soldiers' Joy," "The Triumph," and a ditty, the first line of which runs, "Oh beautiful star in Heaven so bright.".[6]

What little I know of Scan's fiddle style is based largely on the three occasions I heard him play *The Girl I Left Behind Me*, double stopped in G and C, the two occasions he played 32 bars of a schottische, and the advice he gave me.[7] My lasting impression is of a stylist. His tone was flat, with no hint of vibrato, the melody line was broken up rhythmically, and there was more to his right hand than single bowing. His comment, 'I used to use a short bow, not like Reg's' [MP], implied its physical size, not his mechanical method. In the *Heel and Toe Polka* he showed me how on the first two beats he would make heavy down bow strokes right across the fiddle, catching the G and D strings open and the A string fingered as B, and on the first two beats of the fifth bar he would do the same on the open G, a fingered E on the D string and a fingered C on the A.

Mervyn Plunkett heard of Bill Gorringe from both Scan and Jack Norris, and his unexpected, lightning visit to Bill's home in Cuckfield resulted in the recordings issued by Topic.[8] Within about fifteen minutes, with only a few false starts, Bill played the sequence of tunes on the record, together with a rough *Cock o' the North* and an abandoned *Phil the Fluter's Ball*, which have been omitted. No conversation was recorded, except for the comment 'I seem to forget 'em all'. Mervyn took me round to see Bill shortly afterwards but it seemed unlikely that he would ever be persuaded to play the fiddle again. His recorded performances are really quite remarkable, not only as the only surviving recordings of an old Sussex country fiddle style, but as music in their own right. At 87, infirm and out of practice, with his elbow resting on the table to support the fiddle, his mind was alert enough to be able to present a brief cross-section of his early repertoire.

His style conforms to expectations generated by the recorded evidence of a handful of his contemporaries and peers from other parts of southern England. He produces a flat tone with no finger vibrato, occasional droned open strings and a punchy, animated dance rhythm, employing subtle melodic and bowed variations and Scotch snap,[9] and he uses mostly single bowing, with occasional tied bowing on triplets. The tunes, as they appear on the record, are pitched in the keys of F or C, although he fingers as if he were playing in the keys of G or D on a fiddle tuned in concert pitch. Either he tuned the fiddle down a tone, or the tape recorder was running fast. The use of G and D fingering establishes that these keys were used by the Fairwarp fiddlers.

CONCERTINA AND MELODEON

The single-action English concertina, essentially a drawing-room instrument, was patented in 1829. It was some time, however, before the German double-action concertina was designed and subsequently developed in England as the Anglo-German concertina. It is not known for certain how and when the latter instrument, the type Scan played, found its way into popular use in the countryside. Mervyn Plunket tentatively suggested

> ... the sequence of penetration as roughly 1860 - 1885; German rectangular concertinas ... being replaced by British-made instruments from then onwards, but the concertina being swamped quite rapidly by the melodeon from 1885 - 1890 onwards reaching apogee before WW1.[10]

A young lad, the son of a labourer, earning his living playing the concertina in London in 1861, told Mayhew about the popularity of the concertina in the 1850s:

> I was about getting on for twelve when father first bought me a concertina. That instrument was very fashionable then, and everybody had it nearly. I had an accordion before; but it was only a 1s. 6d. one, and I didn't take a fancy to it somehow, although I could play a few tunes on it. I used to see boys about my own height carrying concertinas about the streets, and humming them.... I play entirely out of my own head, for I never had any lessons at all. I learn the tunes from hearing other people playing of them. If I hear a street band, such as a fiddle and harp and cornopean playing a tune, I follow them and catch the air; and if it's any sort of an easy tune at all, I can pick it up after them, for I never want to hear it more than twice played on an instrument.[11]

If the concertina was common on the streets of London in the late 1850s, Mervyn Plunkett's estimation of its arrival in the countryside about 1860 may not be far out. Scan was in all likelihood from the third generation of concertina players. Those he mentioned in tape-recorded conversations were Joe Marten (born 1870) from Chelwood Gate, Albert Browning and Harry Woolgar from Horsted Keynes, and his own brother Trayton, all a generation older than him; and his younger brother, Will, and Tommy and Martha Stephenson from Nutley, who were roughly his own age. Scan implied that, although he admired the playing of Browning and Woolgar, and learnt tunes from them, they were not technically advanced; Woolgar could only play on one side of the instrument.

I suspect that Joe Marten and Trayton took a relatively simple technique - perhaps little more than an uncluttered statement of the melody, based on the established fiddle style - from the first generation of country concertina players, and made something more of it. Joe Marten was good with his hands, inventive and musical, and seems the likely candidate amongst the Chelwood - Horsted lads for exploring the instrument's possibilities. Trayton was in the right position to have been the one who adapted the Fairwarp fiddle stepdance tunes for the con-certina. The articulated melody line, dressed by triplets and fill-ins between phrases and underlined by parallel octaves, (the two notes of each octave played on different sides of the concertina) and harmony represented by the odd, almost accidental use of thirds in place of octaves, characterise the Tester style. These techniques, together with the lift generated by the attack, staccato notes, the sharp intake of air in the bellows and the heavy punctuation at the end of an eight bar phrase, were, in all probability, Trayton's gift to his younger brothers. The recorded duets by Scan and Will of tunes from their childhood are played in near unison. If Scan used his musical creativity in many ways, in absorbing 1920s dance tunes, for example, it was not employed in modifying his old material. It is probably safe to assume that, when we listen to Scan and Will in duet, we are hearing Trayton's music.

Scan heard very few other concertina players, at least not players of the Anglo-German concertina in a country style, although he probably heard English and duet concertinas at the variety theatre and on the wireless.

> **Scan:** I like to hear a concertina played (especially my younger brother; he used to play a lot), especially if I was in another room listening. Well, I expect that was the only time I heard the concertina played. [VS]

> When we used to play together we always used to play in C; nearly always play in C. I used to play a B flat instrument a lot, My youngest brother used to play a B flat instrument with me, and, well, that's what I used to play on Brighton beach ... and that was a jolly good instrument. That was one of Lachenal's make. I sold it about a month or six weeks ago [speaking in July 1966] and it was a five-fold bellows. You see, my wrists are a lot weaker than what they was when I used to play that, and it

was blooming hard work to play it. You know, I had a job to [move] it to and throw [fro]. And then I had this rheumatism as well, so I thought, 'Well, I'll sell it'. I took it down on the coast [to a club] one night with me, and I thought, 'Well, I'll take it down there, and I'll play it, and see if I can sell it.' And blowed me, if I didn't get a buyer come for it directly. I sold it to him. I didn't leave it that night, so I told him, I said, 'Well, I'll bring it down or you can come up.' He says, 'Well, I'll come up to your place and I'll pay you for it.' So he come up and got it and paid for it. [RH]

So I've just bought - well, a week or two back, up London - I bought another one. Only it's a Jeffries and it's a thirty-key instead of a forty-key, but it don't make much difference. I can get what I want to play on a thirty-key alright. I don't need a forty-key, not now. [RH]

Scan played the melodeon as a child and young man, but he much preferred the concertina and fiddle. To a limited extent he was intolerant of some of the rough melodeon players, who had been fairly thick on the ground. The three basic instruments, the fiddle, the melodeon and the concertina were improved during his life time. The earlier instruments had less power and volume. Gut strings were replaced by steel on the fiddle, the brass reeds were replaced by steel in the concertina and the old three or four-stop, rather fragile ten-key melodeon was replaced by the sturdier and louder Vienna button accordion.[12]

Opposite: Scan's musics; 1971

(Photograph: Hamish Black)

KEYS, HARMONY AND PART-PLAYING

On the question of keys, the key of C was imposed on traditional music by the manufacturers of fixed pitch melodeons, concertinas and the Clarke's tin whistle, and thus created a tension between players of the new instruments and the established fiddlers, who were used to the keys of G and D. Scan adapted to the company he was in. He played in C with a tin whistle or melodeon player, most of the time in Testers' Imperial and usually with Bill Avis (piano accordion). He would have used G with a fiddle player, and sometimes with Testers' Imperial to accommodate the bandoneon, which was pitched in G, A and E. He played in B flat on Brighton beach and in duet with his brother Will, who had a B flat concertina and a B flat clarinet. The key of G can sound harsh after a while, but it cuts through a crowd more effectively than C.

> **Scan:** [G] is alright for singing, but C is a bit too high ... You can nearly always get them in G; that's why I play in G a lot, if I'm going to play for anyone to sing. [VS]

Scan used to say he could play in any key, but that claim was based on his experience of the keys other musicians used, rather than on academic theory of music. There is no doubt he could often pick up the key of a singer, perhaps forcing him or her into concert pitch, and then following the course of the song.

The older instrumental music in country pubs in southern England was essentially linear, with the rhythm carried by the emphasis and phrasing of the melody line. Harmony in the form of either parts and counter melodies or chordal accompaniment - prior to the introduction into pubs of pianos, mandolins and banjos - was absent. That is not to say that harmonies are not implicit in the structure of the melodies: harmony was represented by drones on the fiddle and occasional thirds, fourths and fifths added often accidentally and sometimes apparently haphazardly on the concertina and melodeon, and by the grunted, ambiguous basses of the melodeon.

There is evidence of 'bassing' on the cello in Scottish fiddle music, southern English church bands and in Yorkshire, Cornwall and Norfolk.[13] There is also evidence of part singing in Sussex, by, for example, the Copper Family of Rottingdean and Bill Hawkes and Peter Gander from Cuckfield. In Scan's early experience there were some part playing and vamping introduced from brass band and string band music (for example, Trombone Billy and Jack Carr), and during the Edwardian era the influence of the

Brighton variety theatres and the gramophone record would have been felt. In answer to a specific question, however, Scan confirmed he had never seen or heard a cello or double bass played in a pub or dance band.

PERCUSSION

In as far as there ever was an accompaniment - and it may well have been very common indeed - it was percussive, on one or more of four instruments: tambourine, triangle, bones and spoons.[14] Bert Wood and Charlie Bates both volunteered, in reminiscing about the old days, that the tambourine, spoons and bones were common around Danehill. Peter Gander from Cuckfield took his triangle playing seriously, playing along with Jack Norris's melodeon throughout an evening, and late in Peter's life Jack asked the local blacksmith to make him a new one. Similarly, Rabbity Baxter would play the tambourine with Scan at the *Stone Quarry* on all his material, even in waltz-time, double timing on the slow numbers. Mervyn Plunkett heard of a nest of musicians at

Selmeston, including Eric Crouch, who played fiddle, tambourine and spoons, and Art Winter and his three brothers from Hailsham assembled well into the 1950s for their Christmas session in the *Trevor Arms*, Glynde, a family band of melodeon, bones, triangle and tambourine.[15]

References to the tambourine turn up unevenly right through southern England and, although there was a degree of stylistic variation, a common purpose prevailed. Unlike military music and its derivations, where the drums are employed largely to keep time, and art music where they are used for tonal and dramatic effect, country percussion is an integral part of the music, on equal terms with the melody instruments, contributing to the momentum, the dynamics and most of all the rhythmic swing. Scan and Will's tambourine and Bill McMahon's spoons on the Topic recordings illustrate the point.

Bill McMahon had several other percussion devices. He would hold one of his spoons between two fingers, leaving the handle hanging loose, and he would strike it with the handle of the other spoon, producing a triangle-like effect. By clapping his hands in

Bill McMahon (spoons) and Bill Agate (tambourine) at the Half Moon, Balcombe; 1959 (Photograph: Reg Hall)

front of his open mouth and by changing the shape of his mouth, he could create a popping noise with variable pitch. This sort of invention seems to have been endemic. Certainly during the 1950s and 1960s I witnessed in many country pubs various makeshift percussion instruments, always phrasing around and on the melody. There was a certain amount of floor thumping on the beat, but never hand-clapping on the beat (as television and film reconstructions of period rural frolics would have us believe).

The Testers' tambourine technique employed three basic phrases. The most exciting was the beaten tattoo on the taut vellum using the second joint of the right hand middle finger as if it were a drumstick. That was very wearing on the wrist and finger joint; the second phrase - rattling the jingles, with a few odd accented beats - brought some dynamic variation to the music as well as physical relief to the tambourine player. Returning to beating the skin gave a great lift.

The third technique produced a rhythmic propulsion similar to a tailgate trombone glissando in New Orleans music, slightly anticipating the beat on the first beat of a phrase. It required fiddle rosin to be rubbed on the vellum in advance. The player licked his or her thumb, then, pressing it hard against the vellum, pushed it from the bottom of the instrument to the top. The effect was twofold: a dynamic roar, accompanied by shimmering jingles.[16] Bill Agate's method, a relentless four beats to the bar with the back of his hand on the vellum, was outside the mainstream.[17]

NOTES

1. Quoted in Francis W. Galpin, *Old English Instruments of Music* (1910), p. 94.

2. *The Journal of Giles Moore*, Ruth Bird, ed. (1971), pp. 316-18, 320, 322-23, 326, 329, 331, 333, 335, 341, 349-50, 352-53.

3. Keith Thomas, *Religion and the Decline of Magic* (1971), p. 66.

4. Vic Gammon, 'Michael Turner, 19th Century Sussex Fiddler' *Traditional Music*, 4, (mid 1976), pp. 14-22, 32.

5. Playing the fiddle and dancing at the same time is not such a rare phenomenon; it was an essential skill of 18th and 19th century dancing masters. Examples of country musicians include Michael Coleman and Michael Gorman (Co. Sligo), Jinkey Wells, (Oxfordshire) and Emile Benoit, (Newfoundland). Lucy Farr (Co. Galway) says her aunt could lilt, play the fiddle and stepdance at the same time.

6. *Sussex Express*, 19.8.1927.

7. On one of these occasions, in 1958, Mervyn Plunkett recorded 32 bars of a schottische, but the tape is no longer in existence. Scan was also recorded playing Danny Boy on the fiddle. This was several years later and is unrepresentative of his intention, as his bow hand was shaking beyond his control (Mervyn Plunkett Collection).

8. Bill Gorringe lived-in at Miss Turner's dairy at Whiteman's Green on moving from Horsted Keynes. He later lived at Brandsmead, Cuckfield, and worked as a milkman until retirement (Florence Norris).

9. Scotch snap is a rhythmic device - a semi-quaver followed by a dotted quaver - used in strathspeys, schottisches and some Irish hornpipes.

10. Letter, Mervyn Plunkett to me, 16.1.1986. Mervyn did not state his evidence and was offering an informed guess. See also Mervyn Plunkett, 'A Note on the Accordeon, Melodeon and Concertina', *Ethnic*, I, 4, (1959), pp. 4-11.

11. Henry Mayhew, *London Labour and the London Poor*, III (1861), p. 183.

12. Scan probably changed to top-quality steel reed concertinas fairly early in his career. I have no idea when steel violin strings replaced gut; it may be that Scan never changed from gut. Vienna accordeons began to replace the old melodeons in the 1930s, long after the hey-day when 'everybody had a music'. On Topic 12T455/6 Jack Norris and I play Vienna accordeons.

13. Recorded examples of ensembles using a cello:

    Tintagel and Boscastle Players (Cornwall) (1943), Topic 12T240.

    Walter Bulwer (Norfolk) (1962), unissued, Topic.

    Billy Harrison (Yorkshire) (mid 1980s), Musical Traditions 201 (cassette).

14. '[T]he Parish Boyes towards a Drumme 9d.' *Journal of Giles Moore*, Bird, ed., entry for 26.2.1660, p. 322. What kind of drum and for what purpose? Were the Horsted parish boys organised?

    The tenor or side drum does not appear in the evidence of rural social music, i.e., in pubs, etc. The two hobby horse ceremonies currently making use of tenor drums take place in towns (Minehead, Somerset, and Padstow, Cornwall).

15. Mervyn Plunkett and I went to see Art Winter on 10.5.1960, but he could not be persuaded to play. The landlord of the *Trevor Arms* was said to have had a mid-1950s tape of the four Winter brothers.

    Compare F.J. Collings, 'The Concertina in Cornwall around 1890', *Concertina Newsletter*, 7 (Aug. 1972), pp. 9-10. His favourite combination was concertina, bones, triangle and tambourine.

    A common ensemble in early American black-face minstrels consisted of fiddle, single-row accordeon, tambourine, bones and triangle (Hans Nathan, *Dan Emmett and the Rise of Early Negro Minstrelsy* (1962), illustrations p. 148-9 (1844-5), p. 152 (1343).

Ted Duckett (Hampshire), four recorded performances on the bones (1972), Forest Tracks 3001.

16. The tambourine was and still is played in country districts in Ireland, in styles close to those of English players.

    Recorded examples:

    Coleman Country Traditional Society, (Co. Sligo) (1971), Leader LEA 2044.

    Jack Cooley, (Co. Clare) (1973) Gael-Linn CEF 044.

    John Reynolds (Leitrim) (1927), Folkways FW 8821, and (1928) Columbia 3224ZF and 33260F.

    Seamus Tansey/Eddie Corcoran (Co. Sligo) (1967), Leader LEA2005 and Topic 12T184.

    Gerry Wright (Co. Limerick) (1976), Topic 12TS306.

    Gerry Wright/Mary Heffernan (Co. Limerick) (1987), Swilly SWC 005 (cassette).

17. Folktape FTA 102 (reel-to-reel tape).

Father Fletcher's Band, Uckfield, undated. The band was listed in Brooker's Directory in 1888 (but not in 1892) as the 'original Town Band', as opposed to the Town Band which was also listed.

Rev. P. Fletcher, Roman Catholic priest at Uckfield from 1885-93, stands next to James Haestier, the bandmaster (in white hatband). Two of the cornets were already old-fashioned, with valves on the far side of the bell pipe, and there are no trombones.

(Information and photograph courtesy Norman Edwards)

Chapter 7:
Church bands and village bands

The continuum from the 'common fiddlers' of the seventeenth century to the Christmas get-togethers of the Winter family band in the 1950s embraces a broad spectrum of lower class, self-taught, often domestic, usually amateur, music-making. Vic Gammon's academic work on Sussex church bands focuses on other aspects of country proletarian music.[1] The facts are simple enough. The music accompanying divine worship in Sussex churches at the beginning of the nineteenth century was part of popular rather than high culture. For the more than three hundred parishes in Sussex there is evidence of over one hundred choirs, and there may have been many more. These choirs (or quires), ensembles of male and sometimes female voices, often included instruments, sometimes just one, but more often in various apparently arbitrarily chosen combinations. Tenor, alto and bass voices, fiddle, flute, clarinet, cello, bassoon and serpent exploited possiblities for rehearsed and well-practiced orchestration, in the form of solo and repeated chorus lines in the psalm and anthem repertoire and two, three and perhaps four-part harmony. Purchase and maintenance of the instruments and music books were sometimes financed from parish funds.

A degree of musical literacy existed among the players and some would have learnt the basics of their craft from instruction books. Others, probably the majority, learnt on the job by trial and error, listening to and observing others at choir practice or at home. Lining out, the practice of reading out the words line by line in anticipation of the congregation singing them, points to a general illiteracy (or perhaps just a shortage of psalm books), but the survival of some manuscript books indicates that some musicians could make use of written notation.[2]

Contemporary perceptions of the nature of this music are polarised, with two opposing views expressed in the written record. The untrained voices and the exuberance of the performance produced a wide range of tonal texture. Some members of choirs doubled in the community as dance musicians, and there is more than a suggestion that the dance quality came through in the church music, which was characterised by an organic momentum, perhaps even a rhythmic swing.[3] The music may have been raucous, joyful and rough, but it was a source of satisfaction and pride for its participants, inspired by a combination of secular and spiritual motives and emotions. It was their music, expressed in their terms, and for many it was their great joy and the height of their personal attainment. The opposing view was held by the clergy and the squirearchy, whose cultural roots, aspirations and aesthetic judgement came from a quite different value base. They saw rural church music as crude, unrefined and irreligious, quite unfit for association with divine worship.

Church music provided a point of contact for two cultural value systems in conflict; inevitably the more powerful triumphed. Vic Gammon offers a political interpretation. When church bands were secure in their purpose and status they represented an organised power base among working people in rural communities. Pluralism and absenteeism distanced the clergy from their congregations, and parish clerks and choirs filled the vacuum. A movement within the Anglican church in the second quarter of the nineteenth century, based on a twin rationale involving theological redefinition and notions of middle class cultural superiority, reinforced the social class divide. It encouraged the clergy to wrest back from the people their authority as the rightful leaders of the church.[4] The old-style choirs had to be destroyed; working men's organisation within an Establishment institution presented a threat to Church management and middle class authority in general, and was also an affront to its sense of respectability. The clergy and the gentry rallied round; barrel and manual organs were provided, organists and choir masters appointed and a new form of religious music, the hymn, was devised and promoted. Vic Gammon concludes that by the end of the 1860s very few of the old-style church bands and choirs survived.[5]

The church band musicians were faced with a number of courses of action. They could comply with the new order, or find alternative outlets in Nonconformity or in secular working men's organisations. Some gave up music altogether in despair, others perhaps spent more time in the pubs. It would appear that with the demise of the church bands and the social organisation associated with such music-making, there was a consequent decline in their ability to hold together as organised dance bands. Part-playing and bassing among dance musicians became a rarity. However, as one door closed, another opened: the energy that had gone into the church string and wind bands was diverted into secular bands using brass, woodwind and percussion, calling for their participants on the same body of rural and small country town working men, artisans and shopkeepers. The transition can be seen in Horsham, a small country town less than fifteen miles from Horsted Keynes, where the Town Band around 1835 or 1840 used instruments that belonged essentially to the brass band - keyed bugles, trumpet, trombone, french horn and bass drum - and others - fife, flute, clarinet and serpent - that would have been equally at home in a church band.[6]

Village bands caught on far and wide throughout the rest of the century. The early pattern was set down during the Napoleonic Wars, when regimental bands, financed by the officers, provided music for garden parties and receptions, as well as on the parade square. In the four or five decades following Waterloo, civilian patronage produced similar ensembles in Sussex: fully literate musicians capable of satisfying the needs and sensibilities of the county elite. The movement continued with the formation of the Volunteer regiments. Further down the social scale, popular subscription and/or sponsorship by socially-minded members of the gentry made possible the formation of village and town bands as temperate, uplifting and honourable social pursuits for respectable working men.

Musicianship was dependent on limited literacy, rote learning and some ear-playing. Even relatively late photographs of such bands show instruments without music clips and musicians with no pouches for carrying music cards, and seem to indicate an aural approach to musicianship. A defence of ear-playing came from a mid-nineteenth century London street musician:

> The class of men in the street bands is, very generally, those who can't read music, but play by ear; and their being unable to read music prevents their obtaining employment in theatres, or places where a musical education is necessary; and yet numbers of street musicians (playing by ear) are better instrumentalists than many educated musicians in the theatres.[7]

There is little reliable record of how village bands sounded; the exact composition, at least in the early bands, would have depended on the availability of instruments. According to the same London street bandsman, the 'cornopeans or cornet-a-pistons came into vogue' in the late 1840s, followed shortly after by ophicleides and by saxhorns in the late 1850s. Clarinets and valve trombones persisted into this century, and a photograph of Lingfield Town Band taken before the Great War shows euphoniums, drums and mouth organs![8] It was the brass band competitions, regional and national championship events, that regulated the instrumental constitution of brass bands and encouraged development of the style heard today. The sweet, bell-like tone, consistent throughout the whole range of each instrument, is a modern affectation, unknown to the village bandsmen in the years leading up to Scan's introduction to brass band music. Henry Burstow's working man's eye view of Horsham Town Band, around 1835 or 1840, with its alcoholic inspiration and rustic repertoire, makes the connection with Scan's musical world:

> [I]t was as a big drummer to the Old Band that Ike used to afford us the greatest satisfaction. When there was a band job on he would be sure to have sought inspiration in an extra glass or two, and then he would delight us boys by his extraordinary drumstick flourishes, and his industrious accompaniments to the Band's favourite melodies - "Hearts of Oak", "Bonnie Dundee", "Bonnets of Blue", "Rory O'More", "The Brighton Camp", etc.

> These tunes, with perhaps a few others used to constitute the Band's repertoire. Music in band parts being in manuscript only was hard to get and very expensive. It appeared, too, to be the subject of much misunderstanding among the bandsman, and some of the harmonies were certainly rather hard for the public to appreciate, especially towards evening at the Broadbridge Heath and other club feasts where the Band was engaged to play.[9]

HORSTED KEYNES BAND

Horsted Keynes, according to Scan's account, appears to have been late acquiring a band of its own. If there was an earlier version of the band, no record has come to light for the 30 years before 1890.[10] Two tradesmen, Stamford Bish, a bootmaker (born c.1873), and a blacksmith, were the leading lights. Scan's comment that Stamford Bish 'was a good musician, but he wasn't no good till they formed the band' implies that Scan knew him before he learnt to play. The blacksmith was probably Old Tom Murrell's younger brother, who played the bass horn, while other members were Ernie Walder (euphonium), Joe Awcock (tenor horn), his son, Joe, Geoff Wickham and Tommy Briggs (cornets), and a man named Wood on the drum.

> **Scan:** We was living at the *Green Man* when the Boer War was on. I wasn't in it [the Horsted Band] when it started, but they'd got a band here then, when the Boer War was on, because I can remember that well... I think one of the main ones was this shoemaker and this blacksmith. I think, they two got together - what I could understand about it - got one or two in the mind of it, and they had a meeting in the workingman's room to see what they could do and how many they could get. Well, they found out they could get a dozen or more. Well, they could go out with ten, you see, so that's how they formed the band. [RH]

> I went in the band as a drummer. Well, you know, I used to get hold now and then of one of their cornets, and, course, I could pick out a lot of stuff on the cornet by ear. I got hold of the scales quick on it. You know, you've only got three valves, and the bandmaster wanted me to join the band. Well, he wanted me to join like the others to learn music. Well, he give me some music, a sheet of music with scales on, and told me, 'When you think about it, if you got the time, you can keep having a look at that music.' He says, 'You'll get used to seeing it and you'll begin to know.' Well, the man what was the bandmaster of the band, he used to be a shoemaker and used to go down there, and he used to be pointing this music out to me, trying to learn me. He was a cornet player and, course, I couldn't learn that music, you know. I wasn't no good. I tried! I tried hard enough to learn it, but I couldn't,

and they all thought I was going to learn music, because I was good on any music. I was playing a music, but as for to learn the music to read it off, I couldn't, and I never did, and that was the reason why that I come out of the band a lot, because I was no good to the band if I'd got wait to learn the tune [by ear] before I played it.[11] [RH]

> I expect I was with the band two years, 'cause I had a side-drum a long time, but, you see, that was early on. Well, according as the band got on, they started going out to play to clubs and fairs, but I was never in the band when they played to the clubs and fairs. I have known them hire two or three blokes from Ardingly to make up enough for they to go to two clubs one day. You see, they used to get about three pound and there was usually ten of them, so there wasn't a lot of money each, was there? But there was, I should say, about fourteen of them all told. [RH]

> This man, a man name of Grynyer, he lived at West Hoathly station and he had the pub there what they call the *Railway Hotel*, and he was a violin player.[12] He was as good as any pro. He was a good bloke, and he properly understood music. He'd been used to tutoring people music, and they got him to take them over, see, and he got them on well enough that they could go out. Then he used to come down so often, you see, and put them through their paces. But this snob [Stamford Bish] he was a good musician, but he wasn't no good till they formed a band, but blowed if he wasn't a good bloke afterwards. He got hold of it a bit quick, see, and he took interest in it. [RH]

> [It was] that bloke from West Hoathly that taught me a roll and that. It's only 'daddy, mummy, daddy, mummy', you know. It wants a bit of practice, but it's as easy as shelling peas, if you know how. A lot of it why I couldn't learn the music, I think, I was too interested in cricket and that, and I wanted to be off to cricket of a night instead of being banding, you see. I hadn't got sense enough to know different, and that was a lot of my trouble not learning. I'm sure it was. [RH]

Printed music - that's what cost the money! When they had to get music, you had to have a certain amount of copies - enough for a small band. Well, it cost a tidy bit of money, you see. That's where their subscriptions what they used to collect round went for, you see. The blokes didn't have it; it went in the band fund. So that's what they used to buy their music with, you see. Course, you were sure wages weren't very much that time, but they had to buy their uniforms themselves. Mind you they all had uniform. Yes! A blue uniform with a peaked cap and braid round their arms and cross their shoulders and all down their trousers each side. [RH]

Then when they broke up, I don't know what become of their musics. Well, I expect some of them kept them. If you had an instrument belonged to the band, why, you had to take that back when you finished, but a lot of them bought cornets, you know, second-hand cornets ... and that, and a lot of them got their own instruments, you see. The musics what belonged to the band, this bandmaster had them, because he'd got a span roof to his shoemaker's shop, and he put a platform up there, and put these musics up top, and that's where they was the last time I see them. But, course, he's been dead for several years now. I don't know what become of them, bar this big drum, the old drum. The old drum is still about here now what we used to have. They had a new drum and they still kept the old one for bonfire night and rough nights and that, and this new one, it was a posh drum, a later drum, thinner and bigger, see. They had a Church Lads Brigade here formed, so I expect it was this shoemaker told them they could have this drum. They had the big drum and the side drum. [RH]

I've never known where their instruments went to what belonged to the band. There couldn't have been many, I know, but there was some, because a lot of these bass players wouldn't buy a bass instrument, but now a euphonium player - well, they might buy their euphonium, if they was interested, and if they thought about playing music afterwards. Course, a euphonium is a useful instrument, ain' it? And there was a trombone player.

They'd only got one trombone, a slide trombone. They got one, two, three... they got four cornets before I went in. That's first cornets, and a soprano cornet. You know what a soprano cornet is – it's higher! And when they first started they had two clarinets in, but they didn't stick to clarinets long. I expect they wanted too much learning, perhaps. So both of these give up clarinet playing and took another instrument. [RH]

The old drummer, Old Tom Murrell - we used to call him Jolly Beggar[13]... We was on the march one night in the summer marching for practice. We went right up the village and up towards Keynes Place - Birchgrove - up that way, and I was on the left-hand side with the old side drum, and this bloke was beating the drum, and a screw come out the end of his drumstick. The old drumstick, when he put his stick up, flew right out and right over in the field, and he kept hitting with his fist. I didn't know what had happened, and presently he got hold my shoulder and tore me round much as to throw me arse over head. He says, 'Go on, get the head of my drumstick.' Well, I had to run out and go back and over the gate and up the field and find the drumstick. When they got up the road so far, the bandmaster, he rushed forward and give him a nudge and the drum [beat] three times for the stop. That's how he used to signal, see. When they stopped he said, 'What's the matter?' 'Well,' he said, 'I lost my drumstick.' And they had to come back and help me find it. [RH]

There's only one that I know of [still alive in 1964] and he's a very old man. Ninety, pretty well, I'd say, and I ain't seen him now for some time. He was a euphonium player and his brother, a younger brother, and him, they was both euphonium players and, course, that was one of the main instruments in a brass band, because so often they had to play the leading part and, in fact, I think it was one of the finest instruments in a band, because you had more solos on a euphonium than you had anywhere. And they had two baritone players, one tenor and they had one, two, I think they had three or four bass players. Well, they had an E flat and a B flat and then they had a double bass, see, the biggest one of the lot. [There] used to be a blacksmith played this big bass, and the last photograph I see of the band was this bloke what used to play this big bass, and he'd moved to Hailsham. He'd got a business at Hailsham, and when I went to see him one day there, he says, 'I want you to look at this photograph.' And that's the only photograph of the band that ever I see, and this was several years ago now. Course, the bloke's been dead now for a long time, because he was a man when I was a boy, you see. [RH]

I forgot when Horsted Band packed up, but they never had no band after the First War ... I couldn't tell you how many years the band run; it run several years, 'cause I was only quite a boy when I went in it.[14] [RH]

These other bands round about here all was going a long time after this one. West Hoathly was one, Ardingly and Turner's Hill and then the next one was East Grinstead up that way[15] ... Forest Row. I think West Hoathly and Turner's Hill were the top bands. West Hoathly - I can remember them having all new instruments - all silver - and the bloke that took over bandmaster for them used to play with us here. Tommy Briggs his name was, and he was a cornet player. He'd got - I don't know whether it was three or four - brothers used to be members of West Hoathly Band. Well, they got enough they could go out anywhere and play. Mind you, they was good musicians, and then old Tommy, he used to play in Horsted Band. Well, West Hoathly wanted him to come there as bandmaster, so when they had their new instruments, he took them over. Well, then he'd been there a year or two, and he got a job at Crowborough, and he went to Crowborough, and he took their band over, and they all had new silver instruments, and goodness knows what happened to him then.[16] But I know him well, bloke used to wear glasses. He was a little taller than me, but he wasn't very tall. Cor, he was a good musician. All of them were, and I believe there are some of them living up there now this side of West Hoathly. Briggs their name was. They used to have a brickyard there. [RH]

NOTES

1. Vic Gammon, Parochial Music in Sussex: A Study in Social and Cultural Conflict (unpublished M.A. thesis, University of Sussex, 1985).

   Vic Gammon, 'Babylonian Performances: the Rise and Suppression of Popular Church Music 1660-1870', E. and S. Yeo, eds; Popular Culture and Class Conflict (1981).

   Vic Gammon, Popular Music in Rural Society: Sussex, 1815-1914 (unpublished D.Phil. thesis, University of Sussex, 1985).

2. Anne Loughran and Vic Gammon, A Sussex Tune Book (1982), introduction.

3. 'Much evidence suggests the connection between church bands and social dance was strong and widespread.' (Gammon, Popular Music, p. 30).

4. Vic Gammon argues that bell-ringing was also a vehicle for secular, working men's organisation, and a similar movement within the Church sought to crush its independence (Popular Music).

5. Gammon, 'Babylonian Performances', p. 78.

   Vic Gammon's view is that the symbolic ending of the old church choirs was the publication of Hymns Ancient and Modern in 1861 (Popular Music, p. 69).

6. Henry Burstow: Reminiscences of Horsham (1911), pp. 49-50.

7. Henry Mayhew, London Labour and the London Poor, III (1861), p. 163.

8. This photograph was in the possession of Albert Farmer (born 1893), the one-man-band from Lingfield.

9. Burstow, Reminiscences, pp. 49-50.

10. Vic Gammon's newspaper searches revealed no reference to a Horsted Keynes band for this period.

11. Norman Edwards explains that the basic technique is the same for all valve brass instruments. From early on all band parts were written in the treble clef, which made it possible to teach all musicians from scratch together in one group. The exception is the trombone part, written in the tenor clef; 'even then it was customary for the young tenor trombone player to be told to knock off two flats and play in the treble clef'. (Letter, Norman Edwards to me, 16.7.1989).

12. *Kelly's Directory of Sussex* for 1891 and 1901 lists John Grynyer at the *Railway Hotel* (now called the *Bluebell*).

    The East Grinstead Volunteer and Town band under the conductorship of Mr. J. Grynyer played at Danehill Flower Show (*Southern Weekly News*, 29.7.1893).

13. Thomas Murrell (born c. 1865) was a coal merchant, carman and market gardener.

14. Horsted Keynes band played at the Horsted Keynes village sports on Coronation Day, 22.6.1911 (*Sussex Express*, -.6.1911).

15. There was a band in Turner's Hill in 1849 (Gammon, Popular Music).

    The *Sussex Express* referred to Fletching band in 1897 (26.6.1897).

16. 'CORONATION - BRASS BAND free for Coronation Day - Martyn, 7 Croham road, Crowborough.' (*Sussex Express*, 16.6.1911).

Ashdown Forest Friendly Society gathered in front of Nutley Inn, *before making the rounds of the village; c. 1897. Photograph by Daddy Francis.*
(Courtesy Gordon Turner and Phil Lucas)

Chapter 8:
Friendly Society feast days

Friendly societies, organised by working men and encouraged by Rose's Act of 1793, provided financial benefit based on mutuality and principles of self-help, but they also provided a social life closely connected with village bands, and their feast days in late spring and early summer were important events in the working man's calendar. A newspaper report in 1910 gives some idea of the size of the endeavour in Forest Row:

> The Equitable Association is a local friendly organisation which has been in existence for close on seventy years and has accomplished much useful work. During the year 1909 the sum of £82.15s.1d. was paid to sick members. The total worth of the Association is £2,388.1s.5½d. which represents an average of £20.4s.9d. per member. During the past year the Association's income exceeded expenditure by just over £80.[1]

In Horsted Keynes, according to *Kelly's Directory of Sussex* for 1889, 'The Village Benefit Society hold [sic] its anniversary meeting on the last Monday in May'.

> **Scan:** I can't tell you how they started. They started before I could remember, but they used to pay so much a quarter, and they got sick benefit and, I think, when they got so old, if they stopped in the club and retired as a club member, they used to get about one-and-six a week or something of that as long as they lived, you see. They had a burial fund and sick benefit and this pension, that's all you got. Well, that went on like that, and when these other clubs formed - the National Deposit and the Equitable and such clubs as that - the young people didn't join these friendly societies. Well, as a matter of fact, I was a National Deposit bloke... [RH]

You see, all the old members were dying off and it got like that they hadn't got a lot of members and then, of course, what they done where they had got a little money, the club broke up and what members there was in the club, the money went to them. Well, you see, the band money come out of the club, but it got so short of members, you see, there was no money coming in the club... I don't know what they paid. It wasn't a big amount, but every member had to pay so much a quarter... [RH]

When they had their feast days, you see, the money for the band come out of the club. Well, they had a dinner, you see, and that come out of the club, but they all was supposed to attend church - the service at feast days. But if they didn't, they were fined a shilling, so there was ever so many fined a shilling! They'd stopped up in the pubs, because the pubs was open from six in the morning to ten at night that time of day ... Well, then they used to start about 10 o'clock in the morning, and they used to form up at the headquarters - course, there was flags up all at the club. [They used to] march to the church for the service. They used to come out of the service, and all the main subscribers round what subscribed to the club, you see, they used to visit them. The band used to march round ... to their front door, and they used to stand there and play about a couple of tunes, then march round to the next place. Course, soon as ever they'd played about a couple of tunes or whatever they was going to play - they never played long - they was formed up and marching to the next place, you see. Well then, they always strike up a march tune from where they come from till they got away. Then, course, they'd wait till they got a certain distance away from the next house, and then start up playing another march, you see. That's how they used to do it. [RH]

There was a banner in front of the members of the club, the club banner. There used to be two blokes carry that, but that's all there was. And all the club members, well most of them, used to travel round with them, you see, because if they didn't, they wouldn't get no subscription [benefit?] next year. So most of them used to follow the band, and, course, [a] lot of outsiders used to follow as well, you see. It's similar to a bonfire procession in that way. Well, that used to last to over lunchtime sometimes; perhaps, they got somewhere to go after lunch, see, they used to fulfil that, then what time they'd got up to teatime and that, they'd play out at the club ground, you see. Only perhaps, they'd be playing that end of the club ground, and the roundabout would be down this end – the roundabout organ, you see – so they wasn't huddled up close together, and then after teatime they used to have to play for dancing up to ten o'clock. That was what the band had to do. [RH]

The dances were the schottische, the polka, the waltz and the sets.

> Scan: They used to play a rare lot of set tunes ... and they always got plenty of sets out. [DN]

Scan, however, never played in the band for dancing, just for marching. Strangely, little of the band's repertoire rubbed off on him.

> Scan: Well, I know some of them. I've thought about them sometimes. I know bits and pieces of some of the marches, but I've never played them, mind, as I know of. I used to play one old waltz

what they used to play, but I ain't played that for years now. But sometimes I think of a piece of some of the tunes what they used to play. Well, I know one tune - this was when I was in it - *Soldiers in the Park. Washington Post*, I've played that with them. [RH]

The formal notice of Horsted Keynes Club Day in 1901, published in the Sussex Express, throws quite a different light on the proceedings and contrasts sharply with Scan's account.

> The members of the local Friendly Society held their annual feast on Monday. Headed by Horsted Keynes Band, the members marched from the Crown Inn, their head-quarters, to Horsted Keynes Church, where a service was held by Rev. F.D. Smythe, who also gave an address. The Annual dinner was held at the Crown Inn, the Rector presiding and submitting the principal toasts. Mr. B. Clarke acknowledged the toast "The Horsted Keynes Friendly Society", Mr. J.K. Esdaile, J.P., replying to that of the honorary members and Councillor Whittington of Lewes answering for the visitors.[2]

During June and July of the same year, the *Sussex Express* carried reports of the Horsted Keynes Band playing for the friendly societies at Nutley and the *Sheffield Arms*. In June 1905, 'songs were sung by Messrs. Bestie, S. Bish and C. Spriggs' at the club feast at the *Crown*, but there was no mention of Horsted Band in the press report.[3] A month later the *Sussex Express* ran the following notice:

> The Horsted Keynes Benefit Society, which had been in existence for upward of fifty years, has been dissolved. At one time the membership was over 120, and it gradually dwindled down to 23. The share-out to each member was nearly 12s.[4]

NOTES

1. *Sussex Express*, 18.3.1910.

2. *Sussex Express*, -.6.1901.

3. *Sussex Express*, 3.6.1905.

4. *Sussex Express*, 22.7.1905.

Chapter 9:
The 'other' music

During the nineteenth century, and well into the twentieth, elite country society employed professional orchestras from London and Brighton or Army and Volunteer bands of professional standard for their balls and private parties. Further down the social scale, at the level of tradesmen, small-town jobbing, professional musicians were used in small combinations, joined sometimes by local literate musicians, who may have been semi-professional or even amateur. They circulated the latest published material and represented not only fashion, but respectability. These trained musicians did stray into the villages, and appeared at such events as workhouse concerts, even sharing an occasional press notice with a bones player or mouthorgan soloist.[1] They operated mainly in the small country towns of Uckfield, Haywards Heath, Newick and Forest Row and the closed village of Fletching, where the presence of the Earl of Sheffield was felt at formal village festivities.

Among the reported musicians were men otherwise engaged in the music business: T.E. Gearing (piano) from Lewes, R. Whiteside (piano) and Wallace Chisholm (violin) from Uckfield - all music teachers - and Horace Jackson, a piano dealer with a music shop in Lewes. Finch's Quadrille Band was led by a member of a flourishing building and retail firm in Haywards Heath, and W. Bates (violin) was a job master in Newick.[2] Although their identity remains a mystery, W. Allen's Quadrille Band's appearances at Tradesmen's Balls in the *Brambletye Hotel*, Forest Row, in 1897 and 1905 set them very clearly in an identifiable social stratum. The band that played for dancing at the Heathfield Football Club's annual dinner in 1901 consisted of B.H. Naylor and W. Lovell (violins), T. Sinden (cornet) and W. Sinden (piccolo), who were probably all members of the club. Thomas Sinden was an estate carpenter, an artisan rather than an independent tradesman, and he and the piccolo player may well have learnt their instruments in a town or village band.[3]

If Scan was central to the music making and dancing in the countryside around Horsted Keynes, Wallace Randolph Chisholm (1871-1934) held a similar position in the country town of Uckfield. These two individuals operated from very different value bases, however, one an ear-playing countryman, rooted in the oral tradition, utilising what he heard and what he could invent, the other a musically literate small-town working man tied to the restraints of the written score and academic technique. They lived close enough to each other to have had contact, but in the absence of positive evidence to the contrary, it would appear they functioned within different social networks, seldom overlapping geographically. Though both were working men, originally from similar backgrounds, they operated within two separate levels of working society and their social affiliation put them in different musical camps. Wallace Chisholm, perhaps, stood for what Scan meant by 'a posh dance' and what Daisy later called 'a dear dance'. The complete absence of newspaper coverage of Scan's activities indicates that he could function without outside attention, whereas the professionals, perhaps, were de-pendent to some extent on press notices, and may even have been instrumental in making sure the editor received them.[4]

Wallace Chisholm came to Uckfield with his family as a youth from Shipbourne, Kent, where his father, William (1832-1914), had been a gardener. A family story describes Wally sitting on the back doorstep at the age of five, holding a cigar box up to his chin and scraping it with a stick, as if it were a fiddle. The model for this game may well have been his father, who came as an adult from Shetland, where at that time there was a flourishing fiddle tradition. By what means and to what standard he received his music education is not known, but early on he made a career choice between music and Kent County cricket. In Uckfield, by then a member of the Academic College of Violinists, he set up in business as a music teacher, operating from his home at

Above: Uckfield Town Band; c. 1909.

Back row (left to right): G. Dumsday, E. Olive, E. Blackford, H. French
L. Blackford, P.H. Shoosmith, Paul Route, E. Avis; front row (left to
*right): A. Picknell, A. Olive, **Wallace Chisholm**, A. Wren, unidentified.*
Note the valve trombone, flute and clarinet.
(Courtesy Norman Edwards)

Below: Uckfield Town Band, Ringles Cross Sweet Pea Show; 1912.

Back row (left to right): E. Avis, unidentified, M. Grant, unidentified,
A. Picknell, A. Olive, --- Burgess, C. Parsons, E. Blackford,
P.H. Shoosmith, G. Dumsday; front row (left to right): E. Olive, L.
*Blackford, H. French, **Wallace Chisholm**, --- Dumsday, Paul Route,*
Harry Cousins (later bandmaster at Buxton).
(Photograph: Manoah Duplock, Five Ashes. Courtesy Norman Edwards)

136 Framfield Road. His son, Hugh (born 1921), a church organist in demand in and around Uckfield until his death in September 1988, was thirteen when his father died and had only hazy pictures of his father's activities, but he filled in some background. He said his father taught the well-off children in their homes, but every child in all the families in Uckfield took lessons from him. 'If they couldn't afford it, it didn't matter. Mother said, "Where's the Sunday joint coming from?" And he would answer, "Cast your bread upon the waters, my dear." 'Every child' is an exaggeration, in view of the fact that his contemporary and associate, R. Whiteside, was teaching just up the road at number 31.

In addition to teaching music Wallace Chisholm led a band, taught dancing, including the *Quadrilles*, worked part-time as a photographer and was bandmaster of Uckfield Town Band. He is reputed to have been able to cope with any string or wind instrument and also composed organ music for the church.[5]

Respectability characterises the following 1910 newspaper account:

> **Newick Dance.** A very enjoyable dance arranged by Messrs. A.E. Tidy, P.D. Turner, A. Gower and G. Bannister was held at the Reading Room on Thursday night. The room was admirably decorated for the occasion by Mr. William Chisholm and others including Mrs. A. Tidy, Miss Humphrey, the Misses Avery (2), Miss Landridge and Miss Beecham. The attendance numbered almost 60 and thanks largely to the diligence and zeal of the committee and efficient manner in which Mr. G. Bannister acted as hon. secretary, the event was in every way a great success. Dancing was from 8 to 3 o'clock, the music being supplied by Mr. Wallace Chisholm's Quadrille band. Light refreshments were served as required.[6]

Some of the participants can be identified: William Chisholm was a head gardener, Alfred Tidy was assistant overseer and clerk to the Parish Council for Fletching, Danehill and Newick, and kept a farm, while G. Bannister was a shopkeeper.[7]

Wallace Chisholm knew nothing of ear-playing. His large collection of sheet music was destroyed years ago, but in all probability he played from violin and piano scores, the standard items in music publishers' catalogues. A programme survives of the annual ball given by R. Whiteside in connection with

his dancing class in Uckfield Drill Hall in 1914. Chisholm and Whiteside played what looks like a typical selection of Edwardian written material, enlivened by a pseudo-ragtime hit for the *Lancers*:

Waltz .... *The Girl on the Film*
Two-step .... *The Goat's Wedding*
Lancers .... *Everybody's Doing It*
Veleta .... *Chiming*
La favourite
Quadrilles ...... *Welcome Home*
Waltz .... *Little Grey Home in the West*
One-step.......... *Tinkers*
D'Alberts .... selected
Hurndilla
Waltz .... *Nights of Gladness*
Interval
Lancers .... *Marching*
Waltz .... *Flower of the Nile*
Barn dance .... *Spring Flowers*
Quadrilles ...... *Top of the World*
Waltz .... *Smiles, then Kisses*
Two-step .... *Kelly Land*
D' Alberts ...... selected
Waltz Imperial
Waltz .... *Where my Caravan has Rested*
Lancers .... *Gipsy Love*
Waltz .... *Sunshine Girl*
God Save the King [8]

Uckfield Chamber of Commerce Guide; 1924
(Courtesy Norman Edwards*)*

UCKFIELD & DISTRICT

PIANOFORTE TUNING
— AND REPAIRS —
SINGLY OR BY CONTRACT

Wallace R. Chisholm.

ORCHESTRA for BALL ROOM
and
GARDEN PARTIES.

HIGHEST REFERENCES.

136 Framfield Road,
UCKFIELD.

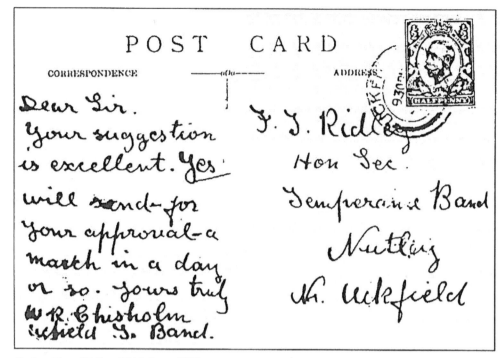

Postcard from Wallace Chisholm; c. 1912.

(Courtesy Norman Edwards)

So much for repertoire, but what about style? There is a family story about the time he put his thumb out of joint at football and went ahead with a planned violin recital at Framfield Church the same night, with the bow attached to his hand with rubber bands. This illustrates the true professional's stance - the show must go on-but what does it say about his bowing technique? Was it, in fact, closer to that of Walter Bulwer than that of Yehudi Menuhin?

Hugh Chisholm was reasonably certain that the final version of his father's dance band was a trio: his father (violin), Mrs Crowhurst from Framfield on the piano and her son, Bertie, on the drums. George Avis, one of Wallace Chisholm's violin pupils, played at a dance with this combination in 1927 when he was about fifteen and he thought the band usually consisted of two violins, piano and drums.

NOTES

1. I have assumed that workhouse concerts were charity events for the inmates; even so, the audience may have included the Guardians and other local dignitaries.

2. A job master ran a carriage and haulage business, with a fleet of varied horse-drawn vehicles.

3. Occupation identifications from *Kelly's Directory of Sussex*. The following are *Sussex Express* notices:

   20.2.1897: W. Allen's Quadrille Band at Forest Row.

   15.5.1897: W. Bates, violin, and T.E. Gearing, piano, at the Ladies' Social Club, Newick.

   5.1.1901: W. Bates at a social, Fletching Schools.

   30.3.1901: Heathfield Football Club Dinner (see text).

   7.1.1905: W. Bates, violin, T.E. Gearing, piano, and George Isgar, cornet, at the village ball, supported by Earl of Sheffield, at Fletching Schools.

   7.1.1905: Finches Quadrille Band at a Fancy Dress Ball in Lindfield.

   28.1.1905: Horace Jackson's String Quartette at Chailey workhouse.

   4.2.1905: T.E. Gearing at a Football Smoker in Lewes.

   8.2.1905: W. Bates, violin, C. Pickett, cello, Kemp E. Brooks, cornet, at a smoking concert in Newick.

   12.2.1905: Finch's Quadrille Dand at the Volunteer's Dall, Cuckfield.

   25.2.1905: W. Allen's Quadrille Band at Forest Row.

   11.3.1905: W. Bates, violin, and T.E. Gearing, piano, at a Cinderella Dance for the Quadrille class at Fletching Schools.

   1.4.1905: W. Bates, violin, C. Pickett, cello, Kemp E. Brooks, cornet, and H. Robinson, piano, at the Hand-in-Hand Slate Club smoking concert in Newick.

4. It is curious that in the period from the 1890s to the 1920s, *Kelly's* listed dancing and music teachers, but made no reference to musicians, bands or orchestras.

5. Hugh Chisholm.

6. *Sussex Express*, 21.1.1910.

The following *Sussex Express* notices place Wallace Chisholm in a variety of contexts:

3.2.1911: a dance at Blackboys.

24.2.1911: with Mrs. C. Van Loock and Miss Eyre, he played 'up to date music' at the second of a series of socials and whist drives at Framfield.

14.4.1911: the Rat and Sparrow [shooting] Club dinner in the *Griffin*, Fletching. Sixty sat down. 'Some enjoyable music was given during the evening, and included violin solos by Mr. Chisholm, recitation by Mr. Parker, and songs by Messrs. Reddich, Weller, Smith, C. Wood, Relf and others. Mr. St. John presided at the piano.'

11.1.1914 and 16.4.1914: Mr. Chisholm's Quadrille Band at the National Schools, Fletching.

11.2.1921: with R. and H. Whiteside at a Fancy Dress Ball in Uckfield.

8.4.1921: with Henry Whiteside, piano, at an Easter dance in Uckfield Town Hall, arranged by R. Whiteside.

11.3.1927, 1.4.1927, 20.5.1927, 14.10.1927 and 28.10.1927: Wallace R. Chisholm's Orchestra at the *British Legion*, Isfield.

6.5.1927 and 10.6.1927: Wallace R. Chisholm's Orchestra at Nutley.

9.12.1927: Mr. W. R. Chisholm's Dance Band at Framfield.

3.1.1930: Wallace R. Chisholm's Dance Band at New Year's Eve function for the British Legion at Framfield.

17.1.1930: with P.G. Ladbrook, piano, at a social, whist drive and dance at Laughton.

7.2.1930: Wallace R. Chisholm's Orchestra at Uckfield Public Hall.

7. Occupation identifications from *Kelly's*.

8. *Sussex Express*, 19.2.1914.

Chapter 10:
Songs and singers

The bias in this text so far has been towards dancing and instrumental music, to the exclusion of songs and singing. Mervyn Plunkett's search for singers barely touched Horsted Keynes and, as far as I can tell, did not extend to Danehill, Nutley and Fairwarp. Scan had spoken to him of his boyhood friend, Harry Knight, who was a good singer, but to the best of my knowledge the only singer he recorded from that area was Scan himself. Mervyn knew the *Sloop* had, or had had, a reputaion for good singers, but he was unable to follow up the lead.[1]

Most of the singers he recorded in neighbouring parts of Sussex were in their seventies and eighties. Some, like Pop Maynard, Jim Wilson, Peter Gander and Bill Hawkes, were active in public, singing in their local pub as and when the occasion was right, on a Saturday night or Bank Holiday Monday. Some, however, like Mrs Lester of East Grinstead, had probably never sung in public in their lives, restrict-ing their performances to home and family. Mervyn went out of his way to speak to a great variety of people about old country songs, and thus in a short time came across many singers and recorded a considerable number of songs. All the indications were that had he had the time and energy, the trawl would have been endless. A real constraint was the limited number of social relationships he could sustain with the singers who gave him their songs.

The problems are threefold in trying to reconstruct the patterns of singing behaviour, repertoires and styles in Scan's experience. The first is the heavily biased reporting of song collectors, essentially people on the outside who occasionally had opportunities to look in. Mervyn, certainly the most radical person involved in this pursuit in the 1950s and 1960s, was critical of the distorted representation of the singing tradition contained in the published work of earlier English folksong collectors.[2] Yet, in the nature of things, Mervyn introduced distortions in his own

A session in the Half Moon, *at Balcombe in 1959.*

Bill McMahon, Snowy Howick and Mervyn Plunkett listen, while Dot Wood of West Hoathly sings.

Opposite: Bill McMahon, Jim Wilson and Mervyn Plunkett. (Photograph: Reg Hall)

work and his collecting was based on his own aesthetic values. Fairly early in his progress as a collector of songs, he drew conclusions and operated from assumptions, particularly about the nature of singing in pubs, which could be challenged.[3]

The second problem concerns the dearth of contemporary documentary evidence. Newspapers, of course, never reported singing in domestic situations or in the taprooms of public houses. They did, however, cover public events of a certain social standing, though in spite of the singers and the songs being listed, there was never any real critical assessment or hard evidence of what went on. The song titles give clues to repertoire, but not to style.

The third difficulty is in taking adequate, reliable oral testimony so long after the event. Those local people I have spoken to recently are either too young, having been born in the 1920s and grown up in the 1930s and 1940s, or, like Daisy Sherlock, seldom frequented pubs. These informants, when they can remember what they heard in their youth, usually mention the titles or a few lines of drawing room ballads and music hall songs. The two polar extremes in the musical culture of country working men and women, the oral tradition and the literate, already discussed in relation to instrumental music, are evident in song and singing. The older, earthier, oral tradition had always operated as a cultural underground, not easily visible to the rest of the world. Singing in church and the performance of the latest, topical, composed comic songs and parlour ballads at formal suppers and smoking concerts carried social kudos. The underground, however, was resilient in the face of a variety of cultural assaults, and was very near the surface, often breaking through veneers of respectability after a few drinks had been taken.

At the musical evenings in the blacksmith's shop in Horsted Keynes before the Great War, Arch Blayber's gramophone provided some of the entertainment; bottles of home-made wine assured the nights were pretty raucous.[4] What, however, went on at the Horsted Keynes Cricket Club concert, arranged by Mrs Noakes, the postmaster's wife, 'which gave so much pleasure to local residents' in April 1910?[5] The same month a newspaper report of a social evening at Heathfield Star Football Club, very much a working men's organisation, listed the patriotic parlour ballads and coon-songs rendered by the members, but among them was a country song, *If I was a Blackbird*, sung by Mr R. Robins, and a stepdance, more commonly associated with the taproom, by Mr J. Porter.[6] Edwardian propriety, sentimentality and jingoism plainly co-existed with the alternative values of many village people.

Sussex Express, *4 June 1914*

The smoker - the smoking concert at slate club shareouts at Christmas-time - was one formal occasion for singing. The share-out at the *Star Inn*, Piltdown, in 1909 was 18s. 6d. - almost a week's wages for its 43 members - and 'during the evening plenty of singers were found and a very enjoyable evening was indulged in.'[7] Arch Sherlock attended the smokers in the *Cross*, Horsted Keynes, which ceased to be held in the 1920s, and he could name the songs and the singers. Bert Gurr (born 1907) has been able to flesh out the bones. Johnny Clark, Lord of the Manor, bought old ale for everyone in the *Legion* at Christmas and he was the slate-club president. Reuben Baker, with his finger in anything in the village where fun was concerned, was the chairman. Bert Gurr thinks of his father as having had the most prodigious repertoire locally. 'Father used to sing all sorts ... They used to pester the life out of him to sing in the *Green Man*.'

> **Arch Sherlock:** When I was in my teens, you know, one of the boys ... old Jack Gurr, we used to get him over the *Green Man* and to get him to sing we used to pull the blinds and get him filled up with beer. Saturday dinner-times. He used to play quoits out in front of the *Green Man*, you see, and you know how they used to mark; they marked the stick by notching it, twenty-one up. Well, he was so bloody drunk, he didn't notch the stick; he notched his finger! That's true! He used to sing that one, *Give Me a Keg or Can*. He had dozens of songs he used to sing. We used to try and egg him on, you know; get him about three parts cut and keep on winding another pint into him.

Among the songs Bert Gurr recalls his father singing were *Dot and Carry One*, about someone with a wooden leg, *The Ivy and the Mistletoe*, *The Mistletoe Bough*, *Brighton's Fine Town*, *Old Queen Victoria's Jubilee Song* and *By Studying Economy I Lived Like a Lord*, the latter to the tune Pop Maynard used for *Shooting Goachen's Cocks Up*.[8] There was also the *Prince of Wales's Ball*, which he got from his father, a policeman, who had sung it on the stage at the Marylebone Theatre in London. Bert's cousin, Freddie Gates, who had come back from the war with experience as a farrier and taken over the smithy, usually sang Comrades at the smoker; Trayt Moore, not generally renowned for singing, used to give *Don't Go Down in the Mine*. Alf Alexander had songs with the banjo, and then years later, a much younger man, George Payne, sang *The Little Pigs Make the Best of Pork*.

Given that Joe Marten was a life-long friend of Scan's - Scan left a concertina with him on permanent loan till Joe died - some sort of understanding of his musical activity is relevant. In common with Will Tester, reconstruction of part of his life story based on the evidence of his children is unbalanced, primarily because the social conventions separated pub life from home life. Children, including Daisy Sherlock, had little first-hand experience of how their fathers behaved in pubs. Joe Marten married in early middle age, in 1910, by which time he had probably ceased being 'one of the lads' (implicit in his association with Trayton and Scan). His children's memories are of his singing at home. His daughter, Mary, confirms 'he had a nice voice' and would 'sing in parts', and his son, Will, recollects he did not sing any of 'the old, real country songs.' If he ever had a repertoire of such material, it did not intrude into his home life.

> **Mary Elphick:** All songs, the time when he was singing, they were all very sad.
> **Will Marten:** They were all based on that sort of thing. All tunes were based on something that was sad.
> **Mary Elphick:** You see, during the last century there was a lot of poverty, terrible poverty and ...

Jack Norris entertains at Cuckfield in the 1960s.
(Courtesy Florence Norris)

> **Will Marten:** It was based on that.
> **Mary Elphick:** The songs, they were based on that sort of thing.
> **Will Marten:** Well, that's the one: 'Father, dear father, come home from the pub/ The clock in the steeple strikes one.' What it was, the old father was in the pub all the time; the boy ran to him asking him to come home, 'cause his son is dying.
> **Mary Elphick:** Yes, and he died in the end.
> **Will Marten:** And at twelve o'clock, he said 'Dad! He's dead,' wasn't it? It went right through the hours, you see, as he sang it. Proper old pub song![9]

Further local snippets come from Christopher Stephens of Fairwarp, who cites his father's party pieces as *The Broom Dasher that Lived in the Wood* and *Buttercup Joe*, and Fanny Lander, who mentioned a singer, Sam Cork, who lived at Birchgrove in Horsted Keynes before the Great War, who 'was a great pal of Tester's.' Around 1910 she used to watch out for a street singer in Chelwood:

> There used to be a man come up from Brighton every Thursday, and he used to sing over the post office. His name was Oliver and he sang that special song everywhere. I can't remember what it was now.

Finally, Polly Marten's father, Mr Pollard, from Danehill:

> **Will Marten:** The wife's dad belonged to the choir ... He was the background to the choir ... Big man, big chested man - bass. Oh, he was smashing ... He really had got a voice ... It was a nice, rich deep voice.

This hotch-potch of recollections, although it hardly amounts to conclusive evidence, does point to a diversity of practices and attitudes towards singing. The piece about the street singer from Brighton poses more questions than it answers, and Joe Marten's 'part-singing' leaves us guessing. However, two pieces of information about Nelson Stephens - first that he was a member of Ashdown Forest Temperance Band, and second that he sang at least two old-fashioned country songs - provide an illustration of the two musical traditions being contained within one person.

Scan, of course, sang a few songs in his time. *Bold Robert Emmett*, probably his father's song, had been his great favourite, but late in life the words and tune eluded him. He had fragments of *Tally Ho, Oxford City* and *They've All Got a Mate but Me*, a ditty remembered from childhood:

> *The last I had, she drove me mad.*
> *In vain I tried to stop her,*
> *For she run away in a very funny way,*
> *And got slowly boiled to death in a copper.*[10]
> [DN]

As an old man, rather surprised to think that anyone would want to hear him sing, his two stand-bys were his brother Bert's song, *The Old Rustic Bridge*, which he delivered with great rhythmic control and dignity, and *The Lakes of Coalflin*, learnt when he was a young man at a wedding party from a young woman who wrote out the words for him. *Barbara*

Allen, which he sings on the Topic record, was not one of his songs. It came to him during the car journey to the *Fox*, Islington Green, and he rehearsed it in his mind, only to forget the last verse during the performance later the same evening.

Scan's singing at the *Fox* in 1965 was a great surprise to Daisy. 'He used to whistle a lot', but she had never heard him sing before.[11] The real singer in the Tester family was Bert, usually known as Tiger, but at this distance in time it is impossible to judge what his singing was like. Scan told Peter Kennedy he sang *Kitty Wells, I'm a Man that's Done Wrong to my Parents, The Sailor's Grave* and *I've been Lonely Since my Mother Died*.[12] Arch Sherlock remembered that his usual songs were *Some Soldiers were Seated around the Camp Fire* and *If Those Lips Could Only Speak*.

NOTES

1. The following singers were listed as having performed at a smoker at the *Sloop*: 'Messrs. R. Setford, M. Setford, Elphick, Marten, E. Hills, jun, Marchant, Tully, W. Farmer and 'Little Jack'.' (*Sussex Express*, 25.2.1905).

2. For discussion of distortion in folksong collecting see Vic Gammon, 'Folk Song Collecting in Sussex and Surrey, 1843-1914', *History Workshop*, 10, (Autumn 1980); David Harker, 'Cecil Sharp in Somerset; Some Conclusions' *Folk Music Journal*, II, 3 (1972), pp. 220-240. David Harker, *Fakesong: The manufacture of British 'folksong' to the present day* (1985).

3. Mervyn left an unpublished book on English traditional singing, which it was his intention to revise and publish.

4. Arch Sherlock.

5. *Sussex Express*, 8.4.1910.

   A similar event was reported in 1911 (*Sussex Express*, 12.5.1911).

   Scan was living in Horsted Keynes at the time of the first of these concerts and probably at Chelwood Gate for the second. Was he included among the entertainers?

   A 1909 press report places a member of the Noakes family in a different social context from Scan: Miss Noakes provided the accompaniment for the songs and dances of 'the girls of Horsted Keynes who took part in the Morris games and rendered folk songs in the Assembly Room the other evening...' (*Sussex Express*, 10.12.1909) While local working people played out their own music and dance tradition, as part of their normal life-style, members of the lower middle class favoured the reconstruction of the English rural tradition represented by the Cecil Sharp/ Mary Neal folk song and dance movement.

6. *Sussex Express*, 15.4.1910.

   At a smoking concert at the *May Garland Inn*, Horam Road, among a list of low-brow composed material, Mr. Godly sang *The Waterford Boys* (*Sussex Express*, 27.3.1897).

   At a Rabbit Supper at the *Bat and Ball Inn*, Chiddingley, Mr. Goldsmith sang *When Jones' Ale Was New* (*Sussex Express*, 6.3.1897).

   A concert at Waldron included material by Gounod and the first appearance of the local minstrel troupe. 'Mr. H.E. Rogers caused roars of laughter with his humourous song, The pantomime and gave an encore The Village Pump.' (*Sussex Express*, 28.4.1911).

7. *Sussex Express*, 24.12.1909.

8. George Maynard, *Ye Subjects of England* (1956, 1962), Topic 12T286.

   The Rt. Hon. George Joachim Goachen, M.P., J.P., lived at Seacox, Flimwell (*Kelly's*, 1895, p. 356).

9. *Come Home, Father* was written by Henry Clay Work in 1864 (W.K. McNeil, accompanying notes for *The Cold Water Pledge, vol 2*, Marimac Recordings 9105 (cassette). This cassette includes a recording by Bela Lam and His Greene County Singers (Virginia), *Poor Little Bennie*, Okeh 45136 (1927)) (Graeme Kirkham and Keith Chandler).

10. Written by J.B. Geoghagan; sung by a music hall artist, Sam Torr, in the 1880s.

    I think Scan learnt *The False Bride* from Jean Hopkins in the late 1950s, although he had heard it before (Folktracks FSA 085 (cassette)).

11. Daisy Sherlock to David Nuttall.

    P.W. Joyce noted the song from the singing of Peggy Cudmore, 13, in Glenosheen, Co. Limerick, in 1854 (*Old Irish Folk Music and Songs* (1909), p. 227).

    Recorded examples include:

    Paddy Beades (Ireland), *The Lakes of Cool-Finn* (1938), Regal Zonophone IZ1081.

    Amy Birch (Devon), *Royal Comrade* (c.1975), Topic 12TS349.

12. Folktracks FSA 085 (cassette).

Chapter 11:
Calendar customs

Christmas received barely a passing mention in the *Sussex Express* at the beginning of this century. In the villages, brass bands and carol singers went round the pubs and big houses, Danehill handbell ringers played at the *Coach and Horses* on Boxing Day and there were servants' balls and long nights into the New Year. In Cuckfield, Peter Gander, Bill Hawks, Jack Norris and their mates had some special Christmas and New Year songs for the pub. *While Shepherds Watch Their Flocks by Night* to the tune *Lyngham* and *The Trees Are All Bare* were among them, and Scan knew and played both tunes.

An old winter custom, Apple Howling, was still practised at the turn of the century. At Danehill the visiting howlers sang:

> *Root fast, root bear,*
> *Every twig, apple big,*
> *Every bough, apples enow,*
> *Hatfuls, capfuls, five bushel sackfuls.*[1]

Giles Moore, rector of Horsted Keynes, paid the 'Howling Boyes' sixpence on 5 January 1657 and again on Christmas Eve, 1659, for their visit to his orchard.[2] Two hundred and fifty years later their descendants were calling on Scan's father:

> **Scan:** When we was at the *Green Man* we used to have a lot of apple trees and that, fruit trees. Well, everybody did that time of day. I mean to say, they don't plant no young trees now in cottages. Every cottage had apple and pear trees, and my father planted a lot of apples. In fact, there's some there now what he planted. [RH]

> Apple howling - that's what we used to call it. They used to thresh the trees till they brought out some beer or wine or something. That was the idea of that.

> That was New Year's time. That happened lots of places; it was a recognised thing like carol singing and I've never seen it except about once or twice, but I know while we was at the *Green Man*, I can remember father coming in and he says, 'You better draw off a gallon of beer, you boys.' He says, 'They'll be just coming round the back now.' But he was artful; he'd had the beer drawed off and called them in. He says, 'You needn't trouble to go down the garden. You can come inside here.' They didn't hurt the trees; they never hit them hard enough to hurt them. You wouldn't see where they'd knocked any bark off or anything. But I dare say some of them [i.e. the trees] used to cop it, you know, especially if they'd had a tidy drink. [RH]

MAY DAY

May Day in Horsted Keynes was marked by a May Queen on a farm wagon and a maypole on the Green, according to Daisy Sherlock, who remembered it around 1923 or 1924. In Fletching it had been a much grander affair, sponsored by the Earl of Sheffield:

> Not withstanding the rough weather on Monday, the village children turned out with their garlands and Maypoles. They started at an early hour in the morning, visiting all the houses in the village, and then journeyed to Sheffield Park, where each one received a small sum of money, special prizes were kindly given by the Earl of Sheffield and Miss Allenborough for the best garlands and Maypoles.[3]

One of the participants, recalling the event in old age, described it as follows:

> The children would decorate small poles with wild flowers and early in the morning of May Day they would form a procession and go all round the village carrying their decorated poles and singing 'the first of May is here today, please remember the May Pole'. People would give them a penny or twopence and things to eat and drink. They would go as far as Searles, then back through the village to Sheffield Place. There they would lay their decorated poles on the lawn and Lord Sheffield would judge which was the prettiest. They would have May Pole dancing on the lawn of Sheffield Place and afterwards came a lovely tea. Grown ups would decorate prams and bicycles and there would be more flowers and Jack o' Greens and the adults would join in the fun.[4]

THE ANNUAL FAIR

Although fairs at Horsted Keynes, Chelwood Gate and Lindfield received a boost from their association with the Friendly Societies' feast days, the fair day was not abandoned with the demise of the societies.[5] In Horsted Keynes, in the years just after the Great War, a handful of volunteers mowed the Green a few days before the last Monday in May, 'for the sake of the children' and for free beer from the parish funds. A collection was taken up round the big houses and village by the schoolmaster, the parson and a few others, which paid for free rides on the roundabout for all the village children until tea-time.[6]

> The gypsies used to congregate in Bonfire Lane during the previous week, under the eagle eye of Mr. Turner, our village policeman; he was a thorn in the side of all gypsies in the district.[7]

> **Scan:** The same people came every year ... They come from Merton, Surrey ... [The man] that had the roundabout, his name was Alf Bond, but I can remember it before ever he came. It used to be Harris's and Bailey's people used to come there with the roundabout, and there was an old man come from this side of Edenbridge. He used to have a big hand roundabout and two blokes ... they used to have one each side of the roundabout and turn this by hand. Only it was extraordinary big roundabout. [RH]

Reuben Baker (1877-1955), a coal merchant, nicknamed the 'Mayor of Horsted', was behind much of the organised social activity among the village people. After Horsted Band disbanded, they hired Ardingly Band and Reuben Baker provided them with free beer. At the end of one fair day they refused to play one more 'last tune'. 'Bugger 'em,' said the Mayor, and that was the last of their free beer.[8]

BONFIRE NIGHT

For many years the bonfire societies in Lewes have dominated activities on November the Fifth for miles around. The importance of Bonfire Night to the working people of the town is illustrated by the extensive newspaper coverage over several weeks in 1900, compared to the passing reference to Christmas. In Lewes the event has an overtly anti-Papist theme, with ritualised declamatory speeches in memory of the Lewes Protestant martyrs of 1555-7 and the burning of a large effigy of a currently unpopular national or international figure. It is also a winter fire festival with trolleys of burning embers pulled recklessly through the streets, firecrackers and a torch-light procession in fancy costume with banners and brass bands.[9]

Bonfire Night was also hazardous in Horsted Keynes in Scan's youth, the result of high spirits and drinking. He once went dressed up in a paper pierrot's costume carrying a real banjo, which ended up on the bonfire when his back was turned, and Arch remembers, when he was young, the lads would 'run through the ashes when they got drunk'. All the shops used to close, but on one occasion the grocer's on the Green stayed open, which was frowned on by local residents. Scan and some of his young mates rigged up a large rocket, a 'Lewes rouser', on wheels and lined it up on the Green. It sped across the road, straight through the open door and into a display of biscuit tins at the back of the shop.[10]

Many villages, including Horsted Keynes, had bonfire societies at one time. By the 1930s, the forces of respectability had triumphed over the disreputable elements essential to the spirit of Bonfire Night. The Fairwarp Band, for example, gave up its annual

'Fifth of November custom at Brighton' by H.G. Hines.
Illustrated London News, *5 November 1853.*

torch-light procession to Maresfield, after the year the hedgerow lining the route caught light. Before the War, bonfire night in most places had become a domestic affair with fireworks and bonfire in the backgarden. Few villages have retained their bon-

fire societies and surviving societies celebrate in the weeks preceding November the Fifth, so they can be free to join the huge crowds attracted to Lewes Bonfire Night.

NOTES

1. Anonymous, 'Memories of My Village' (c. 1956), East Sussex Records Office, ref. W.I. 53/7. Quoted in *Danehill Parish Historical Society Magazine* (Feb. 1987), p. 23.

2. *The Journal of Giles Moore*, ed. Ruth Bird, (1971), pp. 315, 319.

   Moore gave 4d. on Boxing Day, 1661, (p. 323) and 4d. on 20 December 1665 (p. 329).

3. 'May day was celebrated... by the customary exhibition of [4] decorated carts, [15] garlands and [40] maypoles...' (*Sussex Express*, 6.5.1905).

4. Hylda Rawlings, 'A Born Teacher: The Memories of Louise Downer...', *Danehill P.H.S.M.*, II, 10 (1985), pp. 31-2.

5. Horsted Keynes Fair Day used to be on 1 May. Moore recorded the following entries in his journal:

   1 May 1656, 'Giv'n my wyfe for a FAIRING 3s. and the Boy 6d.' (p. 313); 1 May 1657, 'my wyves Boy a fairing 4d.' (p. 315). He also recorded an August fair in 1664, 'Giv'n Philip Godleyes wyfe at Horsted faire 1s.' (p. 327).

6. Daisy and Arch Sherlock.

7. Mrs Coon, 'Memories of my Village: Horsted Keynes' (1956), *Danehill P.H.S.M.*, II, 10, p. 1.

8. 'In the evening there was dancing, the Ardingley Band supplying the music' at a Horsted Keynes garden fete (*Sussex Express*, 9.7.1914).

9. Of the first five bands I heard on the street at Lewes Bonfire Night in 1987, four were playing tunes from Scan's working repertoire: *Sussex by the Sea, Tipperary, Under the Double Eagle* and *Scotland the Brave*.

10. Bob Fry.

The Five Ashes Minstrel Band celebrating the Silver Jubilee in June 1935.

Standing (left to right): John Fenner, melodeon; Lewis Wren, banjo (organizer);

Bert Moore, side drum; Bill Ticehurst, melodeon;

Alf Berwick, landlord of Five Ashes Inn; Wilf Wren, bass drum;

Harry Wicker; Amos Fenner, melodeon.

Kneeling, front: Harold Read.

(Sussex Express, c.1977)

Chapter 12:
Minstrels and carnival bands

Black-faced minstrels appeared in village entertainments towards the end of the nineteenth century, inspired by theatrical troupes and seaside concert parties. The professionals worked within conventions of form and content developed on the London stage during the period from the 1830s to the 1850s, but the rural amateurs were more pragmatic, working with any talent and material available to make a show. American minstrel songs and tunes - *Buffalo Girls*, for example - had circulated previously, but this was not necessarily the material included in village minstrel shows. In the troupe organised to raise funds for the hospital in Forest Row around 1910, Spider Miles sang *To Have a Face Like my Old Woman* and *My Little Jammy Face*, titles that have the ring of the British variety theatre.[1] James Payne's spoons playing in the same show was more than likely practised in the pub on Saturday nights. Fairwarp Minstrels made their second public appearance in January 1935 and at one time there was a troupe of minstrels in Nutley.[2] Whether he was associated with minstrels or not, E. Morley warranted special mention in newspaper reports for his bones playing at concerts in Newick in 1905 and Buxted in 1920.[3]

The Coronation celebrations on the recreation ground at Cuckfield in May 1937.
Jack Norris, melodeon; unidentified, bass drum; unidentified (on the cart), piano accordion.
Could the man on Jack's right be Peter Gander, playing the triangle?
(Courtesy Florence Norris)

Forty years afterwards, Bill Ticehurst recalled his time in the Minstrels Band, which was scratched together for the Silver Jubilee festivities in Five Ashes in 1935. Lewis Wren, one of the local hand-bell ringers, was the man behind it and the band practiced in the clubroom at the *Five Ashes Inn*.[4] The *Sussex Express* reported the fancy dress torch-light procession led by the Five Ashes Silver Jubilee band, directed by Frank Hemsley.[5] Bill Ticehurst mentioned Frank Hemsley as a piano-accordion player, who joined the Minstrel Band sometime later when they played at dances in the early war years. It appears then that the small village of Five Ashes fielded two separate carnival bands for the Silver Jubilee celebration. The organisers arranged an official comic band, while others provided a surprise turn-out from the pub.

Another example of tomfoolery took place at a function in Uckfield in 1920 where:

> The piece de resistance was the performance of the 'Broomfonium Comic Band' whose fearsome instruments gave forth music as weird as their appearance. The audience laughed till they could do so no longer and the bandmaster Mr. A. Corden led his instrumentalists off.[6]

Dressing-up and acting the fool were popular then, as they can be now, on special local and national occasions. Most communities now have no pool of musicians to call upon, but here and there some carnival bands have survived.[7]

NOTES

1. Bob and Mrs Miles.

2. Fairwarp: *Sussex Express*, 8.1.1935.
Nutley: Christopher Stephens.

3. *Sussex Express*, 18.2.1905, 1.4.1905 and 1.10.1920. In the 1.10.1920 edition, he is referred to as W. Hoorley in one report and as E. Moorley in another.

4. Undated cutting, *Sussex Express*, c.1977 (Vic and Sheila Gammon).

5. *Sussex Express*, 3.5.1935 and 10.3.1935.

6. *Sussex Express*, 6.8.1920.

7. See Ronnie Wharton and Arthur Clarke, *The Tommy Tucker Bands of the West Riding: The History and Development of a Working-Class Entertainment* (1979), and Brian Holland, *Here's to the Next Time: Carnival Jazz Bands of the Nineteen-Twenties and Thirties* (1988).

Surviving carnival bands in southern England: The Merry Makers, Padstow, Cornwall, and King's Korner Jazz Band, Pewsey, Wiltshire.

Recorded examples of carnival bands:

King's Korner Jazz band, *March Past* (1982), HD 010 and (1987) KKJB Kassette, no number.

Widnes Star Novelty Band (Lancashire), *Medley of Marches/Great Little Army March* (1932), Zonophone 6158 (second title also on Topic 12TS318).

Chapter 13:
Class and social conflict

The tensions in the social structure into which Scan was born continued in some form or another throughout his lifetime, although the Second World War was a decisive turning point in the demise of the old order. The gentry, in the view of some working people, were divided into the good and the bad, those who were decent and knew their social responsibilities, even if they were patronising, and the nouveau riche who were tight-fisted, elitist and inconsiderate to tenants and employees.

> **Arch Sherlock:** Some of them were gentlemen. Some were real people; others were nothing but bloody gasbags. And that's what the trouble with it was. Those that came up from nothing and made theirself are the worst people there are. The people that are landed gentry are the best people there are ... Not hardly any of 'em left.

The Hardys at Danehill spent money on the community. They built the church and the reading room and provided annual treats and outings for the village children.

> **Bert Wood:** They were jolly nice people, they were. Through the winter, they'd take soup round to the old folks.
> **Charlie Bates:** And the kids used to go down there Christmas.
> **Bert Wood:** I got a new pair of boots, Christmas time, and the girls, they had red riding hoods. [They] used to have a Christmas tree and everything.

The Corbetts, also at Danehill, were of the same ilk and made sure 'every kid had a present at school' and a day's outing to Brighton.[1]

Opposite: Group of workers, including (top left) Philip Thompsett, husband of Scan's eldest sister, Jinny, and Scan's brothers, Fred (front left) and Will (front right); undated.

(Courtesy Daisy & Arch Sherlock)

> **Bert Wood:** We always had a pheasant, Christmas day. The sons used to come round with a pheasant.

The newspaper report of a supper given by Mr and Mrs Stuart of Stonehurst, Ardingly, for their employees and servants spelt out some of the motivation behind such functions. It was 'a very successful affair, and doubtless will do much to strengthen the bonds of good feeling which bind together all on the estate'.[2] Even after the Great War, Sir Walter Scott continued the old ways with a servants' ball at Christmas time in the parish room at Horsted Keynes, with as much food and drink as they could manage and dancing to Gibson's Band from Ardingly.[3]

The Macmillans rebuilt Birchgrove in Horsted Keynes in the 1920s and provided several years work for local artisans and small contractors. They were not held in the same respect as the Esdailes, the Scotts and the other established families, however, and although working men were dependent on them for their living, they did not always stand for any old nonsense, particularly from Harold Macmillan's mother. Scan had a tale of how at Birchgrove he put her in her place. A heavy shower broke up a cricket match and forced spectators and players alike into the refreshment tent. Helen Macmillan fussed around, trying to send the working men home in the rain. 'Well, madam,' he said, looking straight at her, 'I think those that live nearest should go home first.' Many years later Arch Sherlock had a brush with her:

> I did plumbing for Macmillan and I had my plumbing shop out in the stable yard, and she said to me, she said, 'Sherlock,' she said, 'I don't allow smoking. It might burn the place down.' I said, 'If I want to burn your place down, I could do it with my blow lamp in two minutes.' She never said no more to me... I used to walk past her, as if she wasn't there.

Some of the sense of economic injustice was assuaged informally by pilfering, which probably carried more emotional satisfaction than financial reward.

Bert Wood: When they had a shoot at Corbetts or anything, I bet a shilling [Denner Head] was carrying somebody's bag, one of the toffs... and I bet when they got home, they found they'd lost several cartridges.

But if 'everybody used to go beating' for the gentry to earn a few shillings, a good few were also regular poachers.

Arch Sherlock: They [including Scan] used to get half their meals that way when they walked [to work]. They always had a catapult in their pocket and they used to knock over the rabbits and the pheasants on the way.

Charlie Bates: He [Bert Wood] got eye for rabbits and pheasants. He'd pick up a pheasant in a tree at night.
Bert Wood: Yeah, with a catapult. I never reckoned to miss anything... I never shoot but once. I nearly always got him first go. Oh, we had to at that time of day to get something to eat.
Charlie Bates: Everybody had rabbit wire all in the woods and that.
Bert Wood: I used to do a lot of wiring. I got sixteen one night... I used to carry a gun as well. He [Corbett] wouldn't give you permission to shoot pheasants ... but I used to shoot 'em!

Many of those accused of poaching appeared in Uckfield Police Court and were usually fined, although persistent offenders were sentenced to imprisonment.

Will Marten: They used to do a time in prison, you see... but they weren't bad men at all. They'd have 'em up for poaching, you see... The big estates around here kept 'em down, so they didn't get in there and shoot their pheasants.

Crime to the few and economic necessity to the majority, poaching was also covert social resistance, the working man's way of getting his own back. One particular Horsted Keynes man, well-known to be a poacher, had a reputation for more overt defiance. No member of the gentry could expect him to open a gate for them:

Arch Sherlock: Old Alf Pellin, he was one of the biggest poachers that ever walked in a pair of shoes... He had a pheasant. He put a collar round it, and at West Hoathly the police was always after him, you see ... so he says, 'I'll have the buggers!' Gee 'em up, you see. So he put a string round the pheasant's neck and led it up through the middle of West Hoathly, and they couldn't do nothing with him!

Will Marten: They said at Horsted Keynes old Pellin walked down through Horsted one Sunday morning with a rabbit on a string - live rabbit - got a collar on him - just to aggravate the toffs.

ROUGH MUSIC

Differences between villagers, usually involving an issue of morality that could be settled in no other way, had once been commonly dealt with by rough-musicking. It expressed the community's sense of outrage, which may have built up over many years but exploded over a particular incident. Rough music carried with it the legitimacy of tradition, although technically it was a breach of the peace. Since it had popular approval and was more likely to reinforce social order than weaken it, the police usually turned a blind eye. As working men and women gained access to more formal means of redressing grievances, rough-musicking tended to die out.[4]

They all thought it a pretty trick
To play to then some rough music...
When the riot first begun
Beating kettle and the drum,
The old ship bell and the pot-lid, too,
The mortar and pestle that did go.[5]

At Chelwood Common, just after the Great War, local feeling welled up following an unpopular trial decision, and the acquitted man took the full force of his neighbours' expression of their sense of grievance.

Bert Wood: They give him rough music.
Charlie Bates: My mother and the old women went down there - tin cans - and barracked him... miserable old so-and-so... He was never welcome in the village.

Bert Woods: Well, didn't make a bit of difference – that's his life. He was always on his own, so to speak.[6]

There was a rough-musicking in West Hoathly, probably just after the Second World War, and it seems that these two examples and those mentioned by Scan were the only ones in the district in living memory.[7] Scan's story dates from 1893 when he was five or six:

> We had a doctor live here and he had three sons - three boys - and they went to our village school with us, and the house that he lived in belonged to a man name of Field [James Field]. He was a cripple man and he was a nasty old bloke, he was. Well, I don't know what the trouble was about, but anyway this doctor had notice to get out, and so he got out, the doctor did, and he went to Lindfield... His name was Fitzmaurice, Dr. Fitzmaurice - good doctor he was - used to walk all around that time of day; he never had a horse, ride horseback like a good many did. Well, the people was so mad in the village over it, we rough-musicked him. [Field].[8] [RH]

> Now, I was old enough to go to that, so I do know, and I had an old, well, it wasn't exactly a bowl, it was a biggish bowl with a handle to it, and I know I had a stick with a big roll of rag wrapped round it like a drum stick, and I held this bath up and hit it like a drum. They had all sorts of instruments; some had teapots and blowed in the spout and they had anything they could get hold of, and we done it three nights running. You didn't dare to do it no more. There was a police sergeant and two more policemen there stood outside his gate. See, we marched up and down the road; we daren't go round in his place, you see. We marched up and down in the road three times, then we had to leave off, see. Course, a lot of them knew the rules about rough-musicking, and, I'll tell you, that's a tidy row, that is. I should think nearly every workman there was in the village was there, and, I can tell you, there was a tidy gang there. These police was there to see we didn't cause no trouble. Well, that's the law. That was a law, that you daren't rough-music more than three nights. I've heard talk of another man being rough-musicked, because he turned his wife out or something. That was at Chelwood Common, but this one, it's just down the road, the top of Leighton Road, and I can see the old bloke standing there with his crutches now... He owned all that row of houses down Leighton Road. [RH]

NOTES

1. For an account of the Corbett family, see Dame Margery Corbett Ashby: *From the Feudal to the Jet Age* (1982).

2. *Sussex Express*, 7.1 .1905.

3. Arch Sherlock.

   Compare the report of the servants' dance given by T.G. Ashton, M.P., and Mrs. Ashton of Vinehall Place. There were 50 guests, outside catering from *John's Cross Inn*, and dancing till 2.00 a.m. to Mrs Murray's Quadrille Band from St. Leonards. The host and hostess were present at the beginning and then hand-ed over to the butler and house keeper (*Sussex Express*, 7.1.1905).

4. This was not always the case. For example, rough musickers in Bampton, Oxfordshire, in 1900 were arrested; some cases were dismissed and some defendants bound over to keep the peace (*Witney Gazelle*, 15.12.1900 and 22.12.1900) (Keith Chandler).

5. This local song, *Up Turner's Hill*, was recorded in 1957 in Cuckfield from the singing of George Tompsett (born 1876) (Mervyn Plunkett Collection).

6. To respect local sensibilities, I have not given names or dates.

7. 'Rough Music was played in West Hoathly as recently as 1952, when the victim was rather unjustly selected.' (Mervyn Plunkett, 'George Tompsett', *Folksong Research*, V, 2/3, (1986/7) [written in 1957]).

   'The last man to be rough musicked in West Hoathly was ---------- who was a good friend of mine... I never liked to ask him about it but my impression was that it was just after the War, but it might have been in the late 30s.' (Letter, Mervyn Plunkett to me, 16.1.1986).

8. Dr. Fitzmaurice lived in Lindfield from at least 1889 until well into this century (*Kelly's Director of Sussex*), but his name does not appear in the *Parliamentary Register* for Lindfield in 1893. He may have lived in Horsted Keynes briefly in 1893, but not long enough to have qualified for an entry in the *Parliamentary Register*. Horsted Keynes school records for the period are lost.

Scan in 1957.

Chapter 14:
The 1920s and beyond

The pattern and pace of life in the country were transformed by the Great War. To some extent the War accelerated social changes that were already in progress; it broke down country institutions, such as village bands, and created many others, like the British Legion. If the War accelerated 'progress', Roy Dommett has suggested a process by which social change was retarded. He observes that many fathers were killed, some sons looked to their grandfathers for their values, and this could account for some of the old songs continuing long after they might have been expected to have been forgotten.[1]

Fundamental changes had taken place in the character and use of pubs in 1915, when emergency wartime measures were introduced to curb drunkenness. Laws relating to public houses until then regulated little else but the quality of liquor, value for money and sale to minors, and forbade gambling and disorderly conduct; country pubs opened from 6 a.m. to 10 p.m. with no restriction on children in the bar. In 1915, opening hours were reduced to about four in the middle of the day and a little longer in the evening, and children under fourteen were not to be admitted at all. The wartime regulations stayed in operation for the following seventy years or so. The pattern of public house use changed quite considerably, and, not surprisingly, the annual national average consumption of beer fell from 27.5 gallons per head in 1913-14 to 17.3 gallons in 1924-25.[2]

Popular music took on new characteristics after the Great War. Coon-songs, such as *Little Dolly Daydream* and *Lily of Laguna*, had already introduced syncopated melody during the late Victorian and Edwardian era. This was extended to commercial dance music by, for example, the barn-dances and schottisches published by the prolific Glasgow composer, Felix Burns, and similar pieces recorded by the duet concertina player, Alexander Prince. Irving Berlin's pseudo-ragtime song, *Alexander's Ragtime Band*, was the smash hit of 1911-12, and was followed by jazzy post-War songs such as *I've Got My Captain Working for Me Now* and *How Ya Gonna Keep 'Em Down on the Farm (After They've Seen Paree)*.

The new music accompanied new dances; some, like the *Turkey Trot* and the *Bunny Hug* were nine-day wonders, but the fox-trot and one-step became firmly established. On 22 November 1919, the Original Dixieland Jazz Band played at the opening night of the Hammersmith *Palais de Danse* in London. Their particular brand of New Orleans music had very little lasting effect on British popular music, but they did introduce the word 'jazz', and the opening of commercial dance-halls in towns revolutionised public dancing. What had been the preserve of the middle class at private functions and subscription balls was now accessible to shop and factory workers for the price of a ticket at the door. In the country, village halls, more spacious than the old reading rooms, were built to honour the memory of the fallen, and there was local commitment to utilise them. In the early 1920s, the *Sussex Express* reported a rash of whist drives and serials, often fund-raisers for the War memorial, and new Jazz Age village dances.[3]

The increased demand for dancing and the relative sophistication of the new ballroom dance music created more work for professionals and semi-professionals. Local musicians updated their style and material, taking their model from published stock arrangements. Horace Jackson's Band, from Lewes, already noted as playing in 1905, was still active in 1930; Wallace R. Chisholm described his new ensemble as his Dance Band. Other bands active in the area were the Southdown, the Sunny, the Medley and the Manor Dance Bands, Mr Martin's and the Excelsior from Crowborough, the Honolulu from Buxted and the Belgravia Orchestra from Newick.[4] Arch Sherlock danced to a London band, Simon's Syncopators, at Maresfield, and Daisy Sherlock recalled the annual function organised by the member of Parliament for Mid Sussex as 'a dear dance at half-a-crown a head in the Horsted parish room with a

London-based band and dinner jackets'. She 'never used to go to any Conservative dances', but she used to peep in to see what was going on.

New private bus operators, utilising their wartime lorry-driving experience and driving coaches custom-built on ex-army chassis, brought mobility to village dwellers; thus Daisy and Arch were able to follow a number of local jazz bands. They were Picknell's, led by Billy Picknell, landlord of the *Greyhound Inn* at Ardingly, on piano, with violin, saxophone, Jim Dench on the drums and sometimes a trombone; The Gibsons from Haywards Heath, consisting of violin, saxophone, piano and drums, who had a regular tea-dance booking at Boots' Restaurant, Brighton, and did some of the Conservative dances at Horsted Keynes; The Finches, from Haywards Heath, which included a double bass; and The Millses, led by Ren Mills, from Wivelsfield. The Horsted Keynes young dancing crowd travelled as far afield as Ardingly, Lindfield, Cuckfield, Balcombe and Forest Row, packed on makeshift benches in Reuben Baker's coal lorry.

There were gramophone dances and various pianists played at serials and parties.[5] A dance band was formed at Fairwarp from members of the brass band, using the band instruments. The Fairwarp Brass Jazz Band consisted of Charlie Ridley (born 1915), who had joined Fairwarp Temperance Band at the age of seven; Charlie Hemmings, a semi-professional; and Bill Horscroft, a builder at Maresfield, all on trump-ets; Denner Head's son Vernon on piano; and Joe Walters on the Temperance Band's bass and side drums rigged up as a drum kit.[6] Charlie Ridley confirms that, although they could all read, they played by ear and sounded 'a bit American'.

The pre-Great War style could still be heard. At the Freshfields' place at Wych Cross, the housekeeper organised entertainment for the servants - a whist drive on one Monday evening and a dance on the next. The house staff - two nurses, two house maids and two kitchen maids - invited the garden boys and some of the local lads, and one of the kitchen maids, Maggie Ridley (then aged 20), and her brother, Fred Gurr, played mandolins. Their best number for the one-step was not, as might have been expected, *Whispering* or *Pasadena*, but *Onward Christian Soldiers!* [7]

Young men and women, many still in their teens, took up the modern style. Vernon Head (1910-72) was perhaps representative of the children of Scan's contemporaries. He had been taught the piano by Mrs Freeland and then picked up the piano-accordion.[8] He played in the new *William IV* and at the *Foresters*, where it was known for the piano to be wheeled out onto the green after closing time, the police being hotter on licensing hours than breaches of the peace.[9] His cousin, Cicely, was also a pub pianist and accordion player, and other cousins, Rene and Bill Head, played the piano and drums for dancing at Piltdown in the late 1920s.

Frank Awcock (born 1897), nephew of the fiddle-playing Awcocks and brought up by their mother, led the New Crescent Dance Band in Danehill, which from 1929 consisted of Geoff Stephenson from Nutley (trumpet), Frank Awcock (piano accordion), Bert Setford from Freshfields (violin), George Avis (violin, then clarinet and alto saxophone), Ada White (piano), Tom Brunton (drums) and, on odd occasions, Mary Setford (cello) and Charlie Bennett (banjo).[10] Herbert Marten, Joe Marten's son, started out as a self-taught drummer at that time and now plays the saxophone and clarinet regularly in a band called The Stompers at Nutley Club.

Extract from the Fairwarp Band minute book; 1940.

(Courtesy Frank & Jean Gorringe)

George Avis (born 1912) picked up the rudiments of the fiddle from his maternal grandfather, Oliver Martin, a self-taught fiddler living between Piltdown and Nutley. He then took formal violin lessons from Wallace Chisholm. His mother's cousin, a professional London theatre musician, advised him there would be plenty of work in London cinemas, but the trade became depressed shortly afterwards with the advent of talkies. In 1927, at the age of 15, he took his first paid job, with Wallace Chisholm. He knew Scan and remembers hearing Testers' Imperial. In 1928 he played in a trio at the *Star*, Piltdown, with Rene and Bill Head.

He joined Frank Awcock's band in Danehill in 1929, and in 1930 he began doubling at Nutley village hall with a trio at five shillings for two hours. He bought a clarinet in 1930 and an alto saxophone soon after, as the violin was going out of fashion. He was a fan of Roy Fox and Lew Stone and went to see Jack Hylton whenever he appeared in Brighton. He played in an amateur orchestra in Nutley before the War and in another in Horsted Keynes after it. During the War he played with Vernon Head and Canadian soldiers stationed in the area. After the War he played in The Commodores from Burgess Hill and, when he had difficulty with breath control, changed to the string bass. He was a semi-pro musician throughout his working life, combining this with day work in a shop, on a farm and as a groundsman. He could read and transpose at sight, and never played by ear.

Scan's family band, Testers' Imperial, was in keeping with a general movement and existed as a response to a new demand. They took the tag 'jazz band' not simply because they knew the latest songs and played for the latest dances, but also because they had the latest novelty instrument, a set of drums.[11] Scan and Daisy both had a quick ear and experienced little difficulty picking up new tunes. Will, of course, was literate on the clarinet but almost certainly learned the Tester Imperial repertoire by ear.

Scan's formative years and, of course, the most important period in establishing his musical values, brought him in contact largely with diatonic tunes, and his peers played and sang almost exclusively in the major mode, but he had also been exposed to brass bands and fairground organs and all sorts of popular music by way of the gramophone and the variety theatre. The structure of much of this material was quite different from that of country music, with chromatic intervals in some melodies, some chromatic ornamentation and modulations in the harmony. Since he was essentially a melody player, harmony did not really concern him. Confronted with a popular tune where accidentals were a struc-

tural feature of the melody, like the two C sharps in *Bye Bye, Blackbird* played in C, he played them, but, in a song or dance tune where the accidentals were passing or structurally in a weak position, he followed one of three courses of action: he either played them near enough as written, or glossed over them and played the accidentals as if they were naturals, or he reconstructed the phrase altogether. The course he took in any individual case was probably dependent on the source of his material. If he learned indirectly from a written source - that is, from somebody who had the piece from notation - he was more likely to play it almost as written, but if he learned from a mediated source, a melodeon player, for example, or in a pub sing-song, he was more likely to follow the second or third course.

No doubt the band did learn all the latest tunes, but most popular music lasts a very short time and the bulk of their lasting repertoire was what the dancers would have described as 'the good old ones': *Margie, Missouri Waltz, If You Knew Susie*, etc.

> **Scan:** I used to play a variety of choruses, see ... If I was in anywhere now, pub or anywhere, if they was dancing the waltz, I'd play all tunes what they knew, all the songs what they know, see, and the people like dancing to the tunes - and one-steps and such tunes as that.... If you go to play all night, you know, you want a tremendous lot of tunes, if you're going to play three or four tunes for one dance ... With the jazz we always played one tune through and then they had an encore, and we'd play the same tune again, see. Otherwise you'd want any amount. Of course, I knew any amount, but then, if you're going to play six hours, mind you, you got ever so many tunes to play. [MP]

Although all Tin Pan Alley dance tunes were composed with verse and chorus, it was the chorus alone that usually became popular, and many verses were not generally known (with some aesthetic justification!). Scan knew and played some verses, which satisfied his idea that tunes required a first and a second part. In the case of *Down on the Farm*, he added a strain from an Austrian march, *Old Comrades*, to the chorus to make a complete tune, and he composed his own second part for *Alexander's Ragtime Band*.[12]

The piano appears from the early post-War years as the most commonly used instrument among working people, even in country districts, and most village halls and many pubs had one. The piano styles of Daisy Bulwer and Daisy Sherlock make an interesting contrast, as they approached band piano playing so differently, the one rock steady and the other more rhythmically fluid, but both perfect foils for their partners. Daisy Bulwer was musically literate and knew some theory of harmony, and, although this knowledge might have encouraged her to devise a more developed, even fussy style, she chose to keep her accompaniment simple and thus effective. Her usual support for Walter's fiddle was a straight vamp, an open octave with the left hand on the on-beats and chords with the right hand on the off-beats. Her time-keeping was faultless, and subtle shifts of emphasis kept her rhythmically buoyant.[13] Daisy Sherlock, on the other hand, knew Scan's phrasing and fill-ins; she followed him rather than providing a set accompaniment. Sometimes she played the melody on equal terms with the concertina, at others the melody line resolved into a second part. The vamp, usually contained in the left hand, was sometimes divided between the two hands, when right hand off-beat chords were sometimes played staccato and at other times double tapped, giving lift and momentum. Daisy Sherlock slipped from one technique to another as the spirit took her, which ensured constant variation and interest.

Although the drum kit, the invention of black New Orleans musicians around the turn of the century, was seen on the English variety stage just before the Great War, it was first used in dance music in England after the War. There is no way of knowing how Sarah Tester devised a method of playing and constructed a style. She could have heard very little dance band drumming herself before she started the job. Very little detail would have been audible on records or the wireless, and few of the local bands would have had drummers before she started - and anyway, what would their models have been? There are three sources, apart from dance band drumming, that could have influenced her playing. The sound of tambourine beating and the triplets of the spoons and bones would certainly have rung in Scan's head, but there is no certain evidence that Sarah would have heard much of them, especially if she had not gone to pubs. She might well have been familiar with brass band drumming, rolls on the snare drum, clashes on the cymbals and the on-beat bass drum, and she probably saw some flamboyant show drumming in the theatre in Brighton. None of that adds up to 'jazz' drumming. As far as Scan was concerned, she kept good time.[14]

> **Scan:** I sent away and bought a set, only a small set. I think, if I remember right, that was when I used to carry them on my back on push bikes, all the stuff

packed inside the drum, and I got rid of it in rather hurry, because I found hole in the drum. I thought to myself, 'Well, I'm going to get rid of this lot.' So I sold that lot and bought another lot. Well, then I had that lot about twelve months or two year, then I bought ... a mixed lot and that was a jolly good lot, that was, and that was alright - had a 30 inch drum... [RH]

She had a foot-pedal drum, you know, and a side-drum and cymbals and she had a clog-box and one thing and another on top of the drum like. Just the sticks. Never had no brushes, I didn't. No, I had the sticks. She used to do a good job on them. Yes, she could play. Once you started, you know you was going to keep time alright. She was a good one on time. [RH]

Professional dance bands of the 1920s used techniques that had been around for a century or more. Written arrangements involved second parts and counter melodies, solos, the lead moving from one instrument to another, variation in volume and modulations. Jazz introduced to the dance band world stylistic characteristics such as the vocal chorus, hot breaks and solos, the *clip-clip*, relentless four-four of the banjo, the sousaphone *oompah* and swinging rhythm. The members of Testers' Imperial heard all of these on the wireless and the gramophone, yet they followed the minimum of these conventions in adapting to their new repertoire and image. Musicians like George Avis followed one possible route; as professionals they entered the new musical world and absorbed its values. The Testers, on the other hand, did what many ear-playing amateurs would have done; they held to the values of their root culture and made minor modifications in adapting to new demands and fashions.

Scan's approach to commercial popular music remained constant from the 1920s until the day he died. He continued to pick up new songs, but only those that followed the conventions laid down between the wars. Late tunes like *Tulips from Amsterdam*, *You Always Hurt the One You Love*, *Cruising Down the River*, *I'm Dreaming of a White Christmas*, *The Happy Wanderer* and *Edelweiss* entered his repertoire, but *Rock Around the Clock* and *Tutti Frutti* passed him by.

NOTES

1. Roy Dommett in conversation with me.

2. A.M. Carr-Saunders, D. Caradog Jones and C.A. Moser, *A Survey of Social Conditions in England and Wales* (1958), p. 251.

3. *Kelly's Directory of Sussex* listed ten dance teachers in 1922; by 1930 the number had risen to 25.

4. There are numerous references to dance bands in the *Sussex Express* in the late 1920s.

5. Five pianists were named as having played at a British Legion social in Fletching in 1927 (*Sussex Express*, 22.4.1927).

   Cecil Haddock [son of the valet at Dower House] was the pianist at a dance in Fairwarp (*Sussex Express*, 14.1.1927).

6. 'Fairwarp Dance. A dance was arranged for Wednesday evening in the Village Hall from 7.30-11 p.m., the Fairwarp Brass Jazz Band having been engaged.' (*Sussex Express*, 28.1.1927). There was a similar notice in the edition of 23.7.1927.

7. Margaret Bishop (née Ridley).

8. Miss M.W. Cottingham, music teacher, piano, and P.W. Freeland, saxophone, played at Nutley (*Sussex Express*, 29.8.1927).

   Miss Cottingham, piano, Mr. [George] Avis, violin, and Mr. P. Freeland played at Nutley (*Sussex Express*, 7.2.1930).

9. Talking of Christmas in the late 1950s and early 1960s, Frank Gorringe said: 'They couldn't touch you for drinking on the Green' after hours.

10. Ada and Harry White, piano and drums, later formed another band. Daisy and Arch Sherlock took rooms in their house in 1936.

11. Years after, Scan always referred to Testers' Imperial as his 'jazz band', yet by most definitions of jazz it was no such thing. No dance band reported in the *Sussex Express* during 1927 and the first half of 1930 described itself as a jazz band, with the exception of the contingent from the Fairwarp Brass Band. Scan's use of the expression, which went out of high fashion a couple of years before he formed the band, is some indication, that he and his supporters defined 'keeping up with the latest' in their own terms.

12. *How Ya' Gonna Keep 'Em Down On the Farm (After Thev're Seen Paree?)* (Lewis, Young and Donaldson), published 1918 or 1919.

13. Daisy Bulwer may be heard on the following recordings:

    English Country Music (Topic 12T296); *Boscastle Breakdown* (Topic 12T240); and *Scan Tester* (Topic 2-12T445/6).

    I never heard Daisy Bulwer play a quickstep, fox-trot or slow waltz. She might have had a different style for 'modern' dance tunes.

14. George Avis knows of no drummer at that time who had lessons: 'They just picked it up, and some weren't too marvellous!'

Postscript

From a late twentieth century perspective, even for those of us who knew him, Scan's life and times seem very far away. For those seeking values from his world to enrich their own, the cultural gulf might feel too wide for comfort. Yet in time to come, observers looking back at those of us still playing all kinds of music - country and western, jazz, Irish music, whatever - in pubs and clubs and at parties and weddings, might class us together with Scan and his mates as the last knockings of a culture providing live, home-grown music at a human scale for its community's entertainment.

'If I go in anywhere,' Scan said to Alan Waller in 1966,

> don't matter where it is, and there's a chap playing instrument ... I've got ten times more interest in him than I have in any of these here juke boxes or anything of that. I wouldn't have one in my place.

At the Keele Folk Festival; July 1965.
(Photograph: Brian Shuel)

Discography

Scan Tester and some of his relatives and friends appear on the following commercially-issued recordings:

Folktape FTA 102, *Songs and Music of the Sussex Weald*. Reel-to-reel tape issued by the English Folk Dance and Song Society, 1966 (now unavailable).

Topic 12T240, *Boscastle Breakdown*. LP, 1974.

Folktracks FSA 085, *The Man in the Moon*. Cassette, 1975. (Reissued in re-edited form as FSA-45-085.)

Topic 12T258, *Sussex Harvest*. LP, 1975 (now unavailable).

Topic 2-12T455/6, *Scan Tester 1877-1972: I Never Played to Many Posh Dances*. Double LP, issued as a companion to this book.

Scan Tester, concertina.
Recorded by Mervyn Plunkett at Scan Tester's home at Cinder Hill, Sussex, in August 1957.

Waltz: The Man In The Moon	Topic 2-12T455/6

Scan Tester, concertina; Bill McMahon, spoons/effects; Mervyn Plunkett, percussion.
Recorded by Mervyn Plunkett at his home in West Hoathly, Sussex, 24 August 1957.

Stepdance: The Monkey Hornpipe	Topic 2-12T455/6

Paul Gross, fiddle, Michael Plunkett, recorder; Bill Agate, mouth-organ and tambourine, Jack Norris and Snowy Howick, mouth-organs; Scan Tester, concertina; Reg Hall, melodeon; Bill McMahon, spoons/effects; Mervyn Plunkett, percussion
Recorded by Mervyn Plunkett in the *Cat* in West Hoathly, Sussex, 5 October 1957.

I Wish They'd Do It Now	Topic 2-12T455/6

Bill Gorringe, fiddle.
Recorded by Mervyn Plunkett at Bill Gorringe's home in Cuckfield, Sussex, February 1958.

See Me Dance The Polka	Topic 2-12T455/6
The Heel And Toe Polka	Topic 2-12T455/6
Stepdance	Topic 2-12T455/6
Schottische	Topic 2-12T455/6
Polka	Topic 2-12T455/6

A: Scan Tester, concertina; Will Tester and Bill Agate, tambourines.
B: Scan Tester, concertina; Reg Hall, melodeon.
Recorded by Mervyn Plunkett in the *Crown*, Horsted Keynes, Sussex, 22 February 1958.

No. 2 Stepdance (A)	Topic 2-12T455/6
Stepdance (VA)	Topic 2-12T455/6
Polka (B)	Topic 2-12T455/6

Reg Hall, melodeon; Scan Tester, tambourine.
Recorded by Mervyn Plunkett at Scan Tester's home at Cinder Hill, Sussex, 23 February 1958.

Polkas: La Russe/ McCuskers'/ Jenny Lind/ Good Night, Ladies	Topic 2-12T45S/6

A: Scan and Will Tester, concertinas.
B: Art Winter, melodeon; Hilary Burgess, fiddle; Will Tester, tambourine.
Recorded by Mervyn Plunkett at the *Trevor Arms*, Glynde, Sussex, March 1958.

No. 2 Stepdance GA)	Topic 2-12T455/6
Schottische (A)	Topic 2-12T455/6
The Wearing Of The Green IBM	Topic 2-12T455/6

A: Bob Keightley, fiddle; Scan Tester, concertina; Jack Norris and Reg Hall, melodeons; Bill McMahon, spoons/effects; Mervyn Plunkett, percussion.
B: Jack Norris, melodeon.
Recorded by Mervyn Plunkett and Peter Grant at the latter's home in West Hoathly, Sussex, 11 May 1960.

Marches: Scotland The Brave/ The Happy Wanderer (A)	Topic 2-12T455/6
Schottische: Brook Street Polka (B)	Topic 2-12T455/6

Scan Tester, concertina; Reg Hall, melodeon; Daisy Sherlock, piano.
Recorded by Reg Hall and Peter Grant at Scan Testers home in Horsted Keynes, Sussex, 10 October 1960.

The Broom Dance	Topic 2-12T455/6
Polka: Jenny Lind	Topic 2-12T45S/6
Schottische: The Indian Polka	Topic 2-12T45S/6

A: Scan Tester, concertina.
B: Bill Agate, mouth-organ and tambourine.
Recorded by Tony Wales at a folk music festival in Horsham, Sussex, 29 June 1961.

Haste To The Wedding (A)	Folktape FTA 102
Stepdance [No. 1 Stepdance] (A)	Folktape FTA 102
Three Dance Tunes [I Wish They'd Do It Now/ I Love A Lassie/ Polka] (B)	Folktape FTA 102

A: Scan Tester, concertina; Rabbity Baxter, tambourine.
B: Rabbity Baxter, voice.
Recorded by Ken Stubbs at the *Half Moon*, Balcombe, Sussex, 26 June 1962.

Jenny Lind Polka (A)	Topic 12T240
Polka (A)	Topic 12T240
Will The Weaver (B)	Topic 12T258

Scan Tester, bandoneon/concertina/voice.
Recorded by Peter Kennedy at Scan Tester's home in Horsted Keynes, Sussex, 1963.

Waltz No. 1 (The Man In The Moon) /b	Folktracks FSA 085
Waltz No. 2 [Nutley Waltz] /b	Folktracks FSA 085
Schottische No. 1 /b	Folktracks FSA 085
The Jenny Lind Polka /b	Folktracks FSA 085
Schottische No. 2 (take 1) /b	Folktracks FSA 085
(take 2) /b	Folktracks FSA 085
The Heel And Toe Polka /b	Folktracks FSA 085
Schottische No. 3 /b	Folktracks FSA 085
The Step Waltz (Waltz-O'-Vienna) /b	Folktracks FSA 085
Waltz No. 3 [Nutley Waltz] /b	Folktracks FSA 085
Polka No. 3 /b	Folktracks FSA 085
The Broom Dance /c	Folktracks FSA 085
The Monkey Hornpipe /c	Folktracks FSA 085
Country Step Dance /c	Folktracks FSA 085
Barbary Bell [17th of March or St. Patrick's Day] /c	Folktracks FSA 085
Last Figure Of Lancers [Polka /Roaming in the Gloaming/ Horsey, Keep Your Tail Up/Loch Lomond /Polka] /c	Folktracks FSA 085
Oxford City /v	Folktracks FSA 085
The False Bride /v	Folktracks FSA 085
The Lakes Of Coldflynn /v	Folktracks FSA 085

The False Bride /c	Folktracks FSA 085
Interview with Peter Kennedy	Folktracks FSA 085

(There are minor alterations in the titles and some differences in the edited interview on the re-issue, Folktracks FSA-45-085.)

Scan Tester, concertina.
Recorded by Reg Hall at his home in Croydon, Surrey, 8 August 1964.

Schottische	Topic	2-12T455/6
Polka	Topic	2-12T455/6
The Reel	Topic	2-12T455/6
Polka	Topic	2-12T455/6
Schottische	Topic	2-12T455/6
Polka	Topic	2-12T455/6
Polka: Not For Joe	Topic	2-12T455/6
Nutley Waltz	Topic	2-12T455/6
While Shepherds Watch Their Flocks By Night	Topic	2-12T455/6
Schottische	Topic	2-12T455/6
Jig: The Irish Washerwoman	Topic	2-12T455/6
Waltz	Topic	2-12T455/6
The Waltz Vienna or The Step Waltz	Topic	2-12T45S/6
Schottische	Topic	2-12T455/6
Stepdance	Topic	2-12T455/6

A: Bob Keightley, Steve Pennells and Reg Hall, fiddles; Scan Tester, concertina, Paul Gross, piano; Bob Davenport, triangle.
B: Scan Tester, concertina/voice.
Recorded by Reg Hall at the Fax, Islington Green, London, 21 January 1965.

Polka: The Girl I Left Behind Me or Brighton Camp (A)	Topic 2-12T455/6
The Lakes Of Coalflin /v (B)	Topic 2-12T455/6
No. 1 Stepdance /c (B)	Topic 2-12T455/6
Barbara Allen /v (B)	Topic 2-12T455/6

A: Scan Tester, concertina.
B: Scan Tester, concertina; Reg Hall, melodeon; Daisy Sherlock, piano.
Recorded by Reg Hall at Scan Tester's home in Horsted Keynes, Sussex, 21 July 1965.

Polka: Pretty Little Dear (A)	Topic 2-12T455/6
Polka (B)	Topic 2-12T455/6
One-step: Down On The Farm (B)	Topic 2-12T455/6
Waltz (B)	Topic 2-12T455/6

A: Walter Bulwer, fiddle; Scan Tester, concertina; Reg Hall, melodeon; Daisy Bulwer, piano.
B: Scan Tester, concertina; Reg Hall, melodeon, Walter Bulwer, mandolin-banjo.
Recorded by Bill Leader and Reg Hall at the Bulwers' home in Shipdham, Norfolk, 22 July 1966.

The Heel And Toe Polka (A)	Topic 2-12T455/6
Soldier's Joy (A)	Topic 2-12T455/6
The Carnival Is Over (B)	Topic 2-12T455/6

Scan Tester, concertina.
Recorded by Alan Waller at his home in Hillingdon, Middlesex, October 1966.

Waltz	Topic 2-12T455/6
Schottische	Topic 2-12T455/6

Scan Tester, concertina.
Recorded by Tony Engle at the Central Club, Peacehaven, Sussex, 16 May 1968.

Stepdance	Topic 2-12T455/6

Acknowledgements

I am indebted to the following people for their warm and spontaneous responses to my questioning about their own lives and those of their friends, neighbours and relatives:

CHELWOOD GATE: Mary Elphick (nee Marten), Fanny Lander (née Smith, born c. 1896-97), Polly Marten (née Pollard) and Will Marten.
CUCKFIELD: Florence Norris.
DANEHILL: Rose Avis (née Lucas), Charlie Bates, Margaret Lucas (née Awcock), Phil Lucas, Jenny Marten and Bert Wood (born 11.10.1890).
FAIRWARP: Audrey Castle (née Head), Charlie Gorringe, Frank Gorringe, Jean Gorringe, Peggy Head, Charlie Ridley, and Christopher Stephens.
FIRLE: Cyril Phillips.
FOREST ROW: Margaret Bishop (née Ridley), Bob Miles and Mrs. Miles.
HORSTED KEYNES: Bob Fry, Bert Gurr, Edie Heedless (née Tester), Peggy Horton (née Tester), Paul Marten and David Walder.
SHARPTHORNE: Bill McMahon.
UCKFIELD: George Avis, Hugh Chisholm, Norman Edwards, and Sam Hughes.

My attempts to contact relatives of Rabbity Baxter, Tommy Stephenson and Dido Wickham met with no success.

For information, biographical material, references, photographs, practical and technical assistance, encouragement and helpful discussion I would like to thank Chris Addison, Jean Addison, Andrew Bathe, Jim Beard, Chris Brady, Tess Buckland, Sydney Burgess, Eric Byford, Steve Chambers, Bernie Cherry, Bob Davenport, Roy Dommett, Christine Duke, Will Duke, Ian Dunmer, Tony Engle, Claire Gilliam, John Glaister, John Goddard, Sean Goddard, Paul Gross, John Gurney, Claire Hall, Alun Howkins, Ann Marie Hume, Bill Leader, Ann Loughran, Dougie Moncrieff, Chris Morley, Harry Mousell, Steve Pennells, Doë Plunkett, Michael Plunkett, Scott Ramsey, Jim Rea, Mick Reed, Hugh Rippen, Ellis Rogers, Steve Roud, Doc Rowe, Derek Schofield, Christine Smith, Vic Smith, Ken Stubbs, Malcolm Taylor, Mike Taylor, Tony Wales, Alan Waller and Martin Wyndham-Read

I am particularly grateful to Sheila Gammon for word-processing the body of the text, which involved working on several extensively re-written drafts. My thanks are due to her also for copying photographs on location and preparing prints for publication. Similarly, I am grateful to Graeme Kirkham for applying his skills in desktop publishing to the presentation of the text and the illustrations.

Keith Chandler, Sheila Gammon, Vic Gammon, Alun Howkins, Graeme Kirkham and David Nuttall read the penultimate draft and offered criticism and suggestions, most of which I accepted, and which I acknowledge with thanks.

Dave Arthur's book, *A Sussex Life: The Memories of Gilbert Sargent; Countryman*, published by Barrie and Jenkins (London, 1989), gives an account of life on Ashdown Forest and elsewhere in Sussex. There are particular references to Nutley Feast Day, pp. 83-84; gypsies playing the mouth-organ and tambourine, p. 103; Rabbity Baxter playing the tambourine, p. 96; Saturday night dances at *Nutley Inn* with Dido Wickham, Scan and Will (mis-identified by Gilbert Sargent as Fred Tester), pp. 96-97; Joe Marten playing concertina and fiddle ('He could get a tune out of anything'), p. 96; Scan and Joe Marten playing together for dancing at the *Coach and Horses*, p. 96; the *Stone Quarry*, 'a good music pub', p. 97; '...the old singing pub, the *Red Lion*, all the old blokes got in there - no women - for a song.' p. 97; and there are photographs of litter cutting and gypsies on the forest.

Appendix A:
The wider world
Sound recordings by other musicians of tunes from Scan Tester's recorded repertoire

Commercially-available recordings of tunes in Scan's recorded repertoire have been made by many other musicians in Britain, Ireland and the New World. This list, by no means exhaustive, provides comparative material, demonstrating both common and diverse aspects of style, approach and repertoire.

In the case of *Soldier's Joy*, for example, all the versions cited are close to a common melodic standard. The examples given for No. 1 Stepdance, however, are relatively distantly related.

This appendix is intended as an aid to the interested reader, rather than a comprehensive discography, and therefore LP and cassette references are given for material originally on 78 rpm discs and subsequently reissued.

The items are listed in alphabetical order of Scan's usual title for them, with a note of the location on record for those otherwise untitled.

THE BROOM DANCE

Jack Armstrong (Northumberland)	Oyster Girl	1954	HMV B10804	78
Harold Colvill (Cambridgeshire)	Oyster Girl	1972	Topic 12TS229	LP
Fred Pidgeon (Devon)	Quadrilles, Fig.5	1954	Folktracks FSA 087	Cass.
George Tremain (Yorkshire)	Oyster Girl	1946	HMV B9539	78

DOWN ON THE FARM

Bob Cann (Devon)	Old Comrades March	1977	Harvest SHSP 4073	LP
Jim Europe (New York)	How Ya' Gonna Keep 'Em Down On The Farm	1919	Pathé 22080	78
Happy Wanderers Street Band (London)	Old Comrades	1958	Esquire 32-044	LP

THE GIRL I LEFT BEHIND ME

Stephen Baldwin (Herefordshire)	The Girl I Left Behind Me	1954	Leader LED 2068	LP
Walter Bulwer/ Billy Cooper (Norfolk)	The Girl I Left Behind Me	1962	Topic 12T296	LP
Ceilidh Band (Armagh)	The Girl I Left Behind Me	1950s	Folkways FW 8872	LP
Ex-Service Men (Alec Bisset) (Glasgow)	Al'-Get-Ye, Part 1	1931	Beltona 1622	78
Flanagan Bros. (Co. Waterford)	The Girl I Left Behind Me	1928	Regal MR276	78
Patrick Gaffney (Ireland)	The Girl I Left Behind Me	1923	Parlophone E3180	78
John Griffin (Co. Roscommon)	The Girl I Left Behind Me	1925	Bennett 5526	78
Peter Horan/ Fred Finn (Co. Sligo)	The Shirt I Left Behind Me	70s/80s	Comhaltas Ceoltoiri Eireann CL33	LP
O'Leary's Irish Minstrels (Ireland/Boston)	The Girl I Left Behind Me	1926	Columbia 33140F	78
Jasper and Levy Smith (Southern England)	The Girl I Left Behind Me	1975/6	Topic 12TS304	LP
Dan Sullivan (Ireland/ Boston)	The Girl I Left Behind Me	1928	HMV B3613	78

HASTE TO THE WEDDING

Stephen Baldwin (Herefordshire)	Haste To The Wedding	1954	Leader LED 2068	LP
Margaret Barry (Work)/Michael Gorman (Sligo)	Haste To The Wedding	1960s	Prestige Irish 35001	LP
Mellie Dunham (New England)	Mountain Rangers	1926	Victor 19940	78
Paddy Killoran (Co. Sligo)	Haste To The Wedding	1937	Decca 12145	78
William Kimber (Oxfordshire)	Haste To The Wedding	1935	Topic 12T249	LP
	Haste To The Wedding	1946	Topic 12T249	LP
	Haste To The Wedding	1956	EFDSS LP 1001	LP
Thomas Mann (Iowa)	Haste To The Wedding	1937	L of C AAFS L9	LP
Myles O'Malley (Ireland /Philadelphia)	Haste To The Wedding	1936	Decca 12065	78
Mrs Ben Scott (California)	Haste To The Wedding	1939	L of C AFS L62	LP
Dan Sullivan (Ireland/ Boston, Mass.)	Haste To The Wedding	1927	Columbia 33508F	78

THE HEEL AND TOE POLKA

Stephen Baldwin (Herefordshire)	Heel and Toe Polka	1954	Leader LED 2068	LP
Percy Brown (Norfolk)	Heel and Toe Polka	1972	Topic 12TS229	LP
The Eamonn Ceannt Ceili Band (Dublin)	untitled	1975	Outlet SOLP 1025	LP
James Morrison (Co. Sligo)	The Magic Slipper	1936	Viva Voce 001	Cass.
Harkie Nesling (Suffolk)	Sultan Polka	1970s	Topic 12TS374	LP
Ned Pearson (Northumberland)	Heel and Toe Polka	1954	Topic 12T283	LP
Fred Pidgeon (Devon)	Heel and Toe Polka	1954	Folktracks FSA 087	Cass.
Reg Reeder (Suffolk)	Heel and Toe Polka	1970s	Topic 12TS374	LP
Eely Whent (Suffolk)	Heel and Toe Polka	1970s	Topic 12TS375	LP

THE INDIAN POLKA

Flanagan brothers (Co. Waterford)	Highland Fling Medley	1929	Topic 12T365	LP
Tom Morrison (Co. Galway)	Sweet Flower of Milltown	1927	Columbia 33210F	78

Many Scottish country dance and pipe band recordings.

THE IRISH WASHERWOMAN

Stephen Baldwin (Herefordshire)	Irish Washerwoman	1954	Leader LED 2068	LP
Fred Cameron (Elgin)	Scottish Quadrilles, Figure 5	1909	Zonophone 310	78
Peter Conlon (Co. Galway)	Irish Washerwoman	1921	Parlophone E3025	78
Billy Cooper (Norfolk)	Irish Washerwoman	1962	Topic 12T240	LP
Jack Elliott (Co. Durham)	Irish Washerwoman	1960s	Leader LEA 4001	LP
Michael Hanafin (Co. Kerry/ Boston, Mass.)	Irish Washerwoman	1926	Columbia 33115F	78
Thomas Mann (Iowa)	Irish Washerwoman	1937	L of C AAFS L9	LP
Emile Vacher (France)	Irish Washerwoman	1928	Parlophone E6096	78
Emma Vickers (Lancashire)	untitled	-	Vaughan Williams Memorial Library 003	Cass.

JENNY LIND

Walter Bulwer/ Billy Cooper (Norfolk)	Jenny Lind Polka	1962	Topic 12T296	LP
Richard Fitzgerald (Co. Donegal)	Clonmel Races	1960s	Blarney Castle 508	LP
Henry Ford (Michigan)	Heel and Toe Polka	1925	Edison 51699	78
	Heel and Toe Polka	1925	Victor 19909	78
	Heel and Toe Polka	1926	Columbia 555D	78
McCusker Bros. (Go. Armagh)	untitled	1954	HMV BD1326	78
Rose Murphy (Co. Galway)	Last of June	1976	Topic 12TS316	LP

O'Leary's Irish Minstrels (Boston, Mass)	Come Up Stairs and We'll Make a Night of It	1926	Columbia 33139F	78
Reg Reeder (Suffolk)	Jenny Lind Polka	1970s	Topic 12TS374	LP
Jack Rivers (California)	Heel and Toe Polka	1950s	McGregor 10400	78
Pat Roche (Ireland/Chicago)	Doran's Favourite	1934	Decca 12067	78

THE MONKEY HORNPIPE

Walter Bulwer (Norfolk)	Sailor's Hornpipe	1962	Topic 12T240	LP
Billy Cooper (Norfolk)	Sailor's Hornpipe	1962	Topic 12T240	LP
Jasper Smith (Southern England)	Tuning	1975/6	Topic 12TS304	LP

POLKA (Topic 2- 12T455/6 Side 4, track 2j

Orpheus disc piano	Bric a Brac Polka		Saydisc CSDL 359	LP
Harry Davidson (London)	Bric a Brac Polka	1940s	Decca F8782	78

POLKA (Bill Gorringe: Topic 2- \ 2T455/6 Side 2, track 6e)

Walter Bulwer (Norfolk)	untitled	1962	Topic 12T240	
Billy Bennington (Norfolk)	On The Green	1972	Topic 12V229	

PRETTY LITTLE DEAR

Jack Armstrong (Northumberland)	Triumph	1954	HMV 7EG8654	EP
Stephen Baldwin (Herefordshire)	Pretty Little Dear	1954	Leader LED 2068	LP
Walter Bulwer (Norfolk)	Shave the Donkey	1962	Topic 12T296	LP
Donald Cumming & Eddie Holmes (Scotland/ Boston, Mass.)	Triumph	1934	Decca F5473	78
William Kimber (Oxfordshire)	Step and Fetch Her	1956	EFDSS LP 1001	LP
Fred Pidgeon (Devon)	Triumph	1951	Folktracks FSA 087	Cass.
Peter Wyper (Hamilton)	Triumph	1913	Rena 1334	78

THE REEL

Billy Bennington (Norfolk)	Sheringham Breakdown	-	East Anglian Music	LP
Percy Brown (Norfolk)	Sheringham Breakdown	1950s	BBC REB41M	LP
		1972	Topic 12TS229	LP
Walter Bulwer/ Billy Cooper (Norfolk)	Four Hand Reel	1962	Topic 12T296	LP
Billy Cooper (Norfolk)	Four Hand Reel	1962	Topic 12T240	LP
Harry Donnelly (Ireland/ New York)	Dublin Hornpipe	1927	Banner 7023	78
William Hocken (Cornwall)	Boscastle Breakdown	1943	Topic 12T240	LP
MacDonald Brothers (Scotland)	Hornpipe	1970s	Thistle BSLP 80	LP
Eddie Meehan (Co. Sligo) & John McKenna (Co. Leitrim)	Lawson's Favourite	1937	Decca 12014	78
James Morrison (Co. Sligo)	Provincial Hornpipe	1921	Viva Voce 001	Cass.
Frank Quinn (Co. Longford)	Dublin Hornpipe	1924	Vocalion 14899	78
Jimmy Shand (Dundee)	Lancashire Clogs	1930s	Beltona BL2356	78
Phil Tanner (Gower)	Gower Reel	1937	EFDSS LP 1005	LP
Tintagel and Boscastle Players (Cornwall)	Boscastle Breakdown	1943	Topic 12T240	LP
Fred Whiting (Suffolk)	Earl Soham Slog	1970s	Topic 12TS374	LP

SCHOTTISCHE (Topic 2-127455/6 Side 1, track 7)

Stephen Baldwin (Herefordshire)	Schottische	1954	Leader LED 2068	LP
Billy Bennington (Norfolk)	Henry Sadd's	1980s	East Anglian Life	LP
James Brown (Scotland)	Rainbow Schottische	c.1912	Marathon 398	78
Flanagan Brothers (Co. Waterford)	Heart of Man Medley	1926	Zonophone 5157	78
Fred Pidgeon (Devon)	Plain Schottische	1954	Folktracks FSA 087	Cass.
Dan Wyper (Hamilton)	Selection of Schottisches	1910	Rena 1345	78

SEVENTEENTH OF MARCH

Band of H.M. Irish Guards	Regimental Marches of the Brigade of Guards	1914	Winner 2658	78
Billy Cooper (Norfolk)	St. Patrick's Day	1962	Topic 12T240	LP
Pat Roche (Ireland/ Chicago)	St. Patrick's Day	1935	Decca F18014	78
Jasper Smith (Southern England)	Tuning	1975/6	Topic 12TS395	LP
Leo Rowsome (Dublin)	St. Patrick's Day	1933	Topic 12T259	LP

SOLDIER'S JOY

Stephen Baldwin (Herefordshire)	Soldier's Joy	1954	Leader LED 2068	LP
Walter Bulwer/ Billy Cooper (Norfolk)	Soldier's Joy	1962	Topic 12T296	LP
The Cameron Men (Angus)	Soldier's Joy	1934	Topic 12T321	LP
Flanagan Brothers (Co. Waterford)	Soldier's Joy	1929	Columbia 33359F	78
Gargan's Athlone Accordeon Band (Westmeath)	Soldier's Joy	1937	Regal Zonophone MR2563	78
William Hannah (Lothian)	Soldier's Joy	1927	Parlophone E3372	78
		1931	Broadcast S15	78
Willy Henderson/ Bobby Jamieson (Shetland)	Soldier's Joy	-	Tangent TNGT 117	LP
William Kimber (Oxfordshire)	Headington Morris Reel	1948	Topic 12T249	LP
	Four Hand Reel	1956	EFDSS LP 1001	78
George Tremain (Yorkshire)	Soldier's Joy	1946	HMV B9568	78
Dan Wyper (Hamilton)	Pibroch Quadrilles, Figure 5	1921	Regal G7682	78
Peter Wyper (Hamilton)	Reel	1912	Columbia - Rena 1187	78

Many Scottish country dance and pipe band recordings.

STEPDANCE (Topic 2-127455/6 Side 4, track 7)

Bob Cann (Devon)	Uncle George's Hornpipe	1975	Topic 12TS275	LP
John Kimmel (New York)	American Clog	1904/5	Zon-0-Phone 212	78
Jim McHardy (Scotland)	Cliff Hornpipe	1930s	Beltona BL2417	78
Tom Orchard (Devon)	Tuning	1974-6	Topic 12TS349	LP
Leo Rowsome (Dublin)	Higgins' Hornpipe	1948	Topic 12T322	LP
Dan Sullivan (Ireland/ Boston, Mass.)	Wilson Gog	1929	Victor V29031	78
Peter Wyper (Hamilton)	Cliff Hornpipe	1912	Rena 1943	78

NO. 1 STEPDANCE

Stephen Baldwin (Herefordshire)	Liverpool Hornpipe	1954	Leader LED 2068	LP
Bob Cann (Devon)	Tommy Roberts' Hornpipe	1975	Topic 12TS275	LP
Patrick Gaffney (Ireland)	The Southern Shores	1925	Columbia 350D	78
William Hannah (Lothian)	untitled	1930	Parlophone E 3846	78
Gerard Lajoie (Canada)	Reel de Bellechasse	-	Columbia C4006	78
Tom Morrison (Go. Galway)	London Clog	1928	Columbia 33247F	78
A.J. Scott (Ireland)	Plantation Hornpipe	1910s	Pathé 78038/9	78

STEPDANCE (Topic 2-127455/6, Side 4, track 8)

Cyril Barber (Suffolk)	Stepdance Tune	1984	Home-Made Music LP 302	LP
Percy Brown (Norfolk)	Yarmouth Breakdown	1972	Topic 12TS229	LP
William Hocken (Cornwall)	untitled	1943	Topic 12T240	LP
William Kimber (Oxfordshire)	Fool's Dance	1956	EFDSS LP 1001	LP
Tom Orchard (Devon)	Tuning	1974-6	Topic 12TS349	LP
Fred Pearce (Suffolk)	Pigeon on the Gate	1970s	Topic 12TS375	LP
W. V. Robinson (Canada / London)	Freaks on the Mouth Organ,	1924	Regal G8139	78
Phil Tanner (Glamorgan)	Gower Reel	1935	EFDSS LP 1005	LP
Font Whatling (Suffolk)	Pigeon on the Gate	1970s	Topic 12TS374	LP
Oscar Woods (Suffolk),	untitled	1973	Topic 12TS22	LP
Peter Conlon (Co. Galway)	Galway Bay Hornpipe	1912	Okeh 4264	78
Tom Ennis (Ireland / USA)	Rickett's Hornpipe	1929	Columbia 33421F	78
O'Leary's Irish Minstrels (Ireland/ Boston)	Rickett's	1929	Columbia 33122F	78
Dan Sullivan (Ireland/ Boston, Mass)	Rickett's Hornpipe	1926	Columbia 33105F	78

WALTZ (Topic 2-127455/6 Side 4, track 3)

Fred Pidgeon (Devon)	Old Fashioned Waltz	1954	Folktracks FSA 087	Cass.
Rufus Guinchard (Newfoundland)	Granny's Waltz	1982	Pigeon Inlet PIP 737	LP
National Barn Dance Orchestra (USA)	Waltz Quadrille - Part 2	1933	Bluebird B5216	78
Bill Monroe (USA)	Kiss Me Waltz	1970s	Decca 675348	LP

THE WALTZ VIENNA

Stephen Baldwin (Herefordshire)	Varsoviana	1954	Leader LED 2068	LP
Walter Bulwer/ Billy Cooper (Norfolk)	Waltz Vienna	1962	Topic 12T296	LP
Jim Cameron (Angus)	La Va	1957	Beltona BL2692	78
Tony Capaldi (Glasgow)	La Varsovienne	1930	Topic 12T319	LP
Jerry O'Brien/ Joe Derrane (Ireland / Boston)	Varsouviana	1950s	Copley EP9-4	EP
Henry Ford (Michigan)	Varsovienne	1925	Edison 51699	78
	Varsovienne	1925	Victor 19910	78
	Varsovienne	1926	Columbia 683D	78
	Hungarian Varsovienne	1927	Columbia 936D	78
Four Provinces Orch. (Ireland/ Philadelphia)	Shoe the Donkey	1926	HMV B2931	78
Hugh Gillespie (Co. Donegal)	Versevanna	1938	Topic 12T364	LP
Mickie Griffin (Ireland/ New York)	Paddy Canny	1950s	Standard F14005	LP
William Hannah (Lothian)	La Va	1927	Parlophone E3371	78
Paddy Killoran (Co. Sligo)	Paddy Candy	1950s	Colonial 123	LP
Ned Pearson (Northumberland)	Varsoviana (Old and New)	1954	Topic 12T283	LP
Fred Pidgeon (Devon)	Varsoviana	1954	Folktracks FSA 087	Cass.
Frank Quinn (Co. Longford)	The Varsouviana	1923	Gennett 5074	78
Murty Rabbett (Ireland/ Boston, Mass.)	Versouviana	c.1934	Topic 12T366	LP
Jackie Roche (Ireland/ New York)	Shoe the Donkey	1960s	Avoca 33ST101	LP
Jimmy Shand (Dundee)	La Va	1950s	Parlophone F3491	78
Peter Wyper (Hamilton)	La Varsoviana	1910	Columbia-Rena 1438	78

2024 Update

Unfortunately, many of the sources cited for hearing Scan's tunes are currently unavailable and/or out-of-print.

Topic 2-12T455/6, *Scan Tester 1877-1972: I Never Played to Many Posh Dances*, was issued in 1990 as a double LP companion to this book It was remastered and reissued in CD form by Topic Records in 2009 as TSCD581D.

All 55 tracks from this LP/CD, including tunes and spoken words, are now available online on YouTube and can be found here via this smartphone-scannable QR code:

Also recommended:

The Anglo Concertina Music of
SCAN TESTER
by Gary Coover and Will Duke

Over 50 tunes with musical notation and tablature for the Anglo Concertina. (Rollston Press, 2024).

Thanks to Steve Roud for helping coordinate this 2024 re-issue of *I Never Played to Many Posh Dances*, and special thanks to Reg Hall for his diligent research and friendship with Scan that resulted in this delightful and insightful view into rural English village musicians and village life from over a century ago.

Gary Coover
Editor/Publisher

ROLLSTON PRESS